THE BEST
PLAYS
OF 2015

THE BEST PLAYS OF 2015

Edited by Lawrence Harbison

APPLAUSE
THEATRE & CINEMA BOOKS
An Imprint of Hal Leonard LLC

Published in 2016 by Applause Theatre & Cinema Books
An Imprint of Hal Leonard LLC
7777 West Bluemound Road
Milwaukee, WI 53213

Trade Book Division Editorial Offices
33 Plymouth St., Montclair, NJ 07042

Printed in the United States of America

Book design by Lynn Bergesen

Library of Congress Cataloging-in-Publication Data

Names: Harbison, Lawrence editor.
Title: The best plays of 2015 / edited by Lawrence Harbison.
Description: Milwaukee, WI : Applause Theatre & Cinema Books, 2016.
Identifiers: LCCN 2016025280 | ISBN 9781495045813 (pbk.)
Subjects: LCSH: American drama—21st century.
Classification: LCC PS634.2 B49 2016 | DDC 812/.608—dc23
LC record available at https://lccn.loc.gov/2016025280

www.applausebooks.com

Contents

Foreword
by Christopher Burney
vii

Introduction
ix

Eclipsed
by Danai Gurira
1

The Guard
(Black White Ochre Red)
by Jessica Dickey
59

King Liz
by Fernanda Coppel
115

Lost Girls
by John Pollono
183

New Country
by Mark Roberts
233

Nice Girl
by Melissa Ross
287

Foreword

What makes the best play of the year? In a culture so richly diverse with contrasting points of view, can there be a "best play"?

We've seen many try to define "the best"—and the result is a series of thoughtful awards (and their accompanying ceremonies). In the inevitable race to the top, front-runners often seem to be following the critical trends rather than setting them.

In the many theatrical seasons that Mr. Harbison has been editing the collections of "Best Plays of the Year," the brilliance in his anthologies is the range of "best" that has been represented. He has championed plays from distinct voices that capture the variations in contemporary theater. There is not one "best"—there is a generous embrace of many "bests" from both established writers and those new to audience and industry alike.

I have seen the power these books have on the writers included. Whether a nod to a writer with a well-established body of work or a supportive embrace of an emerging writer (who, chances are, has been "emerging" for quite a while), being included in Mr. Harbison's anthology is a significant milestone. Second Stage Theatre is honored to have been represented in these collections by many of the plays first produced in our New Plays Uptown series.

Every year I anxiously look forward to see who has been included. Are they plays I know? Are they surprises? I also encourage writers and audiences to look back over the collections. Who was first discovered? Who has built on that recognition? These collections are simultaneously records and oracles, and we are a field made better by embracing the truth that we have several "bests" each season.

—Christopher Burney
Associate Artistic Director & Curator 2ST Uptown
Second Stage Theatre
February 2016

Introduction

This volume contains six terrific new plays produced during the 2015 calendar year (as opposed to the 2014–2015 theatrical season), which featured a plethora of terrific new plays—on Broadway, Off-Broadway, and in regional theaters—so I had many to consider. I chose the plays which I feel were the most significant. And, let's face it, the ones I liked the best.

Danai Gurira's *Eclipsed* also premiered in New York at the Public Theater before moving to Broadway. It's a gut-wrenching drama set during the Liberian civil war, about the female sex slaves of a warlord, which featured Oscar winner Lupita Nyong'o in its ensemble cast. If ever there was a story that needed to be told, this is it.

Jessica Dickey's *The Guard (Black White Ochre Red)* premiered at Ford's Theatre in Washington, D.C., where it won the National Theatre Conference's Barrie and Stavis Award. Jessica Dickey paints shimmering portraits of Rembrandt, Homer, and those who protect the art we cherish. The play opens in a modern-day art museum where three individuals yearn to experience firsthand the wonder and glory of Rembrandt's work. When a museum guard decides to touch a famous Rembrandt painting, a remarkable journey across the ages ensues. Spanning centuries of human experience, *The Guard* movingly explores the power of creative expression and the sacrifices we make in the pursuit of love and beauty.

Fernanda Coppel's *King Liz* premiered at the exemplary Second Stage Uptown (whose Artistic Director, Chris Burney, has contributed the Introduction to this anthology). It's about a tenacious sports agent, who happens to be African American—and a woman. Under pressure from her boss to sign a local high school basketball star who has been drafted by the Knicks, she lands the kid, but everything goes south when he mouths off at a news conference about his past run-ins with the law. The *New York Times* critic, admittedly not very knowledgeable about the world of professional sports, found it "engrossing," as did I and, I hope, as will you.

In John Pollono's *Lost Girls*, which premiered in New York at the Lucilla Lortel Theatre, produced by MCC Theatre, three generations of women confront their present, and their past, during a raging New England snowstorm. This wonderful realistic drama has one of the best "big reveals" at the end of any play of recent memory. It took me by surprise and knocked me for a loop.

Mark Roberts, the author of *New Country*, is that rarity: a TV writer who also writes plays. He's spent several seasons as executive producer of *Two and a Half Men*, three seasons as creative consultant on *The Big Bang Theory*, and created *Mike and Molly*, but has managed to turn out several wonderful comedies as well, of which *New Country* is my favorite. Country music star Justin Spears is rich, famous, and cavalier, with an ego at the top of the charts. It's Justin's bachelor party on the eve of his wedding day, and his ruthless managers, Paul and Chuck, try in vain to keep an unruly entourage under control. Enter Ollie, the star-struck hotel bellboy with a cock-eyed view of fame; Sharon, Justin's vigilante, scorned ex-girlfriend; and dirty old pig-farming Uncle Jim (played by Roberts himself in an hilarious comic turn), who arrives with an inflatable lady. So how does this raucous rodeo go wrong . . . so fast? Booze, bong hits, blackmail, and a blast. With all of this heat on him, will Justin rise to the top or will his career go pop? Welcome to the *New Country*, where the hits just keep on comin'. One of the things I loved about this play was it reminded me of the kinds of plays that used to be great fun at the Humana Festival, before it started to go all artsy-fartsy. I could even envision several of Actors' Theatre's company members in all the roles. Ah, gone are the days. . . .

Last but not least, Melissa Ross's *Nice Girl* is about a thirty-eight-year-old woman named Josephine (Jo) who lives a dead-end life with her mother, a cranky woman who is not easy to get along with. She makes friends with a co-worker named Sherry, who has just found out that she has been dating a married man and who has decided that a "nice girl" like Jo will help her pull her life together. And she reconnects with Donny, a high school classmate, who works as a butcher and whose life has also gone off the tracks. Tentatively, and touchingly, Jo and Donny find each other. The *New York Times* described *Nice Girl* as a "tenderly drawn drama." That it is. And the *New York Daily News* described it as "a gentle, old-fashioned heart-tugger."

It is my hope that you will want to produce these plays. But I also promise you, these are six great reads.

—Lawrence Harbison

THE BEST PLAYS OF 2015

ECLIPSED

by
Danai Gurira

*To the courageous women of Liberia
and of every war zone.*

*To my auntie Dora,
your light will never dim
in our hearts.*

Production History

This version of *Eclipsed* was first performed at Gate Theatre, London, on April 23, 2015, with the following cast:

Cast

MAIMA   Faith Alabi
HELENA   Michelle Asante
BESSIE   Joan Iyiola
RITA   T'Nia Miller
GIRL   Letitia Wright

Creative Team

DIRECTOR   Caroline Byrne
DESIGN   Chiara Stephenson
LIGHTING DESIGN   Mark Howland
SOUND DESIGN   George Dennis
ASSISTANT DIRECTOR   Rebecca Hill
SCENIC ARTIST   Richard Nutbourne
DESIGN ASSISTANT   Isabella Van Braeckel
PRODUCTION MANAGER   Michael Ager
CASTING ASSISTANT   Cameron Slater
DEPUTY STAGE MANAGER   Surenee Chan Somchit

Eclipsed was produced in New York City by the Public Theater, directed by Liesl Tommy, September 29, 2015–November 29, 2015. The cast was as follows: Pascale Armand (Bessie), Akosua Busia (Rita), Zainab Jah (Maima), Lupita Nyong'o (Girl), and Saycon Sengbloh (Helena).

Scenic and costume design by Clint Ramos; lighting design by Jen Schriever; original music and sound design by Broken Chord; hair and wig design by Cookie Jordan; fight direction by Rick Sordelet and Christian Kelly-Sordelet; and voice and dialect coaching by Beth McGuire.

Biography

Danai Gurira is an award-winning Zimbabwean American actor and playwright. As a playwright, her works include *In the Continuum* (OBIE Award, Outer Critics Award, Helen Hayes Award), *Eclipsed* (NAACP Award; Helen Hayes Award, Best New Play), *The Convert* (six Ovation Awards, Los Angeles Outer Critics Award), and *Familiar*, which had its world premiere at Yale Rep in February 2015. All her works explore the subjective African voice. She is the recipient of the Whiting Award, is a former Hodder Fellow, and has been commissioned by Yale Rep, Center Theatre Group, Playwrights Horizons, and the Royal Court. She is currently developing a pilot for HBO. As an actor, she has appeared in the films *The Visitor, Mother of George, 3 Backyards*, and the television show *Treme*, among others. She currently plays Michonne on AMC's *The Walking Dead*. She is the co-founder of Almasi Collaborative Arts, which works to give access and opportunity to the African Dramatic Artist. Danai was born in the US and raised in Zimbabwe by Zimbabwean parents. She holds an MFA from Tisch School of the Arts, NYU.

Characters

THE GIRL, fifteen
HELENA, early twenties/late teens
BESSIE, mid–late teens
MAIMA, mid–late teens
RITA, forties

Setting

Liberia: Bomi County, a LURD rebel army camp, 2003.

> *It's best to work with the system,*
> *and right now—the system is war.*

It's 2003. Civil war is raging in Liberia. At a rebel army base, four young women are doing their best to survive the conditions of the war. Yet sometimes, the greatest threat comes not from the enemy's guns, but from the brutality of those on your own side. With the arrival of a new girl, who can read, and an old one, who can kill, how might this transform the future of this hard-bitten sisterhood?

ACT ONE

Scene One

[*LURD rebel army camp base.* HELENA *and* BESSIE, *"wives" of a commanding officer, sit. It is a dilapidated shelter. It may once have been someone's decent home. It is riddled with bullet holes and black soot and mortar residue. It is a partially indoor enclosure. Piles of used ammunition litter one corner. The enclosure is well organized, however, with obvious areas for cooking, sleeping, and bathing. A tattered Liberian flag hangs on the back wall.* BESSIE *is six and a half months pregnant. Lights up on* HELENA *sitting on a metal tub, styling* BESSIE's *wig. They look offstage.*]

HELENA   [*Getting up.*] Does dat look like the CO to you?

BESSIE   Sorry! I tought I smell him, he has dis smell, I can smell it, can't you smell it? Maybe it just me who know his smell well well. Let's leave ha for few minute.

[HELENA *pushes her over and lets* THE GIRL *out from under the tub.*]

[*To* THE GIRL.]

Sorry.

[*Pulls her wig off, goes and sits down next to tub again.*]

Can you finish—[*Indicating hair.*]—it making my wig not sit right.

HELENA   Come.

[*Starts to finish braiding* BESSIE's *hair.*]

[*To* THE GIRL.]

So den whot happen when he go back?

THE GIRL   Oh, ya, dere dis one joke I no tell you, one time de servant call him, he say, he say, "You sweat from a baboon's balls."

[*Laughing.*]

[HELENA *and* BESSIE *are quiet.*]

HELENA   Whot dat?

THE GIRL   It baboon sweating in de, de man parts—den he calling him dat.

HELENA   Oh . . . ahh . . . ahh ha, ya dat funny, dat funny.

BESSIE   So in de end he stay wit de African wife?

THE GIRL   Wait! He lovin de American gal, so she say no, den he go back to Zamunda in Africa.

HELENA   Where Zamunda—I neva hear of no Zamunda.

THE GIRL   It not real.

HELENA   Oh.

BESSIE   Why he no be from Liberia?

THE GIRL   I don't know. So he come back and dey have a big, big weddin.

BESSIE   Wit de African gal!

THE GIRL   *Wait!* So we all tinking it wit de African gal and she walking wit de big wedding dress.

BESSIE   African wedding dress?

THE GIRL   Ahhh . . . no . . . it woz de white one.

BESSIE   Oh . . . dose ones borin.

THE GIRL   Ya. So he looking sad sad 'cause he tink it gon be de African one—and den, and den she get to de front and it *not*! It de American gal!

BESSIE   So . . . de American gal win.

THE GIRL   *No!* Dat de woman he love.

HELENA   But he could have been wit me or you or ha—but de American tek him. And you say he prince wit lot o' money. He could have been wit poor African gal den she can hep ha family. You say ha fada have restaurant—so she no need dat hep. I no like dat.

THE GIRL   *No!* It movie—it not real, it just a story.

HELENA   I no like dat story. I goin—

[HELENA *jumps and puts tub roughly over* THE GIRL *and sits on it.* BESSIE *resumes her position. Both look up at a man and watch him. They jump into line as though in an army formation.* BESSIE *responds to him, gestures at herself, puts on her wig and walks out, following him—the audience cannot see him.* HELENA *watches them go, and lets* THE GIRL *out from under tub.*]

THE GIRL   How long I stay unda ere like dis?

HELENA   How long? Don't know right now.

THE GIRL   How long you been ere for?

HELENA   Long time. Long, long time. Dey no let me go after de First World War, dey been keeping me for years.

THE GIRL   Since you was how old?

HELENA   Young.

THE GIRL   Ten years, twelve years, fifteen years, whot?

HELENA   Ten—fiftee—ten years.

THE GIRL   And how many years you got now?

[BESSIE *enters, goes and wipes between her legs with a cloth, comes and joins them, pulls off her wig and sits back down for* HELENA *to finish braiding.*]

HELENA   Lots of dem

THE GIRL   Whot? Whot dat mean?

BESSIE   It mean she old! If she knew how many years she had she would have told you a long time ago.

THE GIRL   You no know how many years you got?

HELENA   I neva say dat.

BESSIE   So how many den?

HELENA   Enough to pull your head bald you no shut your mout.

THE GIRL   Do you wanna know? Maybe we can figure it out.

HELENA   No, dat's fine.

THE GIRL   Don't you want to know? I don know, I just tink we should know who we are, whot year we got, where we come from. Dis war not forever.

HELENA   Dat whot it feel like.

THE GIRL   Ya, but it not. I want to keep doing tings. I fifteen years. I know dat. I want to do sometin wit myself, be a doctor or Member of Parliament or sometin.

BESSIE   A whot?

HELENA   So whot has dat got to do wit how many years I got?

THE GIRL   It go hep you to know alla your particulars.

HELENA   Okay—so how you go figure it out?

THE GIRL   Okay. When did dey bring you ere?

Which war woz it?

HELENA   It de first one—I say. Sodatwoz 1990—no? I tink so, I no know.

THE GIRL   I tink it woz. So—

HELENA   No, but it not happen like dat, I was in Nimba county, and Doe men come and dat when I first taken.

THE GIRL   Ya, dat de same time.

HELENA   Oh, okay.

THE GIRL   So how you get to be wit des rebels when you was attacked by Doe men?

HELENA   Dey find me in de bush when I run.

THE GIRL   And you been wit dem since den?

HELENA   Ya.

THE GIRL   No time you get away from dem?

[HELENA *shakes her head.*]

You remember whot your age when dey catch you?

HELENA   I was small small.

THE GIRL   Before you bleed.

HELENA   Ya.

THE GIRL   So, maybe you had twelve, or thirteen years.

HELENA   Ya.

THE GIRL   So den you now maybe—[*Counting on her fingers.*]—twenty-five years.

BESSIE   Whoaw, see, she old.

HELENA   You not so young. How many year she got?

THE GIRL   You no know?

BESSIE   I tink I about nineteen.

THE GIRL   Why?

BESSIE   Because dat when a woman got de juices to have baby and I got baby.

HELENA   She so stupid oh.

THE GIRL   When dey bring you?

BESSIE   I was living in de nort and Taylor men everywhere, den de rebels come and start de fighting—dats when I woz taken. But I tink I been ere since I woz almost a woman.

HELENA   She been ere not too long time.

THE GIRL   You in de nort—I tink dat fighting woz just few years ago.

HELENA   How you know all des ting?

BESSIE   Ha fada woz in de army.

HELENA   Oh . . .

THE GIRL   I just know when de army go where—I hear my fada and moda talking and—

[THE GIRL *goes quiet, looks away, almost in a trance of silence.*]

BESSIE   So how many years I got?

[THE GIRL *doesn't answer, curls up in a corner, and looks away.*]

Hey, whot ha problem oh?

HELENA   Leave ha. She may be tinking on tings dat happen.

BESSIE   Plenty, plenty happen to me, I neva look like dat.

HELENA   *Shut* it, jus go do sometin, go see—he coming.

BESSIE   He no comin, I tek good care of him. I wanted him to sleep so he not go come back again. I mek sure he finish good and thorough. You gon finish my hair?

HELENA   It not easy oh! You got de original African kink! And look at dis comb—it look like it be run ova by truck! You need a new one oh!

BESSIE   When he go back to war I go ask for one—I need new wig too.

HELENA   You do oh. Dat one more nappy dan your head.

BESSIE   No it not. It still mek me look like Janet Jackson oh.

HELENA   You crazy

BESSIE   It does, plenty people tell me dat.

HELENA   Like who?

BESSIE   Like CO

HELENA   CO neva eva say nice ting like dat. He no know how.

BESSIE   He no say nice ting to *you*. He say it to me.

HELENA   Watch your mout oh. You forgetting who Number One. Just because he jumpin on you alo—

BESSIE   Plenty, he jumping on me plenty.

HELENA   Dat no mean he like you betta.

BESSIE   Whot it mean?

HELENA   It mean—

[HELENA *jumps, runs, and puts the bath over* THE GIRL. *The man enters, the women fall in line.* HELENA *points at herself, goes out and glimpsing at* BESSIE *as she does.* BESSIE *paces, looking agitated.* HELENA *enters.*]

Tought you say you put him to sleep.

BESSIE   Whot he wont?

HELENA   None a your concern. Startin tomorrow, cook only half of de cassava and save de rest.

BESSIE   Why? Who comin?

HELENA   People comin. Dat all you need to know.

BESSIE   Whot he tell you?

[*Sucking her teeth.*]

Who comin to eat all our food? We only have small sma—

HELENA   Jus do as I say. Now come I finish your hair.

BESSIE   [*Suddenly in a huff.*] No! I go finish it myself.

HELENA   Dat fine for me! I love to see dat!

[BESSIE *sits, attempting to finish her hair, can't balance mirror, can't see what she is doing, tries to comb it, comb flies out of her hand.*]

BESSIE   Shit, man.

HELENA   You fine?

BESSIE   Leave me.

[THE GIRL *knocks on tin bath.*]

HELENA   Oh!

[*Quickly uncovers her.*]

I sorry. You okay? I tink he gone for de night now, you sleep under dere, but we put some stone dere to keep it up so you can breathe.

THE GIRL   Tanks.

HELENA   We gon figure sometin betta for you in de morning.

[HELENA *prepares a bed for* THE GIRL *and puts her to sleep under tub, prepares for herself, and starts to get under covers.* BESSIE *still struggles with hair.*]

THE GIRL   Tanks

HELENA   You sure you fine?

BESSIE   I FINE!

HELENA   Good. I gon sleep

BESSIE   So sleep.

[HELENA *goes to bed.* BESSIE *keeps trying to comb her hair.* BESSIE *gasps in frustration.* HELENA *chuckles quietly.*]

Scene Two

[BESSIE *now asleep with hands still stuck in hair.* HELENA *is asleep, the tin bath now upturned.* THE GIRL *is gone. Middle of the night,* HELENA *wakes up, looks around for* THE GIRL, *can't find her anywhere.* HELENA *shakes* BESSIE *awake.*]

HELENA   Where de gal?

BESSIE   Hmmm?

HELENA   Wake up or I go trash you! I say where de gal?

BESSIE   I no know, I sleep.

HELENA   Shit, shit, shit, shit.

[THE GIRL *walks in looking dazed.*]

Whot wrong wit you?

[THE GIRL *doesn't respond.*]

Where you go to?

[THE GIRL *doesn't respond.*]

Whot de matta? I say where you go? Whot did I tell you 'bout going by youself. You know whot dey gon do to you, dey find you? Do you know? Eh! Speak oh! Who dis gal tink she is eh? You know whot I do to protec you? You betta treat me wit respec, I wife Number One to Commanding Officer General. Dat mean he trust me de most—I even tell oda men whot to do—if I tell him about you he go—

THE GIRL   He already do it.

HELENA   Whot? Whot you mean? He already do whot?

THE GIRL   [*Numb.*] He already do whot you talking about—he know I ere.

[HELENA *is silent, stunned.* BESSIE *looks on.*]

HELENA   You meet him?

THE GIRL   Ya.

HELENA   He know I keeping you?

THE GIRL   Ya.

HELENA   Where he now?

THE GIRL   He sleep, he told me to come back and go sleep. He catch me when I go to do wet.

HELENA   Whot I tell you about going outta dis compound eh? Whot I tell you. Shit. We gon get it in de morning.

BESSIE   You go get it, I neva say we keep ha from him.

HELENA   Was it jus him? I say was it jus him?

THE GIRL   Ya.

HELENA   You bleed?

THE GIRL   Ya, I wash already.

[HELENA *and* BESSIE *look on at her, shocked, confused.*]

HELENA   You okay?

THE GIRL   Jus let me sleep, I say I fine, whot number I is?

HELENA   Whot number whot?

THE GIRL   Whot number wife? He say dere is a rankin.

HELENA   Ah, ah . . . Number Four, you Number Four.

THE GIRL   Whot number is she?

HELENA   Tree.

THE GIRL   So who number two?

[HELENA *and* BESSIE *look at each other for a moment.*]

HELENA   She no ere right now.

THE GIRL   Hmm . . . you show me tomorrow whot I do around ere.

HELENA   Ya, I show you.

THE GIRL   Can I sleep ere now? I no have to hide under dat now.

[*Indicating tin bath.*]

HELENA   Ya . . . ere.

[*Handing her a blanket.*]

[THE GIRL *takes blanket and lies down, closes eyes.* HELENA *and* BESSIE *watch her in confusion.*]

Scene Three

[*Next day,* BESSIE *is washing soldiers' clothes in a basin and hanging them on the line.* HELENA *walks in with a bucket of water balanced on her head. She takes it down and pours it into basin and joins* BESSIE *in washing clothes.*]

BESSIE   I tink she a witch oh.

HELENA   Are you stupid?

BESSIE   She go come in ere talking, "Hep me oh!" Den she go lay wit de CO, it not even grieve ha! And she askin whot number is she—she act like he not just jump on ha, and she neva know man before! De first time for me I was crying for two days, he not dere I crying, he come to get me, I cryin, he doin it, I crying, he stop, I crying, I go sleep, I crying, I was vex. She act like she got no problems. Like notin bad jus happen.

HELENA   Coz she not like you dat's all.

BESSIE   No, she got sometin off. Maybe she goin off an she not showing it. I go watch ha close close. Whot you tell CO?

HELENA   I say she woz hiding wit de small soldier.

BESSIE   He believe?

HELENA   He no mind, he got ha now.

[BESSIE *stops suddenly and gasps as the baby moves.* HELENA *watches her.*]

You alright?

BESSIE   No, I no alright, I no want it. I gonna hate it.

HELENA   No you not. It gon be nice to have a small one ere.

BESSIE   Are you crazy? It meking me fat oh! You can have it den . . . why you neva have one, Number One? You been ere for long time. You neva get baby? You can't born?

HELENA   [*She scrubs clothes harder.*] Go check on dat gal, I go finish dis.

BESSIE   Why I go check on ha all de time? She *fine.* I tol you she woz go be fine, you worry bout ha too much—when I first come you no—

HELENA   Jus DO AS I SAY!

BESSIE   [*She stops.*] You too harsh, man. Fine, I go.

[THE GIRL *walks in with firewood, humming a mellow tune to herself.* BESSIE *and* HELENA *look on.* BESSIE *looks over at* HELENA *for a long moment, goes back to scrubbing clothes.*]

[*To* THE GIRL.]

You alright?

THE GIRL   Ya.

BESSIE   You fine?

THE GIRL   Ya.

BESSIE   You sure?

THE GIRL   Ya?

HELENA   Shut it, Number Tree.

BESSIE   I checking. Like you tol me.

HELENA   [*Sucks her tongue loudly at* BESSIE.] You know how to make fire?

[THE GIRL *nods.*]

Good, do dat ova dere.

[*She points at fire pit.* THE GIRL *goes to build fire.* HELENA *goes with her, watches her closely.*]

Is you sure you fine? It betta den whot happen to some of de gals out dere, all de soldier get to have dem. Wit us, it just de CO. I know it no feel good right now, but it gon get betta—you gon get use to it—you alright?

THE GIRL   I fine.

[THE GIRL *succeeds in lighting fire.*]

Scene Four

[*A week later.* THE GIRL *and* BESSIE *are eating.*]

[HELENA *comes in and throws a plate of food away and starts to make a different meal.*]

BESSIE   Whot? He no want dat?

[*Rushing to retrieve the plate.*]

HELENA   He acting like he got a spirit or sometin.

BESSIE   He vex? Whot he saying?

HELENA   He saying de food it taste funny and he tink someone or some spirit trying to kill him. He put a curse on hisself. How God gonna bless a man when he killing moda an chile and stealin and chopping. Den he wonda why he scared of spirits. He want me to make more food and to put dis in it.

[*She holds up small pouch.*]

He really scare coz o de people comin.

THE GIRL   Whot's dat?

BESSIE   It from de medicine man. It go make so dat no bullet can touch him.

[*To* HELENA.]

Whot people?

THE GIRL   How it go do dat?

BESSIE   Dat whot medicine can do—don't you know? You no see de rebels dey got de marks on dere arms where dey put de special juju. Dat whot hep dem not get killed when dey fight.

[*To* HELENA.]

Whot people comin?

HELENA   [*Briskly preparing the meal.*] He gettin more and more mad oh. He actin like bigga devil. And he teking juju den he keep saying stupid ting like, "Oh, de monkey Charles Taylor, he got to die, I gon get him." He don know who Charles Taylor is, whot he done, or whot he gon do when he gone. Just talking a lot o' notin. But I know why he like dis—he scare cos de women comin—dey gon mek him face hisself.

[HELENA *takes food out.*]

BESSIE *Whot?!* Whot you mean? Whot she mean? *Whot women coming?!* Sometin off oh. He tekin his juju and she mekin me cook half de cassava. Sometin off. She no gon tell me dough. I gon watch dem close close. Tink dey can jus be hiding ting from me. I been ere *long* time! I can know all de same ting she know . . . see whot happen I no doin all de ting I do ere, whot dis place gon be like, I—

[HELENA *comes back with several different items in her hands: dresses, shoes, scarves, a radio, a book.*]

[*Dancing with glee.*]

Ohhhh, dat whot I like to see, Number One, dat whot I like. I need some new tings, it been too long. Any high heels, some nice wig or sometin, dis one is finished oh!

HELENA I gon get de rest. Number Four come hep me. DON'T TOUCH! Keep on doing whot you doin, notin happening ere.

[HELENA *and* THE GIRL *exit.*]

BESSIE [*Calling after* HELENA.] Don't be sour oh, I ready for some new tings, just tell me whot I can have and not have. Now dat Number Two gone, I can go second, right? Right?

MAIMA You sound happy I gon, Number Tree, it alright dough, I know you miss me much much.

[MAIMA *enters from the other side of the compound, sharply dressed in tight jeans, a slinky top and a bandana, her AK-47 rifle slung snugly over her shoulder. She carries a sack of rice.*]

BESSIE Whot you doin ere?

MAIMA Where I supposed to be?

BESSIE Somewhere doing some stupid ting.

MAIMA I a soldier and dis an army camp, so where else am I supposed to be?

BESSIE You no solider.

MAIMA Whot?

BESSIE I say you no soldier, you a wife like us.

MAIMA I woz a wife like you. Den I wake up. Ere, I bring special gift.

[*Drags in a bag of rice.*]

BESSIE Is dat *rice*! Oh! Dat so good oh we no have rice in long time oh!

[*Catching herself.*]

But if you want me to tank you, it not happenin—I know where you get it.

MAIMA   You no worry bout dat, just cook it for us.

BESSIE   You no know how to cook now?

MAIMA   I no cook, dat de job you do. I know you missin me while I out dere, fighting for freedom, so I tought I go pay you visit, let you know I okay, we can have some good food togeda.

HELENA *enters with a few more looted items; she sees* MAIMA *and is visibly unnerved by* MAIMA's *presence.*]

HELENA   Whot . . . whot you . . . whot you wont ere?

MAIMA   Ain't you glad to see me? Stop pretending you no glad to see I alive.

HELENA   I not pretending. Whot I want to know is whot you wont.

MAIMA   See, look how we be treating one anoda! I coming, bringing gifts from war and—

HELENA   [*Getting composed again, but still not able to look at* MAIMA.] We no need no gifts.

MAIMA   You talking like you got a spirit oh! I bringing rice. RICE! When woz de last time you see some rice eh?

HELENA   Keep it, we got plenty cassava.

BESSIE   But—

MAIMA   Okay, I tek it to Commando Trigger's wives. I wonted you to have it first—but—

BESSIE   [*Rushing over to* HELENA's *side.*] Can't we just tek it—she not bad no more, she trying to do good, maybe dis gift from *God.* . . . *Please*, Number One, I so sick o' cassava—I so *sick* of it—*please*, just let ha leave it.

HELENA   [*Ignoring* BESSIE, *to* MAIMA.] You still ere?

MAIMA   Okay, I taking it, you wont to act like you loving on God so much, you neva hear of *forgiveness*? Dat when you forget de past and give people new chance. You can't do dat ha?

[*She starts to lug rice out. She glimpses over at* THE GIRL, *who is looking at her intently.*]

Who dis?

HELENA   No one.

MAIMA   Dis de new wife eh? You Number Four? I Number Two. Where you from?

BESSIE   How you kn—

MAIMA   I know evertin that happens around ere, you don know dat by now? Where you from, little gal?

THE GIRL   Kakata.

MAIMA   You likin it ere? Number One treatin you nice nice? She good at dat—in de beginning.

BESSIE   We treatin ha betta dan you would, you have beat ha and shave ha head by now.

MAIMA   Stop talking stupid oh, why don't you beat dis rice like a propa little Commander wife.

HELENA   Don't do notin, Number Tree. Number Two, you ca—

MAIMA   Disgruntled. I have a nem of war now and it Disgruntled.

HELENA   I no care bout whot you call yourself—just go. Go!

MAIMA   Oh, so it still like dat eh? You gon kick me out like dog oh? Okay . . . okay . . . dat fine, I leave de new family be . . . for now . . . but I go come back.

[*To* THE GIRL.]

Little gal, you let me know you need sometin okay? Number One de Great ain't de only one got tings to teach. Dey go tell you, I can do *anything*.

[MAIMA *leaves.*]

HELENA   [*Sucks her teeth ferociously as she makes sure* MAIMA *is gone.*] Tink we gon trow a party for ha or what.

THE GIRL   She got gun.

HELENA   [*Sharply.*] So?

THE GIRL   [*Cautiously.*] Whot she do?

BESSIE   Mmmm, she bad oh.

[*Very quickly, almost manically.*]

When I first come, me and ha we use to be good, good friends, she good wit hair oh, and she used to mek my hair nice, nice—dat woz de nicest my hair eva—

[*She glimpses at* HELENA.]

ah . . . ah . . . den she no like dat she not de one CO trust de most—because he be trusting on Number One because dey been togeda long long—den she start to get not nice—she like to fight too often oh, she no like dat he liking me and calling me first when he come from war—den a *new* gal come—dat when it get ugly oh—

HELENA   Number Tree.

BESSIE   —dis new gal woz cute oh. Even I getting jealous small small. And she have dis long hair, I no know how ha hair it growing like dat when she black like me oh! Maybe she a witch—dat whot I tinking now.

HELENA   Number Tree.

BESSIE   Den, I say oh, she go get CO all de time and all de tings he giving me gon go to dis little ting. But Number Two get too jealous oh. Den one day de CO come back from fighting and he got plenty tings. Den he call Number Four. Dat even vex me oh! Number One she no mind. She no mind noting. Den—

HELENA   *Number Tree*—shut it oh!

BESSIE   She ask—she ask whot happen.

HELENA   You telling ha plenty oda tings dan whot happen.

BESSIE   Okay—I go say it quick—I go say it quick. Okay, so den—where I woz? Oh, so den—

[*Suddenly remembers and laments.*]

Oh de rice, Number One, de rice! Okay, sorry, sorry—so den Number Two see Number Four come back wit alla des tings and she get new skirt, she get new dress, she get des sandals, plenty, plenty tings. Den Number Two vex oh—so she wait till we all sleeping den she jump on Number Four—and remember I say Number Four little oh! So Number Two she beat ha and tek ha tings she give ha sabou! All dat nice hair she got—*gone*—she beat ha face hard oh—in de morning ha face all swollen she looking bad—den when CO call for ha—she scared to tell him it Number Two—'cause den Number Two go really finish ha propa, so den she say it a soldier but she no know who 'cause it dark—den CO tink she loving on anoda soldier, so he kick ha out of dis compound. He no like to see his women loving on oda men. So den she go to anoda compound and in de next compound de women are not for one man in particular—dey fo everyone—so now she in bad way oh, all de soldier be having having ha. Den Number One real vex and Number Two and ha dey be treating each oda bad—so den Number Two, she go get into de army to fight—and me I no know how she do dat or *whot* bad ting she doing to people out dere and—

HELENA   You finish?

BESSIE   Ya I finish oh—she ask.

THE GIRL   She a woman in de army?

HELENA   She devil, dat all . . . devil. You stay away from ha oh. Okay?

THE GIRL   Okay.

[HELENA *sorts all the looted items out and carefully examines each one, folding the clothes with precision after carefully looking them over. Every now and then* HELENA *looks over her shoulder abruptly and* BESSIE *backs up.*]

BESSIE   You find a good wig?

HELENA   Get back, I say I go sort tru it.

[*She picks up a book.*]

Don't know whot he want me to do with dis, it a joke or sometin?

BESSIE   [*Taking it.*] I don't know. It a big ting oh, ere, let me tek it, it go keep de fire burning long time.

[THE GIRL *jumps up and grabs at it as* BESSIE *is about to chuck it.*]

THE GIRL   I want it! If dat okay.

[BESSIE *and* HELENA *look at her long and hard.*]

HELENA   You know how to use it?

THE GIRL   Small small.

BESSIE   Where you learn to use it?

HELENA   Your ma and pa send you to school?

THE GIRL   Ya . . . my ma . . . she mek sure I get book learning.

HELENA   When?

THE GIRL   I start five years ago.

HELENA   So you can read and write and do all dem book ting?

THE GIRL   Ya . . .

BESSIE   Where you go to school? Where you find school in Liberia? She lying, she crazy oh!

HELENA   Shut up ya mout. Dere still are some school left, and she come from near Monrovia, de fighting only been dere small, small time. It about sometin?

THE GIRL   [*Examining the book.*] Ya . . .

HELENA   Whot it about? Book tings or interesting tings?

THE GIRL   I have to look, de front is tore off . . . it about a man.

HELENA   Whot man?

THE GIRL   [*Reading.*] Bill Clint—o

BESSIE   Bill Clinto

HELENA   A white man?

THE GIRL   [*Reading more inside.*] Ya, he white. He from America.

BESSIE   You sho he white? Dere lots of Liberians in America. Maybe he American from Liberia or Liberian from America.

THE GIRL   No, I tink he American from America.

BESSIE   So all dat big ting it just about dat one man?

THE GIRL   I have to read it first.

BESSIE   How you gon read all dat ting. It go tek up all your eyesight, mek you blind.

HELENA   You stupid. You no go blind from too much book.

BESSIE   How you know? You no read.

HELENA   You no read either!

BESSIE   Number Four, you tell us, can you go blind from book?

THE GIRL   I not sure, but I neva heard of dat.

BESSIE   Dat don't mean it not happen.

[*Sucking tongue loudly and goes to her corner.*]

Can I have my clothes, please!

HELENA   Hold on. Are dose pictures?

THE GIRL   Ya, dere lots o dem.

HELENA   Let's see.

[THE GIRL *opens the book and they proceed to look at pictures in the center of it.*] Ya, he white man. He most sure white man. Dis look like it he wife. I wonder if he need anoda.

BESSIE   You want white man now?

HELENA   I no want *no* man but how I go survive I don't have one? If I have one I rather have Clinto and not de one I be having now.

BESSIE   How you know he a good husband?

HELENA   You can tell, he good, he go get his wife nice new ting—see how she dressed? Not old ting he steal from civilian. And he gon go places wit her and hold ha hand. He dances wit ha. Dat a good husband.

BESSIE   You want de CO to dance wit you and hold ya hand?

HELENA   [*Sucks her tongue loudly, ignoring her.*] Read some of it to us, Number Four. I want to hear about Clinto.

THE GIRL   [*Reading.*] Oh, look, he come to Africa, dis him in Uganda.

HELENA   Oh, he holding African beby.

THE GIRL   He is, it say de beby name Bill Clinto—dey nem it afta him.

HELENA   Eh, Number Tree—you nem you beby afta Clinto, maybe he go come rescue you.

BESSIE   [*Sucking her tongue.*] He see me he gon forget dat white wife. She betta not let him come ere.

HELENA   Read some.

THE GIRL   [*Reading.*] Okay, "Bill Clinto—in de White Hos. Presid—ah dat word too hard. Presi-dental work in de—"

HELENA   Oh, it sounding boring oh.

THE GIRL   Wait—it gon get good, just give me a few min—

[*She stops abruptly. They jump into formation.* THE GIRL *is called by CO offstage. She slowly and carefully puts the book in a corner and goes out.* HELENA *goes back to sorting out clothes. She silently puts a couple things aside for* THE GIRL *next to her book and gestures for* BESSIE *to look at the rest.*]

BESSIE   Wait, wait, wait minute. How you go give ha stuff first before me? I have bigger rankin dan ha! How she gon get when I no look yet? I taking whot I want from dere—

[BESSIE *starts to go towards* THE GIRL's *stuff.* HELENA *blocks her.*]

HELENA   Eh, eh, eh, don't you dare. Dat *my* stuff dat I *giving* to ha. So you *is* going second. Tek whot you want. But don't you let me find you taking no ting from Number Four.

[BESSIE *backs up, sucking her tongue. She is thoroughly annoyed, goes over to pile and takes all of the items into her corner.*]

BESSIE   Dis ting was like it was made for me, man!

[*Putting on an African-print top and matching skirt.*]

I look like de First Lady.

HELENA   [*Barely looking up.*] Hmmhmm.

[THE GIRL *comes back in, walking strangely. She crosses, takes water from nearby bucket, grabs cloth, goes to remote corner, and cleans under her skirt.*]

BESSIE   He quick wit you, he be taking too long with me des days.

HELENA   Shut yo mout.

BESSIE   Whot? Dat mean he be liking ha more—or she doing sometin dat mek him feel too good. Whot you do, Number Four? I want him to go quick quick wit me too.

HELENA   LEAVE HA!

BESSIE   I no know *whot* your problem is wit dis little gal. She notin special. She your chile or sometin? We all do it, she used to it now. See, look at ha.

[THE GIRL *is in her corner, reading her book intently.*]

She fine.

Scene Five

[*Two evenings later. Newly looted radio playing.* BESSIE *dancing to a track.*]

RADIO   Dat woz Awilo de jam number one across West Africa! Miss Economic Community of West African States, Miss Ecowas, happening dis Saturday in Accra, Ghana, where we get to love on our West African beauties. *Don't miss it!* Youssou N'Dour and Seun Kuti will be entertaining us all night long!

[*Signal starts to fade out.*]

BESSIE   Oh, shit, man.

[*She frantically turns the dial.*]

Oh, don't stop talking, DJ Jay D! Number One, come hep me get signal, it stop workin—it—

[BESSIE *stops abruptly, sees* MAIMA *watching her in a corner.* MAIMA *is highly amused, with her AK-47 rifle slung around her back.*]

MAIMA   Don stop for me, Number Tree, you having disco all for yourself oh!

BESSIE   Whot you doing ere now?

MAIMA   Can't I visit my sistas wit no reason?

BESSIE   [*Agitated.*] Whot you wont?

MAIMA   Eh, eh! You wont to be harsh like dat oh! Fine, ere, I bring special gift for de new gal.

[*Holds up a pretty cotton dress.*]

She look like she still wearing tings she run tru de bush in.

BESSIE   [*Suspiciously.*] What you want eh? You tryin to do some stupid ting, I know you oh. Leave ha, she don need no dirty dress.

MAIMA   I tryin to tek good care of odas. Dat whot I know to do. Even if you ones don't. You de ones letting ha walk around like she livin wit lizards in de rocks.

BESSIE   You don know how to do notin nice for no one. You betta go before Number One come back.

MAIMA   Oh, ya, where is Number One de great?

BESSIE   She getting wata, she no gon wanna see you.

MAIMA   I no care whot she wont, I my own boss now, I no trying to mek ha happy.

BESSIE   Just go oh, go fight to mek free Liberia or whateva you doin.

MAIMA   Eh, eh, eh, don't talk what too deep for that nice empty head of yours oh. I is fighting for a free Liberia. If you can carry one tought in dere, carry dat.

BESSIE   *Leave me oh!*

MAIMA   Eh, why so vex? Fine, here de dress, you mek sure you give ha. If I see it on you, I gon have to tek it back.

[**MAIMA** *exits.* **BESSIE** *impatiently watches her leave, grabs dress, looks it over, holds it to her body, and places it against herself. She then puts it in her corner and attempts to look occupied just as* **HELENA** *and* **THE GIRL** *enter.* **THE GIRL** *has a bucket of water balanced on her head.* **HELENA** *walks in behind her.*]

HELENA   Whot your problem oh?

BESSIE   *No!* No problem! No problem!

HELENA   [*Staring at her suspiciously.*] We bring wata, Number Tree heat cassava. Number Four, read Clinto.

THE GIRL   Okay . . .

[*Excitedly retrieving the book from her corner.*]

So where we woz? Oh . . . Clinto woz at odds wit de entire government, wit de senate and de house—now both wit Repub-li-can maj-o-ity and seek-ing his blood if possible.

BESSIE   Ahh! Dey gon kill him?

HELENA   *No!* Dey can't kill de big man o' America!

BESSIE   Dey kill Doe.

HELENA   Dat in Liberia oh! Dat no happen in America!

Bessie   Dey kill Doe.

Helena   Dat in Liberia oh! Dat no happen in America!

Bessie   Liberia and America de same oh! Liberia started by America! My great-great-grand mo—

The Girl   I no tink dey talking bout killin killin. I tink dey talking bout stressing him.

Helena/Bessie   Ooooh.

The Girl   President Clinto woz still ad-ada-adamant-ly denying his affair with Monica Lewi-sky, a-nd Congress when—

Helena   Wait, wait, wait oh. Who is Congress and why he want to catch him and whot is affair wit Monica Lew-is-sky?

The Girl   I tink Congress, it like government, like ministers, but dey no have to answer to him.

Helena   Oh, okay—so dey can say whot happen to de big man o' de country?

The Girl   I tink dey vote and den dey can say yes or no to de big man. But dere anoda one—de, where dey now . . .

[*Leafing through book.*]

de Judis-a ry, dey like oda ministers.

Helena   Why dey need so many?

The Girl   I don know. Maybe it to mek sure many people can have say.

Bessie   So who Monica now?

Helena   She Number Two, no?

The Girl   I tink so—but he not supposed to have a Number Two.

Bessie   Oh, that like my pa—he only have my ma, but den dis witch come and mek him look at ha den—

Helena   Number Four—can you keep reading.

Bessie   Oh, wait—why dey want to stress de big man?

Helena   Oh ya?

The Girl   Dey no like him—dey from anoda group—like he LURD like us and dey wit Charles Taylor men.

Bessie   Ooooh.

Helena   Ahh . . . okay.

THE GIRL   [*Reading.*] It seemed de con-se-kence in mind woz to remove him from his pre-si-den-tal role—

HELENA   Wait—

BESSIE   To whot?

THE GIRL   Dey want to mek him no be big man no more.

HELENA   Why? Because he have a Number Two?

THE GIRL   Ya, den he lie.

BESSIE   Why dat gon mek him not be big man no more?

THE GIRL   I don know.

HELENA   Imagine we have dat ere—dere be no one to rule de country oh!

BESSIE   I tell you, if Clinto see me, he gon want me oh.

THE GIRL   My pa only love on my ma.

HELENA   How you know?

THE GIRL   I *know*. He good husband. He tell me only be wit man who loving on me.

HELENA   He no know dis war comin when he tell you dat.

BESSIE   Keep reading. I wan de part when he come to Africa.

THE GIRL   [*Suddenly agitated.*] No, I tired now.

HELENA   Tek dis to dem.

[*Hands her freshly cooked fufu.* THE GIRL *exits.*]

BESSIE   She get sour quick oh!

HELENA   She missing family dat all.

[THE GIRL *returns.*]

THE GIRL   He say he wan to see you.

[HELENA *exits.*]

BESSIE   You miss your pa and your ma?

THE GIRL   Ya . . .

[*Tears brimming.*]

I wan my ma.

BESSIE   I tink mine dead. But I tink I go find my broda when it ova.

[HELENA *re-enters, with a few new loot items.*]

NO! He get more? When dey go fight?

HELENA   Dey been gone two days.

BESSIE   Oh. I no realize. Whot he bring?

HELENA   Tek, I don want anyting.

BESSIE   *Tank you!*

[*She grabs things from* HELENA, *sorts through them ravenously.*]

Oh, dis is *nice!* Oh, I no like dat, whot is *dis!* He crazy oh, he tink we grandmodas, ere, Number Four.

[THE GIRL *takes pile. A packet of hair extensions fall to the floor.*]

Oh, I wont dat! I no see dat!

HELENA   Eyy, you let ha have it, so now it hers.

BESSIE   She no want dat anyway!

THE GIRL   I wouldn't mind—

HELENA   Ah, den it hers, Number Tree, you already have your hair done anyway.

BESSIE   *No!* I need it—I higher rankin dan ha!

HELENA   Ya and you give it to ha, so now it ha's.

BESSIE   I no agree.

HELENA   So whot? I Number One and I say—

BESSIE   If she de big man of dis compound den whot are we?

THE GIRL   Whot are we whot?

BESSIE   We de ministers, no?

THE GIRL   Oh, we de Sen-ate and de Judiciary.

BESSIE   So I as de Sen-ate say no to de big man.

THE GIRL   Okay, den I as de Judiciary I say yes.

HELENA   So whot I say go—de extensions are for Number Four.

BESSIE   Shit, man.

[*Goes to her corner, scowling at* THE GIRL *and* HELENA.]

HELENA   Come, I braid it for you, Number Four.

THE GIRL   Oh . . . okay

[THE GIRL *goes to sit down. When called by* CO, *points at herself and goes.* BESSIE *sulks in corner.* HELENA *leans back and closes her eyes.* BESSIE *starts to inch toward* HELENA, *watching her as she does. She gets close to extensions and attempts to take them.*]

HELENA   Don't even.

[BESSIE *retreats, deflated.*]

BESSIE   It no fair, I *need* those, I having baby and I gon get bigger and ugly, I need my hair to look nice at *least.*

HELENA   You not gon get ugly.

BESSIE   Yes I is, you know how des women look when dey have beby, dey face go big like it got air and dey eyes go small like bird and dey lips go wide like dis and dey look *bad.* I want to use de hair to cova my face small, small.

HELENA   You gon be fine. De CO not gonna jump on you so much.

BESSIE   I know, dat de one ting. He gon be on Number Four *plenty*, coz he no jump on you no more and—ah . . . ah . . . whot I say? I no mean to say like dat whot I—

HELENA   Just go sleep.

BESSIE   Okay.

[*She goes and lies on her mat.*]

You tink Clinto's Number One angry wit him?

HELENA   Ya.

BESSIE   You tink dey all living togeda nice nice now—like us?

HELENA   I no know—I no tink dey do it like us. I tink de women can leave.

BESSIE   Number Two leave. . . .

HELENA   She no leave, she just fightin wit dem now. Dat not de leaving I mean.

BESSIE   Ya. Dat true.

HELENA   Number Tree?

BESSIE   Ya?

HELENA   You been savin de cassava like I tell you?

BESSIE   YA! Tell me whot happening. What you keeping keeping de cassava for?

HELENA   I gon cook it all in de morning.

BESSIE   WHO COMIN?

HELENA   Neva matta. No one you gon find interstin. Number Tree?

BESSIE   Ya?

HELENA   Sleep.

BESSIE   Fine.

[THE GIRL *enters, goes and wipes between her legs, and curls up on the mat.* HELENA *blows out torch.*]

Scene Six

[*Next day. At camp, by the compound,* RITA, *a member of Liberian Women's Initiative, an upper-class, well-educated woman; throughout she occasionally speaks "Liberian English" like the women in the camp, but her proper English often takes over. She is relatively new to the struggle for peace and functions awkwardly in this rough terrain. She approaches* HELENA, *who is pounding cassava with a mortar and pestle.*]

RITA   How tings?

HELENA   [*Surprised.*] How tings? How you come follow me out ere? I got to finish dis.

[*Indicates cassava.*]

You need sometin?

RITA   No, ah . . . I just . . . I . . . I wanted to see how things going out here.

HELENA   Whot?

RITA   And to tank you for de cooking, it was very good, so tank you.

HELENA   You off oh?

RITA   Whot you mean?

HELENA   How you go tank me for cookin? Dat whot I do, dat whot we do ere, how you tank for dat, you off oh.

RITA   That not all you can do—dere much more you could do—no one should expect that from you.

[*Beat.*]

I know I am not really meant to be out here.

[*Looks around cautiously.*]

My colleagues like to follow some rigid protocol when we meet with the COs. But I believe we should take every opportunity to meet you gals. Allow me to introduce myself—I am—

HELENA   [*Loudly.*] I know who you is.

RITA   You do—

HELENA   Ya, he tell me you was coming.

Rita   He did?

Helena   Ya, he say I got to cook good food 'cause de peace women be coming for talks. He always wont us cook best tings for peace women, even when we no have notin.

Rita   I apologize for that, we don't want special treatment—we—

Helena   Eh?

Rita   [*Realizing how she just spoke.*] I say I sorry, we just trying to mek it betta for Liberia.

Helena   [*Coldly.*] Ya, okay.

[*Other side of stage, in the forest,* The Girl *and* Maima *converse.* Maima *holds her rifle in hand.* The Girl *collects firewood.*]

Maima   So you city girl eh?

The Girl   [*Nervously.*] Yah.

Maima   I know Kakata well well. I get supplies from dere all de time. You run for long time?

The Girl   [*Cautiously.*] Some . . . some days.

Maima   Ya, dat hard eh. But you look strong oh. Like you got alota powa!

The Girl   Powa?

Maima   Ya. I can see your eyes, dey got fire! And your arms and legs—dey strong oh.

The Girl   [*Giggling, embarrassed.*] No!

Maima   Yes! You got to tap dat powa oh. You tink God give all dat to you for notin? You tink God let you survive for notin? You got to do de tings you called to do oh. Is dis it? Picking firewood in de bush? Dis whot your powa for?

The Girl   I . . . I don know.

[*Giggles again.*]

Maima   Whot? Whot so funny oh?

The Girl   It just . . . it just . . . Number One say you devil, but you talking like you prophet.

Maima   Number One say dat eh?

The Girl   Hmmhmm!

[*She continues to giggle.* Maima *laughs too, though in a different tone.*]

Maima   Ya . . . ya dat funny oh. Compound, Helena and Rita

HELENA   You betta go.

[*Beat.*]

How you come here?

RITA   Whot?

HELENA   How it okay for you to come here? Why he let you in, treat you good, give you our cassava, not mek you a wife like us?

RITA   Well, we are a part of a large network of women peace-makers, it is our mission to end dis war. Right now we are negotiating with the factions to immediately obey the ceasefire, to put down their guns. The only way to do that is to come to these different warlords and talk them down.

[*Beat.*]

We have been doing this for a long time, we have quite a reputation in de country now, it allows us to come and go like how you see.

HELENA   Why he so scare of you?

RITA   He isn't scared of us.

HELENA   He is! He told no one do notin to de peace women when dey come, he no treat no one else like dat. And he been using his juju a lot just now. Dat how I know he scare de most, when he using dat stuff. It mek his spirit go quiet. So ya, he scare of you.

RITA   Well good. *Good.* They scare of us, maybe we can actually get them to the point where things change and they stop acting like *beasts*, trying to treat us like we village girls they rob from de bush.

HELENA   [*Coldly.*] Is dat right.

[*An awkward pause ensues for a few beats.*]

Why you do all dat stuff?

RITA   Why? Why you tink? You happy with Liberia as it going? You tink dis a nice place? Look at de tings going on, my dear! Look at where *you* are! You tink it normal you wifing some dirty self-proclaimed general in de bush? You tink it normal a boy carrying a gun killing and raping? You think it okay dere no more schools, no more *notin*! I had to *walk* my son from Kakata to the Ivory Coast just so he could stay in school!

HELENA   Okay, you don have to get vex.

RITA   Sorry . . . I . . .

[*A few beats pass.* HELENA *stores ground cassavas.* RITA *starts to look around curiously.*]

So . . . do ah . . . any other gals comin around lately?

HELENA   [*Suspiciously.*] Why you asking me dat?

RITA   If I . . . if I could get you out of ere—would you go—would you go with me?

HELENA   Go where?

RITA   You can go to school, you can—

HELENA   Where I gon go to school?

RITA   I can get you in a camp in Cote D'Ivoire or—

HELENA   Where dat?

RITA   Ivory Coast

HELENA   Oh. So why you calling it sometin else?

RITA   No mind. Why would you not go?

HELENA   I don know.

RITA   Would it be a hard choice? If I could get him to agree, would it be so hard to leave this?

HELENA   No . . . but . . .

RITA   You happy ere?

HELENA   No, but dis is war and I whot else I gon do?

RITA   You know all the things you can do if you go to school, the ways you can improve your life! You can get your own business, own your own house, take care of your children—

HELENA   I no have children.

RITA   But you might have them! You can do betta for yourself! Things could be over soon, you have to think about whot your life can be beyond this bondage you are stuck in now.

HELENA   I no know, I wife Number One. I been wit him for long, long time. I tek care o' him, I—

RITA   The war ends—are you still wife Number One?

HELENA   I . . . I no know who I is out of war—dat not whot I get to tink about.

RITA   I am going to hep you—it is going to end.

HELENA   I got tings to do ere, tings no gon happen propa I go. I tek care o' CO, I know de oda soldier. I have rank ere now. I can tell de juniors and de small small boys whot to do. I care for de oda women, make sure tings run smooth for dem. And dere lots o tings we doin ere now—we even reading book in de compound.

RITA   Whot book?

HELENA   It about de big man of America, Clinto.

RITA   Clinton?

HELENA   Ya. And his government. And Monica his Number Two and how de Judiciary and Senate and Starr trying to stress him.

[RITA *laughs.*]

We no know if he stop being big man because of his Number Two or not—we no get dat far yet. You know whot happen? If you know don't tell me notin.

RITA   I no gon tell you. But you know that happen long time ago oh. Five years or so.

HELENA   We no mind, it still good story, don tell me whot happen.

[*Beat.*]

But, you know, when I look at you, you know all dese book tings—I do wan to learn—I neva go to school—I do want dat. It just . . . I just don know if I can learn now—I getting old to be sometin different.

[THE GIRL *and* MAIMA *enter.*]

MAIMA   So dis stupid little gal go lovin on some oda soldier who beat ha—den she gon tell Number One it woz me and dat it my fault she get thrown out—dat when I have to go. Dey crazy oh.

THE GIRL   Whot about de sabou?

MAIMA   Oh . . . so dey tell you dis already eh? You trust who you want. Like Tupac say, "Only God can judge me." Dey no gon tell you how dey getting all dose tings de CO bring from war eh? Dey no gon tell you how he getting dem. He giving worse den a sabou, but they actin like dey clean o' all sin or sometin.

THE GIRL   So where you get dis den?

[*Tugging on jeans.*]

MAIMA   Kakata

THE GIRL   And dis.

[*Indicating earrings.*]

MAIMA   Dis . . . dis from de big city.

THE GIRL   You get tings from de big city!

MAIMA   Ya . . .

[*Laughs.*]

plenty tings. Didn't you like de dress?

THE GIRL   Whot dress?

MAIMA   What? Dat *stupid* gal. I go fuck ha up good.

[*She sucks her teeth.*]

I brin you dress. So you can look betta dan dis. So you can look good like me. Don worry, let ha have it. Whot you wont? Tell me whot you like.

THE GIRL   Nail varnish.

MAIMA   Ah, which color—you look like you like de red one, or de purple.

THE GIRL   Pink.

MAIMA   [*Laughing.*] Okay. Dat good! You have to decide whot you wont. Dis is war, how you gon survive? Dis is how.

[*Indicating gun.*]

Den you can prospa. You can get every color of de rainbow nail varnish, it no matter whot happening. And most important no man gon touch you.

[*Examines her closely.*]

So de CO he like you ha? He jump on you a lot? You like dat? Look at me. Is dat whot you want? Hmmmhmm? Did you like dat?

THE GIRL   No.

MAIMA   [*Militarily.*] Whot?

THE GIRL   NO.

MAIMA   So whot you gon do? Let me tell you de last time a man jump on me. In fact, I can't remember, all I know is he not know I have gun. He dead now. No one gon jump me again. Now, I chose who I lovin on. Because of dis. Whotever you wan, it's yours. Just go get gun.

RITA   [*Showing* HELENA *how to write her name in the dirt.*] Then the letter "A"—like dis—there—you do it—that's your name!

THE GIRL   I can't . . . I . . .

HELENA   I don't believe oh! I do it? It no lie?

RITA   It no lie.

MAIMA   It easy right now—dey need soldier—dey so desperate for fighter now, dey tek baboon if dey could teach it who to fire. Ere . . .

[*Hands her gun.*]

try it—hold it.

HELENA   It not dat hard!

THE GIRL   I don—

RITA   No, it not!

MAIMA   TRY.

HELENA   I can't believe oh!

THE GIRL   [*Takes gun.*] It heavy oh.

HELENA   It no lie?

MAIMA   Now hold it like dis and you point it forward—now fire.

THE GIRL   No, I scare.

HELENA   I gon tell de new gal—

MAIMA   Scare of whot?

RITA   Whot?

MAIMA   Fire.

RITA   *Whot* new gal?

[*A shot rings through the air.* HELENA *and* RITA *jump up.*]

Scene Seven

[*At camp. Next day.* HELENA *is cooking and intermittently changing the channels on the temperamental radio.* THE GIRL *is painting her nails.* BESSIE *is leaning against a crate, eyes shut, breathing hard.*]

BESSIE   [*To* HELENA *as* HELENA *changes radio channels.*] Wait—dat good song—*wait*—dat music oh! Whot your problem? Let de songs play oh!

HELENA   I not looking for music.

BESSIE   Whot you want den?

HELENA   Neva matta.

[*Beat.*]

I want to know whot happenin

BESSIE   Where? What happen in wit whot?

HELENA   Wit de *war*.

BESSIE   You got a spirit dat too strong oh. So you want to hear does people just talkin and talkin?

HELENA   Yes. It called news.

BESSIE   Who—

HELENA   *Shhhh* your mout oh!

RADIO   . . . as fighting intensifies approximately one hundred women all dressed in white marched to the U.S. Embassy in Monrovia calling for immediate and direct intervention by the U.S. government leading to . . .

[*Radio crackles and dies.*]

[HELENA *sucks her teeth.*]

BESSIE   And we coulda be listening to music all dat time oh!

[*Changing position with discomfort.*]

Was dat one a de peace women I saw you talking to?

HELENA   Ya.

BESSIE   Like de ones who come last time?

HELENA   Ya.

BESSIE   Dat who woz comin?

HELENA   Ya.

BESSIE   Oh dat borin oh. Why she talking to you? I tought dey not talking to us, just to de CO. I tink dey witch oh, dey can talk to CO like dey men or someting.

HELENA   Dey not witch.

BESSIE   Whot? So why dey can do dat? Dey got some strong juju. Dey off oh.

HELENA   No. Dey been workin on dis stuff for long time from de city so de CO have to show dem respec, dat all.

BESSIE   Ya 'cause dey witch.

HELENA   Not everyone witch!

BESSIE   [*She adjusts her position with difficulty.*] Ahhh . . . Senate want to pass bill. It de—"No work when baby coming" bill. I can't do notin—I hate dis, I HATE DIS! I no feel good, Number One.

HELENA   Stop talking like you a small chile, you go *have* a chile, act like it oh!

BESSIE   I shoul neva listen to you, I no want dis ting.

HELENA   You go have it, and you go love it, 'cause dat whot a moda do.

BESSIE   I no want to *be* no moda. You say you go tek care of it. You betta. An you *know* you go tek care of it if it got a face like dat ugly fada of it. Read Clinto, Number Four.

THE GIRL   I no tink he too ugly.

[HELENA *and* BESSIE *stop and stare at* THE GIRL *curiously.*]

THE GIRL   He got a big nose, dat is true, but he no too ugly, his eyes and his mout not too bad.

BESSIE   Dere sometin wrong wit you. Really someting wrong oh.

HELENA   And where you get dat from?

[*She indicates the nail varnish.*]

THE GIRL   Whot?

HELENA   *Don* "whot"—whot you tink? Dat ting you holding in your hand.

THE GIRL   Oh . . . dis wos gif.

BESSIE   Gif from who?

HELENA   *Eeeey!* You no ask ha notin! I wife Number One ere ha? So shut ya mout. A gif from who?

THE GIRL   Dey tol me not to tell.

HELENA   TOLD YOU WHOT? I no tink you understand where you are. You are in my territory, little gal, I am de commanda in chief in dis ere country of dis compound—*everyone* do like dey is tol, dey follow command. You don wanna see wha—

THE GIRL   Dat not whot she tol me.

HELENA   Whot?

BESSIE   Whot she say?

HELENA   Whot you say?

THE GIRL   I *say* . . . dat not whot she tol me.

HELENA   Who? Who tell you *whot*?

THE GIRL   She tell me dat she woz de one de CO love de most even dough you wife Number One /

HELENA   / Oh, of *course*—

THE GIRL   / *Den*, den, she watch how you always mek it so everyting go tru you, jus like when de loot come de oda day and you de one who decide who get evertin firs and you decide who get whot//

HELENA   / HA!

THE GIRL   / *And* she say she bring me nicer tings dan whot you get and Number Tree steal whot she bring me and—

BESSIE   [*Hastily.*] She a *liar* oh! She lyin, Number One, I tell you true—

HELENA   She back again? *Where* she be?

THE GIRL   She go again, wit de soldier, she go to fight.

HELENA   Where you see ha?

THE GIRL   Out dere when I go to get de firewood.

HELENA   So whot? You like ha? You wanna fight now eh? You wanna be in de army?

THE GIRL   I tinkin about it.

HELENA   She tinkin about it.

BESSIE   Tinking!

HELENA   You no know notin, little gal! NOTIN. You tink you can fight, you go do dat, you go see whot happen to you—de ting you go end up doin out dere. You wanna kill a man, a woman, a small small chile? You wanna do dat hey?

THE GIRL   No, but I no gon do dat.

HELENA   How you no gon do dat? You go do whot da commanda tell you go do. If he tell you go kill dat village and bring him tree wives, you go have to do dat.

THE GIRL   She no say dat, she say—

HELENA   She go say good ting cause she wan you to be like ha, but she *lying* to you.

THE GIRL   No, she tell me she get whatever she wont from de civilian, she tell me she only go for Charles Taylor men, not de modas and de children.

BESSIE   Let ha go! She crazy oh!

HELENA   *Shut ya mout!* You no know whot you talking about, little gal. Dey go mek you do all de ting you see when you and you family have to run, all dos ting and worse. Do you know whot she do? Whot des soldier do? Whot dey done in my presence? Dey gon mek you slit a moda's stomach and tek out de beby to see if it boy or a gal. Dey gon mek you—

THE GIRL   [*Explosively.*] I NO GON DO NO TING LIKE DAT! But if I soldier, I no have to stay ere no more!

HELENA   It betta ere den

THE GIRL   *No* it not. Look at ha! She gon have his beby! I NO WANT DAT!

HELENA   We can stop dat, dere is dis leaf you can chew—

THE GIRL   I NO WANNA CHEW NO LEAF! I want him to leave me alone. I just want to get *away from him*! Now she gettin big he gon jump on me all de time, he no want you no more, and I no want dat! If I have a gun, don nobody gonna fuck wit me no more. I wan dat.

HELENA   Dat whot she say? No one fuck wit ha now?

THE GIRL   Ya, dat whot she say. And dat whot I wan.

[*She gets up, walks out.*]

ACT TWO
Scene One

[*Two days later. The middle of a shoot-out.* MAIMA *fires some shots in the direction of random gunfire. They crouch close to the ground.* THE GIRL *holds her gun close to her body and stares on. She attempts to prep her gun and it gets stuck and she falls, struggling to unjam it.*]

MAIMA   Okay listen good oh! Check de ammo for any dents in cartridges. Now, when you put de magazine into dat hole dere—put dat forward lip of de magazine into de hole first. Ya. And be sure de magazine it flat down.

[THE GIRL *dislodges magazine and does as instructed.*]

Good. Now you pull de charging handle to de back, all de way . . . all de way and release. You have to know how to do dat quick quick.

THE GIRL   Okay.

MAIMA   Now come.

[THE GIRL *hesitates, starring at the carnage in front of her in distress.*]

Come.

[THE GIRL *cautiously approaches her.*]

You see dat one dere?

THE GIRL   Ya

MAIMA   Dat de enemy—now fire him.

THE GIRL   Why?

MAIMA   Whot?!

THE GIRL   Why we firing dem? Why . . . why dey choppin de men like dat? Why can't we just let dem go somewhere, run away, why—

MAIMA   I don't know whot you talking about. To me, dat is de enemy. Do you know dey harboring lots of Charles Taylor men ere? Do you know whot dey could do to you? Does are de monkeys who kill our mas and rape our grandmodas.

THE GIRL   But dey just living ere—dey—

MAIMA   EEEEYYYY!

[*Grabs her face and looks deeply in her face.*]

LISTEN TO ME! Does are Charles Taylor's monkeys! Dat who we fightin. We are fighting de monkey Charles Taylor. He eating and drinking and living like a king in a land of paupers. We drive him out. And we gon keep on putting on de pressure. He scare of us. We gon do him worse dan dey do former President Samuel K. Doe. We gon catch him and dress him like a woman before we kill him. We gon restore Liberia to its rightful people. You understand, de enemy, de enemy is no longer human being. Okay?

THE GIRL   Okay.

MAIMA   [*Redirecting their attention to the fighting.*] Now . . . see dat one?

THE GIRL   Ya.

MAIMA   Fire him. Do like I show you, *now.*

[*After much hesitation, she shoots with her eyes closed.*]

Ah, come on—

[*Holds gun in direction of man.*]

Fire again. FIRE.

[THE GIRL *shoots.*]

Good gal. Now you doin sometin, you hepin us get closa to freedom. One monkey at a time. You don't go nowhere. Stay down okay?

[MAIMA *gets up and goes. Moments later* MAIMA *returns.*]

Okay, it's ova. You do good. You do good, good. Round up de young gals.

THE GIRL   Whot young gals?

MAIMA   You'll see dem as you walk around. Round dem up. Dat's your job.

THE GIRL   Where we gon tek dem?

MAIMA   Back to de camp.

THE GIRL   For whot?

[MAIMA *doesn't respond.*]

THE GIRL   Whot? For de generals?

[MAIMA *doesn't respond.*]

No, no, no, no, no, no. How can we do dat to dem—den de same ting dat—

MAIMA   You want it to be you? You want to do it in dere place? Dey won't mind, dey will tek anyting. Dey is beasts and beasts need to be fed. It dat simple. We have to provide dem wit fresh meat or dey go find it some oda way and you don't want to be dat oda way, do you?

THE GIRL   But I thot you say dat . . .

MAIMA   You feed dem, you not get eaten. Dat simple. Go and get de gals or I go have to tell dem you want to replace de gals today. Is it you or dem? Dis is how you survive, you understan? So is it you or dem, Number Four?

THE GIRL   Don't call me dat.

MAIMA   Den go get de gals. If you want a name of war, act like a soldier and *hunt*. Go. Go on gal. Go. GO.

[*They stare at each other for a long moment and* THE GIRL *goes.*]

Scene Two

[*One month later.* MAIMA *leads* RITA *to a makeshift latrine, in the army camp,* MAIMA'*s gun firmly clutched.* RITA *wears a T-shirt with the words "DIALOGUE DIALOGUE DIALOGUE" across the front.*]

MAIMA   So right now I looking to find some sound system. It right ere.

[*Pointing at latrine with rifle.*]

You know does in high demand oh.

RITA   Is dat right?

[*Trying to mask a grimace as she examines latrine, positions herself, and squats to urinate.*]

MAIMA   Ya! See, you women from de city you tink we backward out ere, we know whot is happenin, we got radio, bose, evertin out ere.

RITA   Ohhh!

MAIMA   [*Runs to* RITA, *pulling rifle into position.*] Whot matta?

RITA   Notin. I just almost fall down.

MAIMA   Don't do dat, you gon get a shit bath you fall in dat! I sure you used to betta, you women from de city, but dis all we have ere.

RITA   Dat fine, dat fine.

[*Adjusting her clothes, coming out from latrine area.*]

Thank you.

MAIMA   So. You got some tings to sell from de city? Some rice, some cloth, tings like dat? We can mek our trade on a regular. You come and bring tings from de city den I gon sell it out ere in de bush. One a my men he heping me sell. We can do good business. You got some tings?

RITA   No, noting

MAIMA   Noting? You say you was businesswoman.

RITA   I was. I had businesses in Monrovia and Kakata wit a lot a tings you gon like—

MAIMA   Whot business you got dere? I been to Kakata—I doing business dere too, you got cloths stall or—

RITA   No, my dear, I woz in big business, big, big business. Not whot you tinkin.

[*Almost reminiscent, almost with pride.*]

I had a petrol station, two supermarkets, a hair salon—you know dat woman at all the important events with de big, big head wrap and a lot of makeup? Dat woz me.

[*Beat.*]

I doing different work now.

MAIMA   Whot? Dis peace ting? Dat not gon bring you no profit oh! You woz doing good oh! We could have work togeda! It best to work wit de system, and right now de system it war.

RITA   De war gon end, it gon end soon—

MAIMA   How you know? De fightin getting stronga! LURD is getting bigga! We tekin more an more! We gon out to fight many time in just few days.

RITA   I know, people are dying, for no reason. De fighting getting closa and closa to Monrovia. It real bad now. We was just ere a mont ago and we had to come back again. Your CO got to stop dis. He got to tell his army to stop.

MAIMA   Stop for *whot*?! Dis whot we got to do to get rid of de monkey Charles T—

RITA   Charles Taylor not de only problem. We see de villages you LURD be tekin ova, modas, grandmodas, and children dying. Dat got to end too, don't you tink? Aren't you tired? Don't you want to go home to your family? To move forward? Where you from? Whot is your name, the one your family give you?

MAIMA   See, I know whot you women try to do. You trying to mek us weak. You want us to start to feel like little gals crying—"Ooh, I lost my ma, ooh, ooh, I lost my pa, dey hurt me, dey rape me." I no do dat no more, go to de villages if you looking for stupid gal like dat. I hep mek women strong. Dat whot I do. You want cryin little ladies, go to de commandant wives. Me, I no care about—

Rita   Do you miss your ma? What did she wont for you when you get big?

Maima   *Eh, eh!* Who you tink you talking to? *You*, you women, you come up in ere like you—

[*Gaining her stride.*]

We all know de *real* reason you doin dis—no man wont you, so you got notin else to do but botha us—you need a man? Let me try see I can find you one. It may be hard! You not so fresh no more.

Rita   [*Aghast.*] You rude little ting.

[*Explosively.*]

You who runnin around witout a tought in your head, showing off wit dat stick dat kill people. Trying to act like a business tycoon in de middle of de stinking jungle and using your pussy for profit—

Maima   [*Agitated.*] EH, EH, EH! WHO YOU TINK YOU TALKING TO? You know de tings I go do to you, you not protected by de commanda?

Rita   [*Regaining her composure.*] Okay, okay, okay . . . I apologize for whot I just said. I do. I do.

[*Beat.*]

I ask you about your moda, about your name because you don't wont to lose dat, you must neva lose dat.

[*She reaches out to touch* Maima. Maima *backs up violently.*]

When I lose ha . . . those LURD boys just tek ha. Dey knock me down with their guns and drag ha away. I busy shouting, "Do you KNOW WHO I AM!" Dey didn't care who I woz. I woz just another woman to be abused. And she had tings, tings she wanted to do, to be, she wanted to be a businesswoman like me or something. And it *my* fault because I know that I could have protected her better then that. I should have gone to Ivory Coast or Ghana or something. I stayed ere because I wont to profit from war, tinkin somehow my money gon keep me safe. It didn't do noting for me dat day. How long you tink you can mock God before He mock you back?

Maima   Who you talkin about?

[*Beat.*]

Rita   My . . . my daughter . . . I talking 'bout my daughter. So please, please trust, I ere to hep—I suffering too.

Maima   LURD tek ha?

Rita   Yes.

MAIMA   Ha. So dat why you ere. Actin like you ere for peace talks. Dat why you coming out all de time, talking wit us even though de oda women you wit stay at de CO compound. Actin like you care bout us—you just lookin for your daughta ere. HA! Well, I not ha, so you can get offa me oh.

RITA   No, you not ha. You certainly not.

[*Beat.*]

But *dat not* de only reason why I am here. I am also ere to *hep.//*

MAIMA   Hmmmhmmm!

RITA   I am! And I looking at you right now. And I wont to know—who is your moda and whot is your nem; I gon give you shit until you see whot you do is not whot you meant to be doin, it gon kill you and your heart gon cut and God gon mock you back and—

MAIMA   God not gon mock me! He heping me, 'cause I hep myself. So don't you worry about me. Go look for your daughta and leave us be oh.

[MAIMA *starts to walk out, turns back.*]

Ha, how I gon learn from you oh? Whot you teach your daughta not hep ha. If she had learn wit me, wit dis—

[*Indicating rifle.*]

maybe she still be around.

[MAIMA *mockingly gestures "After you" with rifle.* RITA *after some hesitation starts out, with* MAIMA *following behind.*]

Scene Three

[*The next day. Army camp.* THE GIRL, *rifle in hand, dressed sharp in a tight pair of pants and matching shirt, new hairstyle.*]

THE GIRL   Firm your jaw! FIRM YOUR JAW! You can't be tinking about Mama and Deddy anymore! Listen to me—I am now you moda, your fada, your grandmother, your great-grandfather, your ancestors, your Creator, your Jesus, and your Allah. You belong to me. You will be listening to me all de time. You will do whot I say, when I say do. Touch your nose—I say touch your nose—good. Good. Stand up! Sit down! Stand up again! Good. Now, there will be no crying, no galie talk, and no period cramping ere. I am your superior! You will be doing what I say when I say do!

[*To* MAIMA.]

Den I say some gon be wife and some soldier.

MAIMA   [*Emerging from behind her.*] Dat good! Dat good oh! You get betta about it!

THE GIRL   . . . Ah . . . ya, it getting betta wit de gals. I just remember whot you tell me—

MAIMA   [*Pleased.*] Whot? Whot I say?

THE GIRL   Dat dis is war, and you can't tink too much and God keeping my conscience for me—it gon be clean and new when dis ova.

MAIMA   Dat good oh!

THE GIRL   Tanks!

MAIMA   So where you workin?

THE GIRL   De check point, wit Rambo.

MAIMA   Whot you do?

THE GIRL   [*Excitedly.*] Oh ya! I just tell dem—you can't tek dat big bag a rice all dat way! Den I say, just leave it here, I'll tek care of it. When I see woman wit nice cloth, I just tek whot I like from ha, den I say, "Proceed tru de check point, proceed!" Look, I get some Timberlands—dey a bit small, but I stretching dem out. Dey just do whot I say do! Den dis one man—I fire him. He had too much money—we jokin—we call him Charles Taylor's son! But we scare he got too many connection, so I had to fire him.

MAIMA   Whot you got for me?

THE GIRL   [THE GIRL *hands her half of a wad of money.*] And I save you sometin. Look at dis.

[*Hands her a shirt she took off a civilian.*]

MAIMA   I no like dat.

THE GIRL   Oh, sorry.

MAIMA   But dis is good oh, you acting like solider afta a short time oh! How long you been wit me?

THE GIRL   Ah . . . about a mont.

MAIMA   See! You doing real good job oh! I woz worrying about you, now I see everytin fine oh!

THE GIRL   Ya, I okay.

[*Beat.*]

MAIMA   You lovin on someone?

THE GIRL   Huh?

MAIMA   I say you lovin on someone?

THE GIRL   *No.*

MAIMA   You want to?

THE GIRL   [*Bewildered.*] I . . . I don know.

MAIMA   You need to be lovin on someone—it go hep you be protected. You chose someone you like, high rankin—den I hook it up.

THE GIRL   I tought you say if I have gun—

MAIMA   You have to have someone—it hep. Den you can start your business like me. Right now, I lovin on tree men. If I not lovin on no man I not gon have de tings I want. I just gotta mek sure I wit a man of high ranking. And one of dem he got high ranking. De oda one, he got good business, but de third one, he de one I like, he de one got my heart. De one wit high rankin, he got many women, but I his favorite dough. He give me de most tings when he come home from war. But whot I really want, whot I looking for right now is a four-wheel drive, one a my men teach me how to drive so now I go buy and sell and go back and forth to Monrovia. You need one. We will find you one. Okay.

THE GIRL   Ya . . . okay.

Scene Four

[*Two weeks later.* RITA *and* HELENA *at camp, in compound. The compound looks markedly more sparse, with the cooking station manifesting clear signs of neglect.* HELENA *fiddles with the radio, which now has an elaborate makeshift antenna attached to it.*]

RADIO   . . . The LURD rebels are now closing in on Monrovia, having taken over eighty percent of Lib—

[*Unintelligible.*]

. . . intensive fighting for the past six weeks since early June . . .

[*Unintelligible.*]

. . . displaced citizens in the sports stadium . . .

[*Unintelligible.*]

. . . while the peace talks in Accra are at a deadlock the . . .

[*Unintelligible crackle ensues.* HELENA *finally turns it off.*]

RITA   Da fightin so bad I don't even know how we going to get back. How de CO actin?

HELENA He actin mad oh. He say dey tekin Monrovia den dey gon live in Charles Taylor's hos. Dey talking about Charles Taylor hos an we no got notin ere. Lots a dem in my unit gon and not coming back.

RITA You seen dat gal yet?

HELENA No, but my small soldier been wit ha. He saying she still close, say she looting civilian plenty. She getting de gals for de commandas too, she—

RITA My God. AHHHH! If dese women let me handle dese men—like how I handle dem when I was in business oh! I coulda looked tru dis whole camp propa without sneaking around 'cause of their protocol nonsense. Ahh . . . just wastin time oh! Who she wit?

HELENA Number Two—she calling haself sometin foolish now like Misgruntle or sometin.

RITA Disgrunted?

HELENA Ya

RITA Dat Number Two?

HELENA Ya, you meet ha?

RITA Ya . . . I meet ha.

[*Under her breath.*]

Oh my God.

HELENA She devil, she do bad tings. But Number Four not like ha. Number Four she . . . she special gal . . . she read to us—she tell us tings she wont to do—she—

RITA Where she from?

HELENA Ahh . . . she say Kakata.

RITA Kakata?!

HELENA a, she say ha fada woz in de army dere—but den when de war come she and ha moda run.

RITA She run—wit her mother—

HELENA Ya . . . she talk about ha ma de most, ha ma—

RITA She get caught?

HELENA Ha moda firs den ha.

RITA And she . . . she got book learning?

HELENA Ya.

[*Beat.*]

Who knows where dey be now. I been praying for Number Four.

RITA   [*Turning away.*] Hmm, okay.

HELENA   Whot . . . you no pray?

RITA   Ahh . . . no . . . no I don't. And these women I am working with, they . . . they prayer warriors oh. I'm not into all dat. I'm not . . . good . . .

HELENA   [*Delicately.*] Okay, you wanna to try?

RITA   [*Very hesitantly.*] Ah . . . not . . . not really . . . ah . . .

HELENA   It not gon do you notin harm oh. It mek me feel betta. I see you got sometin heavy on you—praying it mek tings not so heavy.

RITA   [*Stares at* HELENA *for a long moment. Finally.*] Okay . . . okay, you . . . you go ahead.

HELENA   Okay.

[HELENA *kneels and takes* RITA's *hand.*]

God, bring Number Four back, protec ha, keep ha safe in body and mind, convic her heart to come back to sense, show ha your love.

[*Beat.*]

And I pray for Mama Peace, Lord, that she might know ha work it not in vain. We pray in Jesus, His love precious, Amen.

RITA   [*Beat.*] Amen.

[*Beat.*]

Thank you.

HELENA   Tank you.

[BESSIE *walks in, heavily pregnant, with a new but shaggy wig. It covers most of her face.*]

RITA   I have to go—oh . . . hello!

BESSIE   [*To* RITA.] Oh, good, you ere again! You bring cassava?

HELENA   Number Tree—

RITA   No . . . ah . . . no, I don't have anything actually.

BESSIE   NOTING! We no got no food oh! Why you come ere and you no hep—

HELENA   NUMBER TREE!

RITA   You have no food? Noting?

BESSIE   NOTIN!

Helena   [*To* Bessie.] EEEYYYY!

[*To* Rita.]

He . . . he gon bring some . . . we'll have sometin soon.

Rita   Goodness . . .

Bessie   Well, you can read us book at leas! I missin Clinto!

Rita   Ah . . . ah . . . of course, of course . . . oh my goodness how are you—
you haven't been eating—

[*Indicating* Bessie's *belly.*]

Bessie   [*Handing book to her.*] Oh dat.

[*Indicating belly as though it isn't attached to her body.*]

Dat fine! De olda woman from de next compound is midwife. Read, just
small small.

Rita   Okay . . .

[*Opening book.*]

just a little. Do you know where you were?

[Bessie *and* Helena *look at her blankly.*]

Whot woz the last thing you remember hearing?

Helena   Oh, he woz to go to court, den he get to not go.

Rita   Okay . . .

[*Leafing through book.*]

let's see.

Bessie   You tink we send him letta, he gon get it?

Rita   You want to send Bill Clinton a letter?

Bessie   Ya. I just wont to tell him I glad he still de big man and I like his
story.

Helena   She mad oh! She tink de big man of America gon read letta from
us.

Bessie   Why he not? America our fada—we founded by Americans—so he
our big man too.

Rita   That is true but . . . uhhh . . . about that—I should tell you
something. . . .

Helena   About whot?

Rita   About Clinton being the big man. . . .

BESSIE   Oh, ohh, oh oh.

HELENA   Whot your problem oh?

BESSIE   I do wet—but I no do wet.

RITA   Oh my goodness. Where de midwife? We tek ha?

HELENA   Ya, she not far, grab ha arm.

[*They help* BESSIE *up. Her wig falls to the ground as they escort her out.*]

BESSIE   My wig, oh, get my wig! I need it to cova my face small small! De wig oh!

Scene Five

[*A week later.* THE GIRL *rushes in and falls to her knees, weeping and attempting to pray.*]

THE GIRL   Our fada—who are in-sometin . . . hollow your nem, de kingdom dat be yours . . . de kingdom dat be yours come—on eart and in . . . sometin, for de powa . . . you de powa . . .

[MAIMA *enters.*]

MAIMA   You do good work. So you get your nem today.

[THE GIRL *wiping tears away quickly and sitting up.*]

THE GIRL   Whot dat?

MAIMA   De nem dat mek you a soldier.

THE GIRL   Okay.

MAIMA   Ya, so tell me, why are you fightin?

THE GIRL   [*Reciting what she has been taught.*] We are fighting for de liberty of de people.

MAIMA   And who are we fighting?

THE GIRL   We are fighting de monkey Charles Taylor. He eating and drinking and living like a king in a land of paupers. We drive him out. Once he gon, we stop. And we gon . . . and we gon . . .

MAIMA   . . . keep . . .

THE GIRL   We gon keep on putting on de pressure . . . we gon keep on putting on de pressure . . .

MAIMA   He scare of us. He neva gon come out and fight like a man. He want to hide behind all his security. We gon strip him of all a dat. We gon do him worse dan dey do former President Samuel K. Doe.

THE GIRL   //Former Samuel K. Doe.

MAIMA   We gon catch him and dress him like a woman before we kill him.

THE GIRL   Sorry.

MAIMA   Jus keep learning it. If any of de commanders come to you dey go be vex you don know dos tings. So why is you fighting. Choose sometin you want to fight for.

THE GIRL   My moda.

MAIMA   Why?

THE GIRL   I . . . she just who I want to fight for.

MAIMA   Whot you want for her?

THE GIRL   I want ha to be happy, to be blessed by God.

MAIMA   You gon fight for your ma? You go see justice served so you ma and all de mas of Liberia blessed and not in pain no more?

THE GIRL   Ya.

MAIMA   Den dat your nem.

THE GIRL   Whot?

MAIMA   Moda's Blessing.

[Beat.]

THE GIRL   [Searching.] I tink . . . I tink I cursed.

MAIMA   Whot? You tink you whot?

THE GIRL   I CURSED. She curse me, she say, she say, "Devil bless you," and now I, I, I can't remember whot my moda she look like! I can't remember! I go, I go get de gals like I always do afta fighting, but dis one, she looking all nice in ha nice cloth, she acting like she betta dan me, I wanted ha to shut ha mout, to show me respec. She kept saying, "Devil bless you!" Now she keep coming back to say dat to me, in my head, she won't shut up her mouth! Den I say okay, I can fight this ting, I just remember my moda saying, "God bless you"—and dis thing gonna disappear. Den, den, I can't see my moda no more! I can't hear my moda no more! I just hear dis gal!

[Beat.]

I had just wanted to shut ha up. I tought . . . I tought . . . It neva happen like dat before, I got system. De men have to come to me and discuss which gal dey want, I give dem one. I tell dem—dis gal special, she your wife, she only go wit you. But wit dis one—I didn't protec ha like I usually do—I just let dem tek ha, because she woz talking too much.

[*Beat.*]

Dey do it right in front of us at de camp, dey don't care, dey don't care dat God right dere, dat He can see whot dey do. Dey just keep jumpin and jumpin on ha, it five o' dem and I see she too small, she just little, small small den me. I want to say stop but I scare dey gon come to me if I say sometin.

[*Beat.*]

I see she stressed, she start to vomit—it look like rice or oats or sometin, den ha eyes start goin back. I can't move; den, den ha eyes just go still, she starring right up to de sky and she not moving; de fifth one he just keep going till he done.

[*Beat.*]

She got blood everywhere, dey leave ha lying dere and tell one o' de small soldier to go get wata so dey can wash deyselves, dey tell me and anoda small soldier to trow ha in de riva. I just do like dey say, I too scare to say noting. I tek ha arms and he tek ha legs, she still bleedin and bleedin, ha eyes still looking up, I no look at ha no more. We drop ha in de riva and I pray, I pray dat God bless ha soul, dat He no blame me for whot does men do. But it my fault she dead, and she tell me, "Devil bless you," and now I can't even see my moda no more! I cursed. I got dis sin on me and I gon go to de devil straight.

MAIMA   EYYYY! FIRM YOUR JAW.

[*Slapping her.*]

I say, FIRM YOUR JAW! I say firm your jaw, FIRM IT.

[*Hitting her and beating her continuously, passionately.*]

Don't you eva,

[*Beating her.*]

EVA—

[*Beating her more.*]

come to me wit does *stupid* stories—you understan? You got to be *strong*! Dis is war, little gal. And you a soldier.

[*She stops beating her but holds THE GIRL's jaw firmly in her hand.*]

Whot does a soldier do in war? SPEAK!

THE GIRL   Dey fight.

MAIMA   Ya, dey fight. We winning, we even stronga and stronga now. So you betta fight, little gal. You Moda's Blessing now, you *soldier*, you understan?

THE GIRL   I understan.

[MAIMA *releases* THE GIRL *abruptly and roughly escorts her out.*]

Scene Six

[*Same evening.* BESSIE *at camp, with an infant strapped to her back. She sings to herself, as she coos at her baby and sweeps the compound.* THE GIRL *enters and stands silently in the corner, her face obscured by the dark.* BESSIE *finally sweeps at* THE GIRL'S *feet.*]

BESSIE   [*Startled.*] FUCK SATAN, HEP JESUS! Number Four! How you gon come on me like dat.

THE GIRL   I sorry.

BESSIE   Whot you doing ere, Number Four? I not see you for long time. I thought you Commander General by now!

THE GIRL   Moda's Blessing.

BESSIE   Huh?

THE GIRL   My nem, it . . . it Moda's Blessing.

BESSIE   Okaaaay. So whot you wont?

THE GIRL   You getting beby?

BESSIE   Hmmhmm,

THE GIRL   Oh, he sweet oh!

BESSIE   It a gal.

THE GIRL   Oh, ya, oh I see ha betta now, she look like you. She pretty.

BESSIE   Tanks. I like ha. I did not tink I woz go like ha, but I do. She no look like him, she a small small me! How I no gon love ha? I look at ha, and she look at me wit dos eyes and all dat stuff coming out ha mout after she drink milk and I say, If anybody do sometin to my chile, ever—dat de only ting dat gon mek me pick up de gun and fire you, den I curse you, curse you to de devil. Dat when I gon go to de medicine man for true and get some o' de juju dat go hurt someone, dey go wake up with no privates or sometin. Dey go fire dey self—dey be so vex.

[*Beat.*]

I neva felt a love like dat, you know. I kill and curse for ha. And I tink God will be on my side. I sure of dat. How you? You should get beby, it feel good.

THE GIRL   No, I can . . . I don wont dat. Where Number One?

BESSIE   She wit de CO.

THE GIRL   I go wait for ha. Ere, I bring gif.

[*She pulls out a large cassava root.*]

BESSIE   That so good oh, cassava! It been too long oh!

[BESSIE *grabs the cassava root and rushes to cooking station—she searches for a knife to peel and chop the root.*]

THE GIRL   [*Looking around.*] Whot dis.

[*She picks up a tattered piece of paper.*]

BESSIE   Oh, dat dis ting Number One keep doin—she learn to write sometin, she keep writing it ova and ova—she going mad oh! Guess whot we learn about Clinto? He not de big man no more! It a Bush. A bush! Dat his name—a Bush! Like in de bush—you know?

THE GIRL   Ya, I understan.

BESSIE   Dat funny oh!

THE GIRL   Ya. Where Number One?

BESSIE   I tol you she wit de CO. Whot vexing you?

THE GIRL   Notin.

BESSIE   Okay.

[*Goes back to peeling.*]

[RITA *rushes in, excited, looks around for* HELENA.]

RITA   Where's Number One?

BESSIE   SHE WIT DE CO! Whot wrong wit you people oh!

RITA   I have to tell you all something.

[*Notices* THE GIRL.]

Oh . . .

BESSIE   She Number Four.

THE GIRL   [*Automatically.*] Moda's Blessing.

RITA   Oh . . . oh God . . . oh God . . .

[RITA, *trembling and fighting tears, advancing towards* THE GIRL.]

It not ha . . . it . . . it not ha . . . it not.

[*Shaking her head and looking to* BESSIE *in mournful agony.*]

BESSIE   Whot you talking oh?

RITA   Ah . . . ah . . . ahhhh . . . ah . . . noting. Noting.

[*Collecting herself for several beats. To* The Girl.]

Rita Endee, I am a member of the Liberian Women Initiative for Peace—

The Girl   Oh.

Rita   So . . . so whot is your name?

The Girl   I tol you—I—

Rita   Whot is your real name—the name your mother and father gave you?

The Girl   [*Struck.*] Oh . . .

[Helena *enters, a dazed look on her face. She looks over the compound, not even taking* Rita *and* The Girl *in. Methodically, almost robotically, she starts to pick up things and pack them up.*]

Bessie   Whot you doing?

Helena   Hmm?

Bessie   Whot you packing for Number One?

Helena   Helena. H-E-L-E-N-A. Helena. Dat my nem. I not sure about my last nem, I tink it Sowa, Sona, or sometin. I tink it Sowa. I need to remember all des ting now. Where I from? Buchanan? Whot I go do now? Whot I go do now?

[*Starts laughing.*]

Bessie   You go mad oh?

Helena   [*She finally takes in the room.*] He call me over, he say sit down. All de years I be wit him, he neva have me sit down. Maybe sit on him, but neva he sit me down to talk to me like human to human. Den he say, "De war ova, Charles Taylor go to Nigeria, you can go. Pack your tings and go. We going home." Den he get up and walk away. Dat it. All dos years, he tek all dos years, he mek me leave my chile when we running from Taylor men, he, he mek my chile die in de bush, all alone—he mek it so I no get born no more, he mek me so sick my stomach broken, den he go just trow me away like dat. I cook every meal he eat, I know all de secret of his unit, everyting, but he just go spit me out like dat, like I someone he just meet yesterday.

[*Starts to laugh.*]

I scared oh! He say, "You can go"! I can just go, wherever I want—de war it ova! Do I have ma? Do I have pa? I no know, "You can go," I don know whot go means! Whot it mean? I tink, I tink I gon go to Monrovia, sell tings, get a business, but I wont to go to school, I wont to learn to do sometin, to read like you, Number Four—you can be member of Parliament now! Did you hear me? We can all *go*! Let's *go*, Ma Peace! I can go now! You free, Number Four—you no have to fight no more. Don't do no bad tings no more—dat not you, gal, dat not how God mek you. He mek you good gal.

[HELENA *hands* THE GIRL *her book.* THE GIRL *slaps* HELENA *hard, grabs her rifle, and points it at* HELENA'*s throat, pushing her back until the rifle is touching* HELENA'*s throat. She releases almost primal sounds of aggression, her eyes flashing something verging on demonic. She stands there, seeming to will herself to drop the gun and pull the trigger simultaneously.* RITA *stands petrified, then seems to will herself to advance towards* THE GIRL *and speak to her softly.*]

RITA   Gal . . . gal . . . listen to me. I am a member of Liberian Women for Peace. I gon hep you, gal, I gon hep you—you don't wan to do this. Dis is not you, dis not whot God make you for.

THE GIRL   Whot he mek me for?

RITA   Good tings, he mek you for so many good tings. Look at her, she wants to read now—why? Because of you, because of you, my daughter.

[THE GIRL *looks over at* RITA, *searching.* THE GIRL *breaks down, drops her rifle, and drops to her knees and weeps.* RITA *removes rifle, drops to her knees also, and gently strokes her back.* THE GIRL *crumples into* RITA'*s arms.* RITA *clings to her with yearning compassion. Silence ensues for several beats.* BESSIE'*s baby starts to cry.*]

[RITA *stroking* THE GIRL'*s back, to* BESSIE.]

How is she?

BESSIE   She fine.

RITA   She's just a few days old huh?

BESSIE   She young, young.

RITA   Whot's her name?

BESSIE   Clintine

RITA   Oh, Clementine—that's Fre—*no*! Clintine. Clintine?

BESSIE   Ya.

RITA   Okay, that, that's lovely. We need to move. The Commander General is letting you go—these camps are dismantling, so I can get you all some help. There is a truck we are catching—about fifteen minutes from ere. We rounding up as many of you women as we can, but there is no time! We have to go now. There is still some fighting, so we have to get to the main road really carefully. But the major crisis is over. Taylor is gone! So I am going to take you gals to a camp—further north, near Guinea—

BESSIE   I tink I go stay.

HELENA   Whot you say?

BESSIE   I go stay wit CO.

HELENA   Stay to do whot?

BESSIE   He de fada of my chile, he de only man I know to be wit for long time. Whot I go do out dere? I can't learn to do tings, dat not me.

HELENA   So you go follow CO around wherever he go?

BESSIE   Ya, I go home wit him. He like lovin on me, he no gon mind.

[MAIMA rushes in.]

MAIMA   Moda's Blessing, so you run ere like beby eh? Let's go.

RITA   Where are you trying to take her?

MAIMA   Dat not your problem—she soldier.

RITA   Taylor is gone.

MAIMA   I know dat. Dat don mean it ova. His monkey soldiers still everywhere. Whot dey tink? Dey tink we go just stop now?

RITA   You got to stop, it ova! The ECOWAS forces are killing any rebels still fighting. They are going to have disarmament and you have to turn in your weapons—

MAIMA   Dey can turn in dey modas! I not letting my gun go for notin. Moda's Blessing—LET'S GO!

BESSIE   Leave ha! She gonna stay wit Ma Peace and Helena.

MAIMA   Wit who?

HELENA   Wit me. It ova oh. Just stop, you should just stop it while you can.

MAIMA   Shut your mout. Stop for whot? Den whot? No way. And since when you care about whot happen to me eh?

HELENA   I always care about you. Dat why I can stand to see de tings you doing. But you can stop now, it ova.

MAIMA   [Stares at HELENA for a long beat. Finally.] FUCK YOU! Moda's Blessing—

HELENA   Leave ha, Maima.

MAIMA   Whot you call me?

HELENA   I call you your name.

RITA   De war ova, get back to who you woz. You go back out there fighting you not gonna make it.

MAIMA   You God? NO! So you no know notin about whot gon happen to me. YOU NO KNOW. DIS WHOT I KNOW TO DO.

[*Breaking*]

WHAT YOU TINK EH? WHAT YOU TINK? YOU TINK I GONNA BE LIKE MY MODA begging at de refugee camps, pleadin around for a cup a rice, den dey just jump ha till she dead when dey supposed to be protecting ha? Tink I gon let dem treat me like I is notin! NO WAY! DAT NOT MY STYLE, DAT NEVA GON BE ME!

[*Desperately.*]

MODA'S BLESSING, COME ON! COME WIT ME! LET'S GO!

THE GIRL   . . .

MAIMA   You gon stay?

[*Beat.*]

You stay, you gon wish you come. You stay, you no gon have *notin*. You just go back to being weak little gal.

[*She leaves sucking her teeth.*]

[*Silence for a few beats as they watch* MAIMA *go,* RITA *shaking her head.*]

RITA   [*To* THE GIRL.] You gon be okay. You can find your family now

THE GIRL   I don't tink I have any, my pa dead and my moda, dey, dey tek ha and den dey

[THE GIRL *stares at* BESSIE—*her face immobile. The women all stare back at her in a prolonged silence, absorbing all that isn't said in full understanding. Finally.*]

RITA   We have to go.

HELENA   Okay—

BESSIE   Okay. Bye.

HELENA   Bye. Stay wit God eh, don't stay wit CO forever—he gone waste you.

BESSIE   I be fine.

RITA   Whot is your name, my daughter? The one your mother and father gave you?

BESSIE   Oh, dat? It . . . it Bessie.

RITA   Good, okay, Bessie, I cannot just leave you—please, come, you can—

BESSIE   I be fine. I be fine. I *wan* stay. Dat whot I wont.

RITA   Okay. . . .

[RITA *gives up. To* HELENA *and* THE GIRL.]

Come, we have got to go now. Here, let me help you.

[*She helps* HELENA *gather up her things.*]

[RITA *and* HELENA *exit.* THE GIRL *goes and grabs her book, stumbles on her gun, stops, picks it up, and looks at it and looks after where* MAIMA *exited. She stands there with book and gun in hand behind* BESSIE, *who sits on the floor with her daughter, cooing her and singing to her gently.* THE GIRL *doesn't move, seemingly transfixed to the floor, unable to walk in either direction. Random gunshots can be heard in the distance. As* BESSIE *sings, the lights fade out.*]

BESSIE   Clintine, Clintine, you so pretty like mama—Clintine, Clintine!

THE GUARD
(BLACK WHITE OCHRE RED)

by
Jessica Dickey

Photograph by Paul Smith

Production History

Original production by Ford's Theater, Washington, D.C., September 25 to October 18, 2015 (Part of the Women's Voices Theater Festival)

Cast

ACTOR ONE   Mitchell Hébert
ACTOR TWO   Josh Sticklin
ACTOR THREE   Kathryn Tkel
ACTOR FOUR   Tim Getman
ACTOR FIVE   Craig Wallace

Creative Team

DIRECTOR   Sharon Ott
COSTUMES   Laree Lentz
LIGHTS   Rui Rita
SOUND DESIGN & ORIGINAL MUSIC   Rob Milburn & Michael Bodeen

Biography

Jessica Dickey is an award-winning American actor and playwright most known for her play *The Amish Project*, which opened at the Rattlestick Playwrights Theater to great acclaim from audience and critics alike and continues to be produced around the country and the world. Jessica's play *Charles Ives Take Me Home* premiered at Rattlestick Playwrights Theater in June 2013, for which she was hailed as a "talent to watch" by Charles Isherwood of the *New York Times*. *Charles Ives Take Me Home* went on to be produced at City Theatre in Pittsburgh, Strawdog in Chicago, and Curious Theatre Company in Denver. Jessica's play about Civil War re-enactors, *Row After Row*, was commissioned by Rising Phoenix and had its official world premiere with the Women's Project in January 2014 at the City Center in NYC, followed by a regional premiere at People's Light and Theatre. *Row After Row* was recently nominated for an Ovation Award for Best Play after its Los Angeles run at Echo Theatre Company. Ford's Theatre commissioned Jessica to write a play for their Women's Voices festival in Washington, D.C., the result of which was her newest play, *The Guard*, for which she won the prestigious Stavis Award. *The Guard* recently completed its run at Ford's Theatre. Over her career, Jessica has been thrice nominated for the Susan Blackburn Prize. Other awards and recognitions include Writer in Residence at the New Harmony Project, the

Sewanee Writers Conference Walter Dakin Fellowship, a Playwrights of New York fellowship nomination, a semi-finalist and publication for the Emily Dickinson Poetry Contest, a finalist for the Kahn Award Career Scholarship, and a winner of the Bell Atlantic Leadership Award. She is a proud new member of New Dramatists and a board member of the New Harmony Project. Visit: www.jessicadickey.com

Five Actors

ACTOR ONE   Male, 50s–60s
  HENRY   museum guard, bookish, grieving but in denial
  REMBRANDT THE PAINTER   brilliant, grumpy, soft-hearted

ACTOR TWO   Male, early 20s (to play 13–24)
  DODGER   training to be a guard, subversive, tattooed, seeker
  TITUS   Rembrandt's son, clever, loves his father, pragmatic

ACTOR THREE   Female, early to mid-20s
  MADELINE   art student, forthright, grieving, not afraid to argue
  HENNY   Rembrandt's partner, loving, practical, grounded

ACTOR FOUR   Male, 30s–40s
  JONNY   guard, military background, carries a gun, caring in his way
  MARTIN—hospice care nurse, strong, knowing

ACTOR FIVE   Male, 60s–70s
  SIMON   Henry's husband, poet, an inherent grace and toughness
  HOMER THE ANCIENT POET   visionary, crude, crazy, brilliant

Please don't make everyone white.

Setting

A large, spacious room with walls that can change color to reflect—

White—Present day, a major art museum in the United States
Red—1653, a luxurious home in Amsterdam
Ochre—Roughly 800 BC, a temple in Greece
Black—Present day, the death bed of a poet

The following four sections connect like four paintings curated next to each other. Distinct but connected.

Aristotle with a Bust of Homer by Rembrandt (1653)

WHITE

[*A spotlight illuminates a man's face. This is* HENRY. *His face shines out from the dark.*]

HENRY   One of the greatest painters of our civilization
Rembrandt
Preferred only four colors of paint:
black, white, ochre and earth red.
Because these hues best highlight the color of the skin.

For example
In Rembrandt's *The Man with the Magnifying Glass* . . .
The clothing is dark ochre and shades of maroon
His hair is brown and black with flecks of light
The space around him is an earthen black.
So that there
floating in the middle of all that darkness
Is the pale and luminous specter
of his face.

I love that.
That set against an immense and layered darkness
The human light is most visible.

[*Florescent lights start popping on around him. Morning in a large room in a major American art museum. High ceilings, clean light. The walls are a crisp linen-white color.* JONNY *and* HENRY *are opening for the day.*]

HENRY   Good morning, Jonny.

JONNY   [*Startled.*] Fuck me. What're you doin' here in the dark, ya nutball?

HENRY   Have you ever been to Tucson?

JONNY   What?

HENRY   Have you ever been to Tucson?

JONNY   Arizona? No.

HENRY   Me neither. But the indigenous people of Tucson believe that the saguaro cactuses—cacti?—walk at night. Simon wrote a poem about them (in his second book, I believe).

JONNY   The what?

HENRY   The saguaro—you know, the tall cactus that grows in the Southwest?—they sort of lean a little—they really do look like people. . . . Simon called them "disciples of the sky."

JONNY   Okay.

HENRY   Anyway I've always thought that it was true here. That at night the paintings come alive, expand somehow. And then when the lights go on in the morning—on the Manet, the Vermeer, the Renoir—it's like there's a secret alive in the room, as if something vital and mysterious is pretending to be asleep, their inner life tucked beneath a frame.

JONNY   Why are you saying this?

HENRY   Because that's what I'm doing here. In the dark. I like to be here when the shift happens. From "alive" in the dark to "asleep" in the lights.

[*Beat.*]

JONNY   You say weird shit in the morning.

[HENRY *goes about prechecks for the morning shift.*]

Anything interesting in prechecks?

HENRY   Not yet.

JONNY   That's too bad. You heard about that umbrella that got left here last month, right?—had pictures of naked cowboys in it once you opened it up? People are crazy.

[HENRY *keeps doing prechecks.* JONNY *just hangs around—clearly likes* HENRY, *finds him comforting or something.*]

JONNY   Supposed to rain.

HENRY   Mmmm.

Jonny   You gonna do the Anna Wintour birthday dinner? You know, in the Asian wing?

Henry   Uhhhhh, I hadn't thought to. Why, should I?

Jonny   Oh yeah, man, she's big in the fashion world. Big. I love fashion. The Kardashians? Love that shit.

Hey—so Twyla asked me to invite you to supper for the holiday. If you're free. I think she's gonna do a lamb or something. If you don't already have plans. I know it's still a ways off, but she told me to invite you. . . . To Easter . . .

Henry   Oh . . .

Jonny   I hate Easter. The bunny shit? Hate that. Anyway. You have plans? Or—?

Henry   Uhhh, no, no, not yet. . . .

Jonny   [*After a beat.*] Okay. I don't mean to pry. I just know she'll ask.

[*Ala Twyla.*]

"Did you ask if he had plans? People get shy when their partner is dying."

[*Maybe he shouldn't have said that.*]

You know Twyla, she's always mother-hen-ing everybody. I mean, of course Simon is welcome to join, if—you know . . .

Henry   That's very kind.

Jonny   . . . How is Simon?

Henry   Uhhhhh. Still Stage Four.

Jonny   Yeah, that's a shame.

[*Chuckling.*]

You know Twyla and I still laugh about that staff holiday party two years ago when Simon kept doing that squirrel voice?—you remember that?—he kept hoppin' around talkin' about *nuts. Nuts, nuts, nuts!*

Henry   Ah, yes. My poet husband and his unusual flair for theatrics.

Jonny   It was hilarious! The staff parties always make me feel like such a jackass, the tie and everything, but Twyla likes 'em 'cuz they're fancy and there's free champagne. Simon got points in my book 'cuz he asked me about Iraq. Not many people do that. . . .

[*A sad pause.*]

So how's he doing? I mean, how are his spirits?

HENRY   Uhhh, it's hard to say. He sleeps a lot. Or so I'm told. By his nurse.

JONNY   That's—yeah, that's some real shit. I don't know how you're doing it, man.

HENRY   "Doing it"?

JONNY   Yeah, like, how you're keeping your shit together. If Twyla were dying, I'd be a fucking *mess*. I'm saying you're strong. You gonna take any time off, or . . . ?

HENRY   Well, I suppose I'll have to. For the funeral.

JONNY   . . . Yeah. But I mean, like—don't you wanna be home? With him?

HENRY   I don't think either of us would like that very much.

JONNY   Really? You guys aren't the chicken noodle soup types?

HENRY   I don't know what that means.

JONNY   You know, chicken noodle soup types. Like if one doesn't feel well, the other makes them chicken noodle soup. Don't you guys like chicken noodle soup when you're feelin' bad?

HENRY   We do. We just prefer to put it in the microwave and eat it ourselves.

JONNY   Got it, got it. Well, listen, you should take some time, buddy. Looking at these walls all day can't be good.

HENRY   I like these walls.

JONNY   Not me, man. End of each day I am ready to *bail*.

[*Small pause.*]

Well, look, if you're in the leave-me-alone part of it, I get it, but if not you should come to dinner. Seriously. We don't have to talk about it. Or we can.

HENRY   That's very kind of you, but—

JONNY   Well, just, you know, just—give it some thought. Holidays can be tough. Even with the bunny shit.

[MADELINE *enters with her easel and paints. Beat.*]

JONNY   Ma'am, this section is closed today.

MADELINE   Oh. I mean, they let me in. . . . I'm a copyist? I'm going to be working on the Rembrandt?

JONNY   You sure you got your dates right? They're painting the hall out there for an installation.

MADELINE   I have my approval letter.

[*She offers her approval letter, which he checks.*]

JONNY   [*With a wink to* JONNY.] Alright, well. We're gonna have to check your measurements.

MADELINE   [*"Measurements"?*] Okay.

HENRY   That's fine. I'll check her, Jonny, it's fine. Go ahead and set up Miss. I'm almost done here with the prechecks. I'll be with you in just a minute.

MADELINE   Okay. Thank you.

[HENRY *continues prechecks. She sets up her stuff.* JONNY *has sauntered over her way.*]

JONNY   So you're a painter.

MADELINE   [*No interest.*] Ish.

JONNY   Ish?

MADELINE   It's just a class.

JONNY   That's cool.

[*Re: the Rembrandt, down front.*]

You're gonna copy that one there? That's a tough one. The light . . . his eyeballs . . .

MADELINE   . . . Uh-huh.

[*He peeks at her canvas, which is blank.*]

JONNY   [*Trying to make a flirty joke.*] Got a long way to go.

MADELINE   I haven't started yet.

JONNY   No, I know, I'm just messin' with ya.

MADELINE   . . . Uh-huh.

JONNY   So is that where the hot chicks go nowadays to meet dudes? Painting class?

MADELINE   [*Back the fuck off.*] Actually it's where the hot chicks go to *grieve* a loss.

[*Beat.* HENRY *looks up from his clipboard.*]

JONNY   [*Getting the message.*] I got you. That's cool. Respect.

[*Trying to recover, and also probably actually trying to be helpful.*]

Hey, Henry, maybe you should take a painting class.

[HENRY *and* MADELINE *make eye contact, recognizing they have something in common.*]

HENRY   [*Gently, taking* MADELINE *in.*] Yes, perhaps I should. Thank you, Jonny.

[HENRY *turns and almost runs right into* DODGER. *He makes quite a picture with his rad-ass Mohawk.*]

Oh my!

DODGER   Is one of you guys Henry?

HENRY   [*Recovering.*] Good morning. Yes. I'm Henry. You must be Bernard.

DODGER   Dodger.

HENRY   Sorry?

DODGER   Dodger. Bernard is my grandfather.

HENRY   Oh, I thought they said—

DODGER   I go by Dodger.

HENRY   Alright then. Dodger. It's nice to meet you. Uhhhh. This is Jonny.

JONNY   'Sup.

HENRY   Welcome to your first day.

DODGER   Thanks.

HENRY   I'll be training you. Come in, come in, let's get you oriented with prechecks and such.

DODGER   How do smoke breaks work?

HENRY   Smoke breaks? Uhhhh—I believe they work like all the other breaks—every twenty minutes you'll rotate and depending on your section and team size, you'll rotate out every hour forty or so. And of course your lunch, which is forty-five minutes.

JONNY   Just make sure you smoke twenty feet from the building. That's a thing.

DODGER   Okay.

JONNY   I'm serious. And show this guy some respect. Been here longer than most of the art.

DODGER   What the fuck, man?

HENRY   Alright, let's begin, shall we?

[*Brief standoff, but* JONNY *decides to let it slide for* HENRY'S *sake.*]

JONNY I'll check in with you later buddy—Twyla makes a great lamb . . .

[*Exiting, maybe for* MADELINE's *benefit?*]

I'll be the good-looking man with a gun. If anyone needs me.

HENRY [*As* JONNY *leaves.*] That's very assuring, Jonny, thank you.

[*Once he's gone—*]

Sorry about that. Jonny is what we call an SPO—Security Protection Officer. Different unit than us. They carry guns. We're the GPOs—General Protection Officers. I don't know why we can't just be called museum guards. It seems simple enough to me, but there you have it.

There are basically three types you'll encounter on staff with you here at the museum. There are the retired military and government agency types. You can tell who they are right away. It can be a little unsettling at first—guns, metal detectors—but you'll get used to it. Most of them mean well and just try to do their job.

Then there are the retired teachers, people who want to do something simple, something that allows them to be around the art and people without too much responsibility. And then of course there are the artists, like yourself. There was even a year when the guards got together and produced a show of their work. It was really interesting, I can tell you.

DODGER How do you know I'm an artist?

HENRY [*Surveying the tattoos, the hair.*] Just a hunch. Now, I think first—

DODGER So which are you?

HENRY I'm sorry?

DODGER The three types. Which are you?

HENRY Oh. I guess I'm an amalgamation. I taught art history in a small boarding school and at one time I fancied myself a painter. Anyway.

So! Welcome to the museum! It's a quiet morning, which is nice, gives you a chance to get the lay of the land.

[HENRY *plows through the following with quick pace.*]

I assume they showed you our entrance by the loading dock? You'll use that to enter and exit the museum. We'll make sure you know where your locker is. You leave your uniform here, you know, where it is laundered for you, and then every morning you'll attend the team meeting—they're easy—just covering any events going on in the museum, opportunities for overtime, which you'll find you want since the pay is rather *dire*. So let's walk through the morning procedure.

[*Throughout all of this* MADELINE *has been seated, getting herself ready, preparing her canvas, studying the painting.* DODGER *may occasionally steal a glance over to her.*]

Oh, I almost forgot about you! We have a copyist here with us today. You'll see them around the museum from time to time. It's rather lovely—having someone here *painting* reminds our patrons that once upon a time all the paintings they see now *were painted*! An artist sat in front of a blank canvas and tried to communicate a truth from the human condition in the language of composition and color. . . . Lucky for us, our job today is simply to make sure their canvas is the proper size.

[*They stand by* MADELINE'S *canvas.*]

So they went through her bag at the door of course, so we'll just do this quickly and leave you to it. It cannot be the same size as the original; so in this case the Rembrandt is 143.5 by 136.5 cm, so less than that. Here you are—

[HENRY *produces a little tape measure from his pocket and hands it to* DODGER.]

You can do the measurements.

[DODGER *awkwardly maneuvers around* MADELINE.]

DODGER   Hi.

MADELINE   [*Taking in his whole Goth situation.*] Hi.

[*He measures the canvas.*]

HENRY   Alright, my lady.

[*With a reverent little bow—*]

Bonne chance.

[HENRY *hops back to his instruction.*]

So. Prechecks. Just making sure there is nothing new—no tiny scratch or discrepancy of texture on the painting or the frame. If we find anything we are unsure about, we write it on our sheet and report it immediately, and someone from Restoration will come examine the piece. After a little time of doing this every day with the paintings, this intimate encounter at the beginning and end of each shift, you start to realize what a privilege it is.

You'll find your eyes continue to find something new. Something—you didn't see before. And that's an interesting phenomenon, no? How you can look at a piece a million times and suddenly see . . . it's mysterious. Because, of course, the painting is exactly the same. It's *you* that's different.

It's happening even now. Even now you are no longer the same. You know? Even now—you are changing.

[*A beat between them. Then* HENRY *suddenly whips an Officers' Inspection Report of Objects sheet for the morning prechecks out of his pocket.*]

So! This is the Officer's Inspection Report of Objects! Wheee! Pretty self-explanatory—just fill in the top section, date, gallery number, this is Room Thirty-Nine. . . . Uh-huh, right there. . . . Uh-huh. You see, they list the different items that might be in the room—paintings and works on paper get tallied together, sculpture, furniture, etc.—so you just count them for this top section, and then down below is where you write any notes. So first just count and we'll go from there.

DODGER   Okay.

[DODGER *counts the items in the room.* HENRY *looks at* MADELINE *and then at the Rembrandt, with a familiar smile.*]

So the bust is a sculpture?

HENRY   Correct.

DODGER   And the sketches?

HENRY   Works on paper, up there with the paintings.

DODGER   Okay. We've got thirteen paintings and works on paper, one sculpture, one piece of furniture. (Do I count the bench?) . . .

HENRY   No, but you do check the ceiling for any leaks.

DODGER   Okay. Done.

HENRY   You're a natural! Now. Something you'll hear an awful lot about, at team meetings and such, is protection. You see, we're not just here to protect the art, we are here to protect the space *around* the art.

DODGER   The space around the art.

HENRY   Correct. We have an estimated four million visitors per year, in peak season that's roughly eight to nine thousand visitors per day, and it is our job to ensure that the art (and the space around the art) is safe. So that is why we rotate every twenty minutes. The idea being that by keeping a shifting façade—

DODGER   Do the guards ever move up?

HENRY   Sorry?

DODGER   Like, do the museum guards ever rise in the ranks so they can affect policy?

HENRY   What an interesting question. Uhh, not that I know of. Though I've only been here since *ancient Greece*, so perhaps before then. Who knows—maybe you'll be the first!

[*Re: the prechecks sheet.*]

Alright, I'm going to run this down to the office. It's your first shift! Don't be nervous. It's a museum. Nothing happens.

[HENRY *leaves.* MADELINE *stands down front, facing the audience, looking at a large painting. Her hands are on her heart. She is rapt.* DODGER *stands at his post by the archway. Several moments pass. . . .*]

DODGER   If you want to touch it I won't tell.

[*Beat.*]

MADELINE   What?

DODGER   You heard me.

[*She takes a beat, decides mental illness might be at play, or that she misheard, goes back to the painting.*]

I'm serious.

[*She looks at him.*]

You can touch it.

[*She looks around, then back at him.*]

Touch it.
Touch the art.
I won't tell.

[*She looks at him.*]

You know you want to.
Go on.
Touch it.
Touch the art.
Quick.
I can't protect you long.
Go on.
This is your moment.
Touch the art.
Touch it.
Become part of its history.
Go on.
Touch it.

Touch it.
Touch it.
Touch—

MADELINE   [*Shaming him, very firm.*] Stop. Stop that. I'm not going to touch the art.

[*She feels a little bad.*]

Thank you anyway.

[*A beat. She tries to go back to enjoying the painting. Even puts her hands back on her heart. She almost succeeds, but then—*]

DODGER   I understand.
You don't feel worthy.
It's the art.
You're in the space around the art.
You're under the spell!
I get it.
It's cool.

I think you'll regret it.
Later.
In the bathtub.
You'll think, Dammit.
I should've touched the art.
Just saying.

MADELINE   I'm not going to touch the art. What's wrong with you?

DODGER   What's wrong with me? What's wrong with *you*? That's the question. You get a perfectly good opportunity to touch the art and you blow it? Do you realize what I'm risking for you? I see you, your hands on your heart, and I think, There, there is a person who would appreciate an opportunity to touch the art. So I take that risk, I make that leap, and you shame me? Shame on *you*, that's what I say.

MADELINE   Are you mentally ill? I'm serious, do you have a diagnosis? Because later tonight "in the bathtub" (whatever *that means*) I will *not* feel bad for not touching the art, but I *will* feel bad for bawling out a developmentally challenged bipolar who had a bad day with his meds, you know what I'm saying?

DODGER   [*A little cowed.*] My mother was bipolar.

MADELINE   Don't tell people to touch the art. Are you going to tell people to touch the art? Don't do that. Are you going to do that?

DODGER No.

MADELINE Don't lie to me.

DODGER I'm not. You just seem like someone who deeply loves art—

MADELINE I do, I do deeply love art.

DODGER Okay, and I think it would be good to bring art and people together, not further apart, break down the divide so that people won't feel—so—alienated.

MADELINE That "divide," as you call it, is not there to make people feel alienated. It's there to protect the art from the grimy shit on our fingers, like chicken grease, which, yes, maybe I just had because maybe I've been a feeling a little sad and unmoored lately and I thought fried chicken would help, because I used to have it a lot as a child, which is not the point. The point is that we don't touch the art because it will *harm* the art, and then *no one* will be able to become "a part of the art's history" because the art will be *ruined*.

DODGER I never thought of it that way.

MADELINE How did you get this job?

DODGER Please don't report me. I wanna rise up the chain of command so I can effect change.

MADELINE Well, you're off to a bad start.

[MADELINE *stares back at the painting, suddenly consumed with the possibility of touching it.*]

Have you ever touched the art?

DODGER No. I haven't, I swear to God, I haven't. I just want to. I just want someone who seems worthy to do it so that I can, I don't know . . .

MADELINE And I would be worthy why?

DODGER I don't know—because you had your hands on your heart and you're so pretty. Please don't report me. I'm not mentally ill. I'm artistic.

[*Beat.*]

MADELINE Alright, I'm not going to report you. *Don't* do that again. No one should touch the art, do you understand? Unless they are trained professionals. Okay? Okay?

DODGER Okay.

MADELINE Okay.

[*Beat.*]

And thank you.

[*Beat.*]

For saying I was pretty.

[*Beat.*]

DODGER   You're welcome.

[*Long beat. She stares forward, unable to stop thinking about touching the painting. What that would mean. And why that feels so connected to her hands on her heart.* MADELINE *stands lost in thought for a moment, looking down, brow furrowed.* DODGER *watches.*]

DODGER   Are you okay?

MADELINE   Stop watching me.

DODGER   Sorry.

MADELINE   Don't you have something else to do?

DODGER   No. . . . You look—*peaked.*

MADELINE   Stop watching me.

DODGER   I have to watch you; it's my job.

MADELINE   Well, stop.

DODGER   Sorry.

MADELINE   *Peaked?*

DODGER   . . . Sorry.

[*She continues to stand there in front of the painting, facing the audience. She seems unable to move—to sit back down and paint—or to cry—or to make a friend—all of which would probably help her.*]

MADELINE   There's nothing wrong with rules.

DODGER   Did you really just say that?

MADELINE   What? There's not.

DODGER   Of course there is.

MADELINE   No there's not.

DODGER   Rules *suck.*

MADELINE   *Rules suck?* What, did you like read that on a T-shirt?

DODGER   Don't tell me you think rules are *good*?

MADELINE   Of course I do. Rules tell you how to live, what's wrong with that?

DODGER   Rules don't tell you how to live, *morals* tell you that. And you already know how to live. You're here communicating with art. You're ahead of most of the world.

MADELINE   You're the weirdest person I have ever met.

DODGER   Thank you.

MADELINE   It wasn't . . . a . . . compl—

[*She get a wave of lightheadedness.*]

DODGER   Are you okay?

MADELINE   . . . No—I need—to just—I'm—

[*She sits down right where she is, right in front of the painting, down center.* DODGER *comes to her.*]

DODGER   Okay, okay, just sit right there. Sit right there. Yeah, you look— you're still very pretty but you do look a little—sweaty—like your eyes are watery and your pupils are dilated.

MADELINE   I need to just. Sit. For a moment.

DODGER   Okay. Uh. Do you want me to go get you some water?

MADELINE   No.

[*He looks around for a moment. No one is around.*]

DODGER   Should I go call someone?

MADELINE   I have some water in my bag.

[*He gets it out and hands it to her. She takes a sip. He crouches next to her.*]

DODGER   Is that better?

[*She nods. A quiet beat. Her eyes are closed.*]

MADELINE   Will you just hold my hand? For a moment?

DODGER   . . . Sure. Yes.

[*He takes her hand. They stay like that for a moment.*]

MADELINE   Do you ever feel . . . like your whole life is ahead of you . . . and you're not sure . . .

DODGER   . . . You're not sure what?

MADELINE   [*searching*]

I don't know—you're not sure . . . *why.*

[*They sit for another moment.*]

DODGER   What's your name?

MADELINE   Madeline.

DODGER   Madeline. I'm Dodger.

[*He gives her hand a little bob up and down.*]

Nice to meet you.

[HENRY *re-enters.*]

HENRY   Oh dear.

DODGER   Sorry. She got—she felt—

MADELINE   I felt dizzy for a moment—it's nothing really—I can get up now.

DODGER   You sure?

HENRY   No, no, just stay here for a moment. Dodger, we have to file a report. (Forgive me, madam, I'm going to use this as a teaching moment.) We can't let her get up and walk around until she's cleared.

MADELINE   No, really, I'm totally fine now.

DODGER   She seems totally fine now.

HENRY   I'm sorry, my lady, I have to ask you to rest here for me.

[*To* DODGER.]

What if she gets up and staggers around and knocks over the sculpture over there? This is the protocol. Go notify Jonny.

[DODGER *reluctantly lets go of* MADELINE's *hand. He exits.* HENRY *and* MADELINE *sit quietly for a moment.*]

HENRY   Thanks for your patience. This won't take very long. We'll have you back up to your work in no time.

[*Beat.*]

So how long have you been a painter?

MADELINE   Uhhhhh, about a week?

HENRY   Oh. A novice.

MADELINE   Yeah. What's that quote? *If you're sad, the best thing to do is learn something . . .* ? My grandmother and I used to come here when I was little, before her MS got really bad. . . . So I found this painting class. I'm terrible at it, but I like it. It's soothing or something.

HENRY   It was Merlin.

MADELINE   I'm sorry?

HENRY   Merlin said that. T. H. White, I believe, *The Once and Future King*: "The best thing for being sad . . . is to learn something. . . . You may grow old and trembling in your anatomies, you may lie awake at night listening to the disorder of your veins, you may miss your only love. There is only one thing for it then—to learn."

MADELINE   Yes. While my grandmother was dying, I read to her. Mostly I don't remember what, but that passage stayed with me.

HENRY   You must have spent a lot of time with her.

MADELINE   She took care of me. Well, the last few years I took care of her.

HENRY   You're very young to have been a caretaker.

MADELINE   I guess so, but . . . she was my person. She died. Just last week actually.

[*She touches a small ring on her finger.*]

 She left me this ring.

[HENRY *takes her in.*]

HENRY   You know, there are three types of people who come to the museum.

The most obvious are the tourists. Kind folk who feel they should see that famous Van Gogh or Monet, so they zoom through the rooms to find them, and then look around a bit forlornly before they wander out again into this strange thing we call a city.

Then there are the old white-haired ladies (and their dutiful husbands) who have been coming to the museum for years. You know who I mean—this brave, blessed generation of men and women who go to the theater, who buy memberships, who understand what it means to participate in the cultural institutions of our country—and who are frankly keeping those institutions alive. And who themselves will soon die, leaving the rest of us to *catch on.*

And finally there are the seekers. Souls on the verge of an *understanding.* They look at each painting, at each sculpture, like it's going to reveal exactly what they need. As if any moment it's going to look back at them and say . . . *"I know you"*. . .

[*She nods. Something between them. Then she rubs her leg, her brow furrowed.*]

Are you alright?

MADELINE   My leg is tingling. This has been happening all week—I keep—having symptoms of MS—I can't tell if they're just—psychosomatic or—I get dizzy, a tingling in my legs. . . .

[*She starts to panic a bit, rubbing her leg.*]

I need to get up. I need—please, I need to move my legs.

HENRY   I'm sorry, I, uh—

MADELINE   Please. I can lean on you. I just have to get up right now. My leg needs blood. I need to get up. I need to get up right now.

HENRY   Alright. Alright. Let's . . .

[*He helps her stand. He steadies her as she moves her legs tentatively, getting feeling back into them.*]

How is that, is that better?

MADELINE   [*Trying to calm down, or not bawl.*] A little. Sorry. I don't really know what to do with myself. . . .

[*A beat as* HENRY *figures out how to help/distract her.*]

HENRY   [*Looking at up at the Rembrandt before them.*] It's a wonderful painting you're working on, *Aristotle with a Bust of Homer.*

MADELINE   [*Still recovering a bit.*] Yeah.

HENRY   There are so many rich details that make it unique, don't you think? Like the hands.

MADELINE   What about the hands?

HENRY   Oh, have you not noticed? The hands are different sizes! Look at that front hand—it's abnormally large, while the other hand is quite small.

MADELINE   Wow. I've never noticed that.

HENRY   I don't particularly know what to make of it, but I love it.

MADELINE   [*Appreciatively.*] Huh. And look at that little ring. It's just *glows.*

HENRY   Did you choose this painting? For your class?

MADELINE   Yeah. My grandmother was the second type you mentioned— the old ladies who support culture?

HENRY   Ah, yes. God bless her!

MADELINE   Yeah, right? So it just seemed right to do a classic.

HENRY   Well, you picked a good one. Rembrandt was at the height of his powers when he painted it.

MADELINE   Why did he pick Aristotle?

HENRY   It's debated whether he did! It was commissioned by a rich Italian named Ruffo, and all we know is that he requested "a philosopher." There's some pretty good scholarship out there that asserts it was actually Apelles, the ancient painter. Do you notice anything funny about his clothing?

MADELINE   His clothing . . . Oh! It's not historically accurate. He's not dressed like an ancient Greek or whatever.

HENRY   Yes you're very clever! It's true—Rembrandt put Aristotle (or Apelles) in clothing of his own time. Apparently *historical accuracy* is a relatively modern notion!

MADELINE   I love the way he is touching the head of Homer. . . . As if he's trying to connect to the past, find something he can *hold on to.* . . .

HENRY   Mmmm, I like that. And see the way his other hand is touching the chain he wears? That refers to the Golden Chain of Being—from Homer's *The Iliad*—the Chain that connects the earth to the heavens. Wonderful poet, Homer.

[*Beat.*]

How's your leg feeling?

MADELINE   It's better. Thank you.

[*Suddenly there is "ding" from* HENRY's *pocket. He pulls out his cell phone.*]

HENRY   I'm so sorry.

MADELINE   That's okay—

HENRY   We're not supposed to—but my partner is *not well.*

[*He reads the text. Doesn't respond.*]

MADELINE   Is everything okay?

HENRY   Hm? Oh, just a grocery request. No one's dead. At least not yet. (Ha-ha.)

MADELINE   What's your partner's name?

HENRY   Simon. Simon Noth (speaking of wonderful poets).

MADELINE   Oooh, a poet. I'd love to marry a poet. Or at least sleep with one.

HENRY   Oh, they're terribly dashing as a breed, aren't they? Shall we walk you a bit? Would that help your leg?

[*They walk in a loop around the room, her on his arm.*]

MADELINE   You met in school?

HENRY   Oh no, he was fifteen years older than me, although we were in a school (technically). He was giving a reading at the school where I taught, and I was *very* young, mind you, I'd never been in love, and I saw him read his work and he was—lit from within or something—I just wanted to touch him.

MADELINE   An older man. I'd also like to sleep with one of those.

HENRY   [*Re: her long list of people to sleep with.*] My lady, you have much work to do!

MADELINE   Yeah, I guess I really do!

HENRY   Oh, nonsense, you have plenty of time. But I have to tell you, after our first date I thought, *Oh, don't love someone so much older. He'll die before you; you'll have to watch him—decay. . . .* But what can you do? . . .

[*Small beat.*]

Sorry I'm being macabre. Yes, hang out at poetry readings! Great way to meet a—what do the youth say now?—a "hottie"! Great way to meet a "hottie."

MADELINE   My grandmother always said, Whatever blows your skirt.

HENRY   Oh my!

MADELINE   [*Laughing with him.*] Oh yeah!—and she knew how to blow her skirt, believe me. She said, Madeline, you'll find most of the time the *braver* choice is the *better* choice. She was deeply cool.

[*They've arrived back in front of the painting, which she now considers in a new way.* DODGER *re-enters with* JONNY.]

JONNY   How are we doing here?

HENRY   Much better it seems.

JONNY   Ma'am, are you sure you should be standing?

MADELINE   Yeah. I just felt light-headed.

JONNY   I can call an ambulance for you if you'd like.

MADELINE   No, seriously—

DODGER   Maybe a little orange juice? It's vitamin D–fortified.

MADELINE   No. No orange juice, I'm really fine.

JONNY   Okay, I'm going to get the paperwork for you to sign saying you declined the ambulance.

[JONNY *leaves.*]

MADELINE   Jesus.

HENRY   It's the era of lawsuits.

DODGER   [*Gentle, to* MADELINE.] How are you?

MADELINE   Better. Much better.

HENRY   [*Noticing their connection.*] Dodger, what's your station in life?

DODGER   Uhhh. I'm a street artist.

HENRY   What do you mean?

DODGER   Depends on who you ask. If you ask the establishment, I vandalize public buildings.

HENRY   If we ask *you*—

DODGER   Then I create art right on the very walls of public life. Not separate, but right on the side of your bank. Your train. Your favorite deli.

MADELINE   So, in the Rembrandt, who do you think that is—Aristotle or Apelles?

DODGER   Oh, Apelles.

HENRY   Interesting!

MADELINE   Why?

DODGER   Rembrandt was saying artists are the real philosophers. We're the ones really studying and communicating the human condition. Poor sonofabitch.

MADELINE   Rembrandt?

DODGER   Oh yeah. Lost everything. His money, his fame, his family. But here he is.

[*A thoughtful pause between all of them.*]

MADELINE   What is it about museums? They just make it better somehow.

DODGER   Do you think? I think they make people feel more alone, more separate.

MADELINE   But that's why they make it better. The aloneness is the truth.

DODGER   The aloneness is the truth. Rules tell you how to live. Listen to you!

MADELINE   Listen to *me*? Listen to *you*! Museums make people feel more separate? You're a *museum guard*. You *work* in a *museum*!

DODGER   It's my first day.

MADELINE   Somehow I'm sensing it's not gonna work out.

DODGER   Not with *that* attitude it's not.

MADELINE   *Not with that attitude?* You are so annoying.

DODGER   Thank you.

MADELINE   It's *not a comp*—

HENRY   Can I say something?

[*They had forgotten about him.*]

MADELINE/DODGER   What?

HENRY   You two should go on a date.

[*Beat.*]

MADELINE/DODGER   What?

HENRY   A date. You should go on a date.
Just do it.
Go on a date.
You're the same age!
You're both lovely!
You seem to—um— *engage* one another?
Go on a date!

[*They look at him like he's crazy.*]

Listen:

[*To* DODGER.]

She's grieving.

[*To* MADELINE.]

He can pull off a Mohawk.

[*To them both.*]

It's a match!

[*They stare at him—that makes no sense. Another "ding" from his pocket.*]

Excuse me. Dispatch from the House of Death.

DODGER   House of Death?

HENRY   That's our nickname for our apartment.

[*He reads the text. Doesn't respond.*]

MADELINE   Henry's partner is dying.

DODGER   Really?

HENRY   [*Putting his phone away.*] Uhhhhh. Yes.

DODGER   I'm sorry to hear that.

HENRY   Well. I mean we're *all* dying, in one way or another. Some of us are just doing it a little faster than others.

[*Beat.* HENRY *escapes by looking closer at the painting.*]

Look at that chain. Did Rembrandt really intend for it to be Homer's Golden Chain of Being? Or did he paint it just because it was fun to paint? I mean, look at the thick, voluptuous paint. It's very bold. It *shimmers*. Makes you just want to . . . touch it.

[Madeline *and* Dodger *make eye contact.*]

Madeline   Maybe you should.

[*Beat.*]

Henry   What?

Madeline   Maybe you should touch it.

[Henry *nods, not sure if he misheard or mental illness might be at play, tries to go back to the painting, but then—*]

Henry   What?

Madeline   Maybe you should touch the painting. Maybe you should touch the Golden Chain of Being.

Henry   Maybe I should touch the painting?

Madeline   Yeah.

Henry   Have you lost your mind?

Madeline   Yeah.

Dodger   I'm with her. I think you should touch the painting.

[*Beat.* Henry's *brain just won't compute.*]

Henry   What?

Dodger   Touch it.

Madeline   Touch the painting.

Dodger   Touch it.

Madeline   Touch the painting.

Dodger   Touch it.

Madeline   You're worthy.

Dodger   You really are.

Madeline   You're the most worthy human being in this room.

Dodger   Well.

Madeline   What?

Dodger   You're worthy too.

Madeline   No I'm not.

Dodger   Yes you are.

MADELINE   I'm really not.

DODGER   You're wrong.

MADELINE   I wanted my grandmother to die. Believe me I'm not worthy.

DODGER   What do you mean?

MADELINE   Like I stood at her bed and I said, *Please just go.*

DODGER   Everyone wants their grandmother to die.

MADELINE   What?

DODGER   Grandparents are scary. Right? Eventually? Not when you're little, not before you understand that Death is going to devour everything you love. But then you start to understand these things and you watch your grandparents get older and lose their dignity and who wouldn't want that to end? It's a major buzz kill.

MADELINE   You're not helping.

DODGER   [*Back to* HENRY.] You should touch the art.

MADELINE   You should.

DODGER   And so should you.

[*Beat.* HENRY *looks back at the painting, like it's suddenly calling to him. It has never occurred to him that he could touch the art.*]

HENRY   Touch the art. . . .

[*Something opens inside him.*]

[JONNY *re-enters with the forms.*]

JONNY   Okay, buckarooneys. Here's a form for you, and a form for y —.

[*He stops, sensing he's interrupting something large.*]

What's goin' on?

[*Beat.*]

HENRY   [*Still with the painting.*] Grief is mysterious.
It's the sunlight.
Or certain street corners.
A sudden sense that you're dreaming.
Like you misplaced something of immense value and have no idea where.
Or how.
Grief is
A profound sense of failure.
Terrible, terrible failure.

MADELINE [*Recognizing it for herself.*] Failure . . .

HENRY It's so hard . . . to love someone.
Because inevitably it's not going to be enough. Or work.
Eventually they're going to—

[*He makes a gesture that mirrors the Golden Chain in the painting.*]

Ascend their own Golden Chain
and there's nothing you can do.
Except hope that you helped them, somehow.
And live with the fact that you couldn't.

[*Beat.*]

JONNY Well, now I'm depressed.

HENRY So am I. . . . Which is why I'm going to touch the art.

[MADELINE *gasps!*]

JONNY Wait, what?

HENRY Jonny, we're going to touch the Rembrandt. You should join us.

JONNY Are you joking?

HENRY No.

DODGER Let's do this.

[MADELINE *and* DODGER *and* HENRY *prepare.*]

JONNY Wait, guys, guys, what's goin' on?

MADELINE How should we do this? Like a three count?

JONNY What's happening?

HENRY I love that.

JONNY Guys, *guys*, come on, let's just—

HENRY [*Totally unfazed.*] I say we only touch a specific spot, reduce the impact.

JONNY Step back.

MADELINE I'll touch the ring.

JONNY Come on.

HENRY I'll touch the chain.

DODGER Alright. Homer's hair.

[JONNY *suddenly draws his gun.*]

JONNY GUYS. GUYS. STEP AWAY FROM THE PAINTING.

[*They stop and look at him, but don't move.* JONNY *stands there with his gun, very uncomfortable.*]

Goddammit this is the worst day ever!
I just drew my gun on my friend!
Because he's lost his mind with *grief*!
And said all this depressing shit that I'm never going to forget.
And now I have to go home and ask Twyla if I've remotely helped her up her Golden Chain.
Fuck me!

MADELINE   [*To* HENRY.] Thank you for saying all that. I feel better.

JONNY   This is really awkward right now. Henry, we've been friends a long time—don't make me tackle you.

HENRY   I'm sorry, Jonny.

MADELINE   You only live once, right?

DODGER   We do realize this won't change anything. We're still going to be . . . whatever we are.

JONNY   Guys.

MADELINE   But maybe not. Maybe something will *get in*.

HENRY   Let's do this.

DODGER   [*In response to "something will get in."*] What?

HENRY   One.

DODGER   What will get in?

JONNY   Guys!

HENRY   Two.

MADELINE   [*Twinkling with the mystery, the potential.*] I don't know.

HENRY   Three.

[HENRY, MADELINE, *and* DODGER *reach out to touch the art.*]

[*Blackout. End of scene.*]

RED

[*Lights up to reveal a large, spacious room in a luxurious home in Amsterdam. The year is 1653. The Rembrandt paintings that were on the wall in the museum are now resting on the ground, covered in sheets. The walls are now a deep red. The bust of Homer is still in the corner.*]

[Rembrandt Van Rijn *is getting ready to paint. He has had too much wine. He holds a letter from Ruffo, his patron.*]

Rembrandt   [*Reading Ruffo's letter.*] A *philosopher?* Oh, he's got to be joking.

[*As Ruffo.*]

Dear Rembrandt—Paint me a *philosopher.*

[*As himself.*]

Dear Ruffo—No.

[*Mutters.*]

(Jackass.)

And then he'll write me back—

[*As Ruffo.*]

Dear Rembrandt—Why not?

[*As himself.*]

And I'll say, Dear Ruffo—Because you're a greasy headed *putz.*
A *philosopher* is someone who appreciates the dark edges of humanity.
And *you*, sir, make *biscuits.* You're a *biscuit* guy.
What kind of asshole has a family fortune in *biscuits?*
And he'll say—

[*Ala Ruffo.*]

Me.

[*An impotent Ruffo laugh.*]

Hehe hehe hehe.

[Rembrandt *as himself.*]

(I bet that's how he laughs: Hehe hehe hehe.)

[*Back as Ruffo.*]

Dear Rembrandt—I am paying you five hundred florins to paint me a *philosopher.*

[*As himself.*]

Dear Ruffo—I don't give a pigeon's pecker. Hehe hehe hehe!

[*Suddenly passionate, furious.*]

A philosopher
investigates their own face
over and over again,

searching for the bare, miserable, elemental *truth*.
A *philosopher*
reveals not what you *want*,
but what you *are*.
You wouldn't know a *philosopher*
If he *shat* on your *face*!

Actually don't mind if I do.

[REMBRANDT *plops the canvas on the floor and squats to take a shit.* HENNY *enters on* REMBRANDT, *mid-squat. She's brought bread.*]

HENNY   [*Unfazed, also unamused.*] What are you doing?

[*Beat.*]

REMBRANDT   [*Caught.*] Prepping the canvas.

HENNY   Is this a new technique?

REMBRANDT   [*Still squatting.*] Yes.

HENNY   And who might this new technique be for?

REMBRANDT   Antonio Ruffo. The Biscuit Guy.

HENNY   Sounds benign.

REMBRANDT   Don't be fooled. Putzes like him will destroy us all.

HENNY   He's employing *you*, so he can't be that bad.

REMBRANDT   Well.

HENNY   What does he want, this putz?

REMBRANDT   A *philosopher*.

HENNY   Not bad.

REMBRANDT   [*Loud fart sound.*] *Pfffffff.*

[*Beat.*]

HENNY   My love.

REMBRANDT   What?

HENNY   Get up.

[*Beat.*]

REMBRANDT   I can't.

[*Beat.*]

HENNY   Why not?

[*Beat.*]

Rembrandt   I'm stuck.

[*She goes to him.*]

I hate getting old!

Henny   You're not getting old.

Rembrandt   Yes, I am, that's why they hate me.

Henny   Who?

Rembrandt   The annals of my fickle public.

Henny   [*Restoring his pants.*] Annals? Don't say annals, my love. Your public loves you.

Rembrandt   But eventually they *won't* love me and I'll be bankrupt and destitute, with little gray patches on my sleeves, the cries of my dead children clanging in my head like hungry coins in—in—in tiny metal cups.

[*Both struck with the sudden darkness of this image.*]

Henny   Why do you drink in the morning, my love?

Rembrandt   (I know.)

Henny   It makes you so maudlin.

Rembrandt   I knooooooooowwwwww.

Henny   When I hear you doing voices in here I know you need some bread.

Rembrandt   And so you brought some.

Henny   And so I brought some.

[*He takes her hand.*]

Henny   Shall I sit for you?

Rembrandt   I'm not painting a woman.

Henny   [*Starting to undo her blouse.*] That's never mattered before. You need company.

Rembrandt   No, no let me work. There's a certain Italian putz that needs a painting. I hate him.

Henny   You don't.

Rembrandt   I do.

Henny   You hate needing him. It's not the same thing.

Rembrandt   Yes, it is.

HENNY   Do you have an idea?

REMBRANDT   Oh, whatever—it's always me in the end. It's like a curse. With the lace, the fur, I can get away, crack into something *beautiful*—and then I get to the face and there I am—mucous-y eyes, thirsty lips, worried brow. Me. Every time. And eventually they'll see it. The *Fashion* will see it and I'll be ruined.

[**HENNY** *has been listening, like a good friend. She perhaps has also been tidying, like a good partner.*]

HENNY   How much is the commission?

REMBRANDT   Five hundred florins.

HENNY   Very good.

REMBRANDT   Says you.

HENNY   Yes, says me. Says the *annal* of your fickle *pubic.*

REMBRANDT   [*An old joke between them.*] Oh, ha-ha-ha-ha-ha.

HENNY   Ha-ha-ha-ha-ha.

REMBRANDT   [*She made him laugh.*] You're charming.

HENNY   And you're grumpy.

REMBRANDT   Well, bring your annal over here and improve my mood.

HENNY   I'll do no such thing, leave my annal out of it. Eat your bread. I checked your pigment last night—you're fine on red and ochre, but you needed charcoal, so I sent Titus.

REMBRANDT   Well, we know how Titus loves a good *errand.*

HENNY   Be nice to poor Titus, he's had a very bad morning.

REMBRANDT   And why's that?

HENNY   A package arrived.

REMBRANDT   So what?

HENNY   So you promised Titus no more packages for a while.

REMBRANDT   Oh God. That's a present for you, you know.

HENNY   I don't need any presents.

REMBRANDT   Don't say that, I love giving you presents.

HENNY   My love, the very fact that I will never again be someone's maid is all the present I shall ever need.

REMBRANDT   Did you hate being my maid?

HENNY   Well, obviously being *your* maid had its perks, but I'd been many many maids before I was yours and, yes, I hated it. You saved me.

REMBRANDT   [*Dead serious.*] No, no. It was you who saved me.

[*She touches his face.*]

HENNY   Nothing will save you from Titus, so you'd better eat some bread. I'll have tea for you in a little while when you hit your slump.

REMBRANDT   My slump. What slump?

HENNY   You know, when you come into the kitchen and pick things up and put them down.

REMBRANDT   What?

HENNY   Every day at about noon. And tea always helps.

REMBRANDT   My Henny. What would I do without you?

HENNY   Stay drunk and run out of pigment. I leave you to it.

[*She starts to go.*]

REMBRANDT   [*Stopping her, very serious.*] My love. I dreamt it again last night. I was on a dark ship, like some Odysseus. You were naked on the bow, shivering. There was a light on half my face, like here, and I could hear Titus crying in the dark. . . .

HENNY   My love—

REMBRANDT   . . . and there was an angry god down in the water. . . . And then you were gone.

HENNY   [*Warning.*] My love, stop—

REMBRANDT   Everyone was gone—

HENNY   [*With love, his face in her hands.*] Stop this. There is nothing to be afraid of. There is no dark ship. There is only you. And that canvas. Nothing more.

[*A beat. He nods.*]

REMBRANDT   A philosopher . . .

HENNY   [*Holding her breasts.*] Oof, I'm going to wake the baby. My breasts are killing me.

REMBRANDT   Good God—the baby! I always forget we have one! What's her name again?

HENNY   Cornelia.

REMBRANDT   Cornelia, lovely that.

HENNY   She's quite enchanting actually. And hopefully hungry.

REMBRANDT   Bring her in here, I want to eat one of her fat legs.

[*The sound of the front door.*]

HENNY   I will in a bit. I believe your other child just arrived home.

REMBRANDT   [*Back to his canvas.*] Titus? Good, I need the charcoal.

HENNY   Be nice to him. He worries about you.

REMBRANDT   [*Not really listening, working.*] Mm.

[*She starts to go—he looks up.*]

Henny.

[*She stops.*]

You're beautiful.

[*She smiles. Then leaves. He works.* TITUS *enters, very pissed.*]

TITUS   You have got to stop.

REMBRANDT   There you are. I need that charcoal.

TITUS   How could you?

REMBRANDT   How could I what?

TITUS   You know what.

REMBRANDT   I don't actually, the charcoal.

TITUS   [*Putting the charcoal on the table.*] How could you buy this damn pot?

[REMBRANDT *continues working.*]

REMBRANDT   Pot, what pot?

TITUS   This Asian pot, this pot from Asia.

REMBRANDT   Oh that.

TITUS   (*Oh that*, he says.)

REMBRANDT   That, my dear boy, is a *vase*.

TITUS   (A *vase*.)

REMBRANDT   An Asian *vase* and a very *elegant* one at that.

TITUS   Elegant? I believe the "e" word you're looking for is "expensive."

REMBRANDT   [*Taking the vase from him, sets it aside.*] Well, of course it was *expensive*; beautiful things of quality usually are. (I make my living on this principle, lest we forget.)

TITUS   It's precisely your living that I'm talking about.

REMBRANDT   Is it? I thought we were talking about a pot.

TITUS   You can't keep spending like this.

REMBRANDT   Like what?

TITUS   Like an emperor or something. You just bought this huge house in the most ridiculous part of town.

REMBRANDT   Which you don't seem to mind living in.

TITUS   Of course I don't mind living in it, it's not the house I take *issue* with—

[*He has pronounced "issue" with the "ss" sound rather than "sh."*]

REMBRANDT   *"Issue"?* Is that how the youth are saying it nowadays?

TITUS   [*Ignoring him.*] It's the buying of the house and then proceeding to spend as if said house was not purchased!

REMBRANDT   (*"Issue . . ."* It's like putting a moustache on a *wig.*)

TITUS   You're always complaining about having to hound people to pay you, and yet you spend like you're on salary with the royal crown!

REMBRANDT   Titus, you're your mother's son.

TITUS   And a lot of good it did *her.*

[*A stunned beat.*]

I'm sorry. I didn't mean that.

[*A pained silence.*]

I just want you to be more careful.

REMBRANDT   If it were up to you we'd live like monks.

TITUS   That's not true.

REMBRANDT   Yes it is. Titus the monk. Except I don't know what you pray to, Titus, what is your aim?

TITUS   You, you are my aim, you're what I pray to, do you know how that feels? Oh, Rembrandt the genius, and it's like yes but have you seen our bank book? I'm the child. Not you. It's not fair.

[REMBRANDT *studies him.*]

REMBRANDT   You're right, my boy.

TITUS   Oh God.

REMBRANDT   You are, you're quite right.

TITUS   Now you're humoring me.

Rembrandt   Humoring you?

Titus   Yes.

Rembrandt   What's the difference between humoring you and *agreeing* with you?

Titus   If you *agreed* with me you'd *change*.

Rembrandt   [*Struck.*] Jesus. I either need to get smarter or hope my family gets dumber.

Titus   [*Softening slightly.*] Maybe Cornelia will be dumb.

Rembrandt   You think?

Titus   I hope. Right now she's the only one I can boss.

Rembrandt   I know how you feel.

[Rembrandt *coughs.*]

Titus   [*Still mad, but wanting to be close, softer.*] Can I sit on your lap?

Rembrandt   [*Huh.*] Of course you can.

[Titus *sits on his father's lap.*]

Titus   You stink.

Rembrandt   Well, I'm old. Part of the deal.

Titus   That if you're old you stink?

Rembrandt   Indeed.

Titus   But I'm young and I stink.

Rembrandt   You don't stink.

Titus   How do you know? You're so old you can't smell.

Rembrandt   I can too smell.

Titus   What do I smell like?

Rembrandt   [*Smelling his wonderful son.*] Like sweat and bad vegetables and hair. It's lovely.

Titus   Henny says I stink.

Rembrandt   What does she know?

Titus   Everything.

Rembrandt   It's true.

Titus   Lucky us.

Rembrandt   [*Chuckling.*] Lucky us.

TITUS   Do people think I'm Henny's son?

REMBRANDT   Why do you ask?

TITUS   Master Thomlin told her to mind her son when we were in the shop. 'Til he realized who we were and then he sucked up because he knew we would buy something.

REMBRANDT   Do you want to be Henny's son?

TITUS   [*With a shrug.*] I like what I am.

REMBRANDT   And what's that?

TITUS   I'm like her helper that she hugs and tells they stink and then let's have warm apples with cinnamon.

REMBRANDT   Ah, lovely. She's lovely, our Henny.

TITUS   Am I crushing your leg?

REMBRANDT   A bit.

[TITUS *gets off his lap, sits down next to him. Softly.*]

TITUS   Do you think about Mother?

REMBRANDT   Saskia? Of course. Every day.

TITUS   What do you think about?

[*A painful beat.*]

REMBRANDT   Mostly I think about the end. . . . . I wasn't very there for her. In the end.

TITUS   Where were you?

REMBRANDT   [*Far away, like a bad dream.*] Anywhere I could be. Anywhere but next to her gaunt, sad face.

[*They both remember her gaunt, sad face.*]

TITUS   Do you tell Henny you think of her?

REMBRANDT   Of course. Henny knows grief and love aren't mutually exclusive.

TITUS   What do you mean they aren't mutually exclusive?

REMBRANDT   They're opposites that can coexist.

TITUS   Like that I stink but I'm lovely?

REMBRANDT   That's right. Or like light and dark.

TITUS   Or love and death.

REMBRANDT   Yes. Well done, little monk.

[*Sometime in the last beat or so* TITUS *has started mixing pigment for his father. They work together around the table. Throughout the following* REMBRANDT *begins to paint.*]

TITUS   [*The bust of Homer.*] Who's that?

REMBRANDT   That's Homer. Great poet. He wrote *The Iliad* and *The Odyssey*.

TITUS   They were poems?

REMBRANDT   More like stories. With speeches. *Lots* of speeches.

TITUS   [*Crinkling his nose at the bust,*] He looks weird. Was he weird?

REMBRANDT   Oh, I imagine so. We don't really know. Kind of like now. No one really knows who anyone is.

TITUS   I hate when you talk like this.

REMBRANDT   It's true. We're all just standing in front of one another, perceiving the basic composition, but the real core of it, this human being in front us, is a mystery. Like a good painting.

TITUS   I know you.

REMBRANDT   Oh, do you?

TITUS   Yes.

REMBRANDT   What do you know?

TITUS   I know you like bacon.

REMBRANDT   I do.

TITUS   And it gives you diarrhea.

REMBRANDT   It does.

TITUS   I know your cough in the morning sounds like the wheel at the mill getting stuck over and over again. . . . And you hate rich people and you're ticklish under your arm pits and your favorite color is blue.

REMBRANDT   How do you know my favorite color is blue?

TITUS   You always want Henny to wear her blue dress.

REMBRANDT   There's a lot of reasons I want Henny to wear that dress.

TITUS   And you never paint with blue.

REMBRANDT   So what?

TITUS   So that's how I know it's your favorite.

REMBRANDT   You think it's my favorite because I *don't* paint with it.

TITUS   Yes.

[*Beat.*]

Rembrandt   Does my cough wake you?

Titus   Yes. I always hear your cough. Even when I'm at school I feel like I know exactly when you're coughing.

[*They both think about* Titus *thinking about his father's cough.*]

Rembrandt   [*Struck, then redirecting.*] You can't paint with blue because it steals the show. These colors keep the person, the human being, focal—put blue on the canvas and suddenly we don't know where to look.

Titus   Why?

Rembrandt   Because blue is the color of divinity, the heavens. We don't need to see the heavens; we need to see *each other.*

Titus   I told you it was your favorite.

Rembrandt   [*Smiling, quietly satisfied with his wonderful son.*] . . .

Titus   [*Re: the painting.*] Who is this for, by the way?

Rembrandt   This, my dear boy, is for a certain Italian penis. In Italy.

Titus   That's generally where Italian penises live.

Rembrandt   And may it stay that way.

Titus   It is going to be of Homer?

Rembrandt   (That's an idea.) Homer—huh—I hadn't planned on it.

Titus   [*Back to Homer.*] He looks so old.

Rembrandt   He is old.

Titus   Older than you?

Rembrandt   Older than all the books you know.

Titus   Older than the Bible?

Rembrandt   Older than the Bible. When I was your age my father read him to me.

Titus   [*Ala gruff Harmen, a joke between them.*] Harmen van Rijn.

Rembrandt   [*Chuckle, ala gruff Harmen.*] Harmen van Rijn. Haven't they started Homer at your school? I'm going to read him with you tonight. And then someday you can read Homer to your son or daughter.

[Titus *approaches the bust of Homer. Pats his head.*]

Rembrandt   [*A hint of his terrible dream.*] Met a very bad end, poor Homer. No family or friends. Disgraced.

TITUS   Homer.

[*He suddenly sees* TITUS*'s hand on Homer's head.*]

REMBRANDT   Look at your tiny hand. How strange.

TITUS   It's not tiny.

REMBRANDT   It is. Look at mine.

[*They compare hands.*]

TITUS   Mine isn't tiny. Yours is just *big*. Your painting should have one of my hands and one of your hands.

REMBRANDT   Why's that?

TITUS   Then we'll be together. In the painting. Can I touch it?

REMBRANDT   The canvas? Sure, why not.

[TITUS *goes to the canvas, gently touches his fingertips to it. He stays there touching it for a long time.*]

Titus? What's wrong?

TITUS   [*Still touching it.*] Someday you'll be gone and we'll only have your stupid paintings.

REMBRANDT   That's not true.

TITUS   [*Quietly.*] Yes, it is.

REMBRANDT   [*Trying to make a joke.*] You'll have the Asian pot.

[*More serious.*]

You'll have your memories.

TITUS   I don't want memories. If you're not here I can't sit on your lap. Or smell you in the kitchen. And if you keep buying stupid Asian pots we won't have any money for your cough and you'll die.

[*Ah. There it is.* REMBRANDT *stops working.*]

REMBRANDT   Ah.

[*Beat.*]

Oh, my boy.

[*A moment of having no idea what to say. Gently —*]

I see it the other way. I won't die someday because I buy the Asian pot. I buy the Asian pot because someday I will die. Money is the opposite of beauty. And beauty is all we have.

TITUS   Well, some of us don't care about beauty and would rather have *you*.

REMBRANDT   Alright. Alright, Titus. No more Asian pots.

[*Beat.*]

TITUS   [*Quietly.*] You've said that before.

REMBRANDT   I have not.

TITUS   Yes, you have. That's how I know you're humoring me.

[*A kind of despair comes over* REMBRANDT. *He puts his hand on* TITUS's *smelly head.*]

REMBRANDT   My boy. Your old man is a very flawed creature. You have to forgive him for it.

[*A beat.*]

Go on now, let me work.

[TITUS *leaves.*]

A philosopher.

[*Blackout.*]

OCHRE

[*From the darkness—*]

HOMER   I don't want it written down!

[*Lights up to reveal the ochre wall of a large temple in ancient Greece. It is sunset. The poet* HOMER *is ranting about poetry.*]

I keep saying over and over again—
Don't write the damn thing down!
That'll fuck it all up!
If it's written down someone can sit and read it *by themselves,*
And that's a terrible idea! Terrible!
They won't understand it.
Not unless it's in front of them in image.

[*He looks up and suddenly sees the audience.*]

Holy shit.

[*He stands there and adjusts to this new given, this large group looking at him from the dark. . . . And then he decides to roll with it and continue his point.*]

Well, why not. . . .

Do you know what I'm saying?
They need to *hear it*—with their neighbor's smelly armpits and their child's

hiccups and some stranger's hair twisted up off their neck from the hot sun.
It needs to wash over them in the air—through their ears, around their
thoughts. . . .
You need to be able to zone out on the boring bits.
The Iliad is a long goddamn poem!
I should know, I wrote it, and believe me not all of it is *compelling*—
So let them think about the evening meal
or what it was like to touch their first breast
and they can't do that if it's written down, if it's written down
they have to *read* every word. *It's a terrible idea.*
I may be old and useless but I know a few things about poetry
and it's meant to be *heard.*

[*Calming himself, still eyeing the audience warily.*]

Alright, squirrel, slow yourself. Steady. Steady now.

[*Chuckles to himself.*]

Squirrel.
That's what my wife called me, you know.
Livia.
Ooooh she was a *pox.*
But I adored her by the end.

It takes a long time for people to learn to live together. And some people
never do, I've seen that. But if you can get through all the awful stuff, being
separate people and all that, domesticity can really work. Once you've done
the procreation bit and you can just let yourselves be the siblings you are—
siblings with a sordid past, if you will—you can just sleep with whomever
you please and enjoy a nice meal together at the end of the day. It's a boon.

I always found it quite interesting actually, who she'd take for lovers.
I remember when she took up with the Hyram, the baker.
Oh, he's terribly plain, terribly dull, I never would've thought.
But I saw them one day. He was wrapping her bread, *literally*,
and there was something in the way she took it from him, smiling,
that I knew he was wrapping her bread *metaphorically* . . .
and that fascinated me!
I spent the next few weeks watching him. . . .
It was a bit weird of me, I admit, but I wanted to *know*!
I was *curious*, you see?
I was curious about him, but really I was curious about *her.*
Why she liked this plain little baker with his paunch and bald head.

People cross paths at particular moments in their lives and it's a fascinating thing—ten years ago you'd have never dreamt it and then something about the thing they are and the thing you need. . . . I watched the way he worked the dough in his shop, the pale thick yeasty-smelling flesh, and I thought . . . *Huh.*

It's such a shame really—that by the time you're able to really see another human being, not as you know them, not as they pertain to you, but just as they are—which of course is an unknowable thing, a mystery—your life is basically over. It's like it's all about to get a lot more interesting, and *poof.* You're out.

I want to put my hand on your head.
Lay my images before your brain through the soft furry mess of your hair.

[*Suddenly very earnest, to the audience. Trying out a poem—maybe playing a lyre.*]

Bring your eyes to mine.
Let's start the climb—up the Chain
link by link—
scene by scene—
'Til we can feel the gods.
'Til we *are* the gods.

[*Beat. He makes a face.*]

Meh.

I like the idea, though.
Climbing the Chain.

A good poem should make you look down and suddenly see yourself.
Your fragile, freckled hands and toenails.
Your puckered rear.

[*Maybe he plucks the lyre again, gently, unconsciously.*]

I was by the river the other morning
And there was a large heron in the stream.
Slender, like a reed of light and mist
I watched it glide from one leg to the other for a few minutes—
When suddenly it turned and saw me—
I saw that we could see each other—and I thought—that—
That—is what it is to be *alive!*

We have no idea what the other is thinking, what's it's like to be them. . . .
We barely perceive what it is to be *ourselves!*
We are constantly encountering wild animals!
I'm a wild animal called Homer!

This temple belongs to a wild animal called Jove!
And you're a—well, I don't know, what are you?—
See, it's happening even now! . . .

[*He acts this out a bit, like he's the heron, the audience is him.*]

You and I are in a great stream, gliding from one leg to another,
We sense another is there,
and so we turn and see. . . .

[*He stands in the moment when we turn in the stream and see one another.
Then moves on.*]

You know madness isn't so bad.
One day you're ranting about poetry and then you look up and there's a
legion of—what?—mysterious creatures looking back at you and you think,
Well, alright.

Maybe that's what this whole business is about—art.
It's practice for the real thing.
If we can bear to listen to a poem, or a whatever,
we just might stand a chance of seeing another person. . . .

[*Suddenly frustrated, or filled with despair.*]

Or—I don't know.
I shit in a pot!
Can you believe it?
Shit? In a *pot?* It makes no sense.
But this will never change!
From now 'til eternity man will shit in a pot!
Death will await each of us.
Stop now—think—you're going to die, and you have no idea *how!*
It's a mystery that floats ahead of us all our lives.
How will you die?
Your mouth full of blood, your organs gasping?
Your legs crushed, the infection set in and unstoppable?
A broken heart?
Old age?
• Drowning as your child waves to you from shore . . . ?
Or a chicken bone—like a sharp exclamation point
stuck in your pink throat. . . .

I don't mind it really.
Death.
I don't want to *suffer.* I don't want boils on my flesh

or to fall into a ditch and break my leg and die ripped apart by buzzards.
But the dying itself bit? I'm good with that.
I try to look at it positively.
There are so many things I'm finally going to get to *find out.*
For example—
What on earth did Livia see in that Hyram?
I'm going to *ask her.*
(I'm also going to make love to her good and proper, rather than the drab
routine I did the last two hundred times or so she indulged me.)
I'm going to kiss her more.
Ooooh, that'll shock her!—she'll swat my arm and tell me to go jump in the
river (that's what she did when I was cheeky, which was always).

I'm going to see the heavens.
See what's really going on in all that blue up there. . . .
What a god really looks like.

[*He looks back at the audience. Suddenly struck by a possibility . . .*]

Or

Has that already happened?

Am I here already?

Did you watch me pull myself up,
Grasp the final golden link in that long long Chain. . .
And start raving about poetry
Not knowing
that I am here . . .?

[*He steps toward them, palms open, truly humbled.*]

Is this the heavens?
Are you . . .
the gods?

[*He stands there, searching their faces. Throughout the scene the sun has been
slowly setting, the light getting cooler and darker.* HOMER *slowly, gently, drops
to his knees, palms up.*]

Did I write anything of value?
Was I anything more than a poor, blind fool?
Did anyone hear any of it and
Miss their son,
Or plan a delicious evening meal,
Or tell their wife they adored her . . .?

You'll let me know.

Ye gods.

You'll let me know.

[*The sunset completes. Blackout.*]

BLACK

[*A dark room in the apartment of an old building. There is not much furniture left in this room, just the hospice bed, maybe the couch, an IV stand, a bedpan.* HENRY *enters. The hospice nurse,* MARTIN, *gets up, meets* HENRY *near the door.*]

MARTIN   Shhh.

HENRY   Hi.

MARTIN   He's sleeping.

HENRY   How was he today?

MARTIN   Did you get my texts?

HENRY   Sorry.

MARTIN   Would it hurt you to send a reply?

HENRY   We're not supposed to have our phones. On the job.

MARTIN   Mm-hmm.

HENRY   Did he eat?

MARTIN   Some pudding.

HENRY   Chocolate?

MARTIN   Mm-hmm.

HENRY   Good.

MARTIN   He wanted pistachio.

HENRY   And?

MARTIN   We're out. Thus my texts.

HENRY   Right. Yes. Sorry.

MARTIN   Mm-hmm.

HENRY   His fluids?

MARTIN   Pretty good. His spirits have improved. He told me to suck his dick.

HENRY   . . . No.

MARTIN   Oh yes.

HENRY   No!

MARTIN   Suck my dick.

HENRY   He hasn't said that since 1989!—a cop arrested him for holding my hand at a restaurant.

MARTIN   Well, he said it today. Suck my dick. Right in that bed.

HENRY   Jesus. Well, I'm sorry.

MARTIN   [*Affectionately.*] Don't be. Simon makes even "suck my dick" sound like poetry.

HENRY   Amen.

[*A beat.*]

MARTIN   You should know. . . .

HENRY   Yes?

MARTIN   He's in and out.

HENRY   In and out?

MARTIN   Of consciousness.

HENRY   . . . Oh.

MARTIN   He has moments of total lucidity, where he's his old self, and then the next moment he's gone.

HENRY   Okay.

MARTIN   Just so you know. So you're prepared . . .

HENRY   I understand.

[*Beat.*]

MARTIN   Alright I'm off.

HENRY   Thank you, Martin.

MARTIN   Sure thing.

HENRY   See you tomorrow.

MARTIN   I'll be here.

HENRY   So will I. All day. From now on.

[*He stops.*]

MARTIN   [*No judgment, just surprise.*] Really?

HENRY   Yes.

MARTIN   Alright. See you then.

[*He leaves.* HENRY *stays by the door, contemplating the sleeping* SIMON *across the room. A beat.*]

SIMON   [*Eyes still closed.*] Fuck you.

HENRY   [*Startled.*] Oh Jesus. You're awake.

SIMON   [*Mocking their exchange.*] The living bonding over the dead.

HENRY   Martin said you were asleep.

SIMON   "Amen." Assholes.

HENRY   You scared me, you know; "Fuck you" coming from the dark like a ghost.

SIMON   Oh, just you wait. I'm gonna haunt you like the "Cask of Amanti-fucking-llado."

HENRY   Simon.

SIMON   [*Making haunting ghost sounds.*] Ooooooooooh.

[SIMON *coughs. His voice is weak, but he's himself.*]

HENRY   Simon, stop.

SIMON   You didn't get the pudding.

HENRY   You had chocolate.

SIMON   Chocolate tastes like plastic now.

HENRY   I'll run out first thing in the morning. You'll have pistachio pudding before you can say "Suck my dick."

[HENRY *gives him a look.*]

SIMON   He deserved it.

HENRY   I doubt that very much.

SIMON   He was trying to make me shit in that thing again—that plastic pot—and I told him I was *done*—he said I wasn't dead yet and I still had to behave and shit where people can handle it, so I told him what he could do.

HENRY   Suck your dick.

SIMON   Indeed. I can't believe you didn't bring the pudding. I'm dying, you know.

HENRY   I do.

SIMON   No, you don't. You don't know I'm dying. You just think I'm smelly and sickly and shitting in a pot.

HENRY   When you've spent thirty-five years failing someone, it doesn't seem right to suddenly turn into Partner of the Year. Right at the end.

SIMON   (Failing someone. . . .)

HENRY   Right at the home stretch.

SIMON   What are you talking about?

HENRY   All the times I came home from work and you just wanted to go on a walk together.

SIMON   Well, you know how I love to creeper our neighbors.

HENRY   And all the dinners I finished first and left the table to read the paper because you eat so *interminably slow.*

SIMON   (My delicate constitution.)

HENRY   And left you sitting at the table . . . alone. . . .

[*He shakes his head with the pain of that thought.*]

Or how I always drank too much at your writing parties and accused you of flirting . . . or hinted you were a burden or . . . I could go on and on.

SIMON   Don't be dramatic.

HENRY   I have been vain. And petty. And eremitic.

SIMON   Eremitic? Don't say eremitic.

HENRY   And *mean.* And *cowardly.*

[*Beat.* SIMON *really takes him in.*]

SIMON   Well. I'd forgive it all for some fucking pistachio pudding.

HENRY   Would you now?

SIMON   Yes.

HENRY   Well then.

[HENRY *pulls out some pistachio pudding he picked up on the way home.* SIMON *gasps.*]

Ta da.

SIMON   Add manipulative to that list. And *dishonest.*

HENRY   I shall.

SIMON   And *sneaky.*

HENRY   Done. Shall I also add *forgiven*?

SIMON   Get me a spoon, you cad.

[HENRY *does.*]

Were you just going to keep that in your fucking pocket?

HENRY   I don't know, I was just trying to find some way to surprise you.

SIMON   [*Chuckling, pleased.*] I should have died while you still had it in your pocket! *That* would've haunted you good and proper.

[*Ala tortured* HENRY.]

"Oh, he never knew I had the pudding! I was too *eremitic*."

HENRY   [*An old joke between them, laughing like this.*] Oh, ha-ha-ha-ha-ha.

[HENRY *sits next to* SIMON *while he eats the pistachio pudding. He himself has opened a chocolate.*]

SIMON   [*Joining in, an old joke between them, laughing like this.*] Ha-ha-ha-ha-ha.

HENRY   I like the chocolate.

SIMON   Well, you don't have stage-four cancer.

HENRY   Neither do you. You're just smelly and sickly and shitting in a pot.

[*They eat.*]

SIMON   So how was your day at the House for Dead White Men? Did you bring home any umbrellas with naked cowboys in it?

HENRY   No.

SIMON   Then get out.

[HENRY *chuckles then pauses, trying to process his day.*]

HENRY   [*Almost vibrating with it.*] I think—I think I had an amazing day.

[SIMON *stops.*]

SIMON   Really? Pray tell.

HENRY   *Pray tell?* Don't become Emily Dickinson.

SIMON   What do you mean *become*? Emily and I have been *one* for many years, you know that.

HENRY   (Pray tell.)

SIMON   [*Falsetto, ala Emily Dickinson, an annoying one at that.*] *Because I could not stop for Death—*
He kindly stopped for me—
The Carriage held but just Ourselves—
And Immortality.

HENRY   You sound like a fag.

SIMON   I am a fag.

HENRY   How do you know?

SIMON   You suck my dick.

HENRY   [*Spitting up a little pudding.*] Ha!—not for many months now.

SIMON   Oh, rub it in.

[*They eat together for a few moments.*]

Lucky Emily.

HENRY   Why do you say that?

SIMON   Here we are, over a century later, quoting her poems.

HENRY   You've published eight books.

SIMON   Well.

HENRY   Well what?

SIMON   Will anyone *read it*? Will anyone quote it while eating pudding with the love of their life?

HENRY   . . . They may.

SIMON   Oh, shut up.

[HENRY *watches him, not wanting to break the spell.*]

HENRY   You're very spry tonight.

SIMON   How do you know? Maybe I'm this spry all day long.

HENRY   You know what I mean. We haven't talked like this in weeks. Usually when I get home you're out cold. . . . I've missed you.

SIMON   Oh God, don't.

HENRY   Don't what?

SIMON   Don't start in with some simpering "don't die" crap.

HENRY   I'm not.

SIMON   Well, good.

HENRY   . . . But don't.

SIMON   Don't what?

HENRY   Die. . . . Don't die.

SIMON   Ha-ha-ha-ha-ha.

HENRY   I'm serious. . . . Don't die.

SIMON   Come on.

HENRY   Don't die. Don't die.

SIMON   Henry.

HENRY   [*Heartbreaking, simple.*] Please.
Don't die.

. . .

Please don't die.
Please.
Don't die.
Please don't die.
Don't leave me here without you.
I don't want to be here without you.
My love.
My heart.
Please.

SIMON   [*Taking his hand, a whisper.*] Henry. . . .

[*Gently, but firmly.*]

Enough.

[*He holds* HENRY's *hand a moment longer, until he's recovered, then he pats it.*]

SIMON   So come on. You were out there today, the world beyond these walls—tell me everything. Any mental illness on display? Did Jonny let you touch his pee-pee in the boys room?

HENRY   [*Laughing, wiping his tears, but recovered.*] Oh, you're terrible to Jonny!

SIMON   Well, he's ridiculous.

HENRY   He's alright.

SIMON   Of course he's alright (if you drop every aspect of his personality besides the fact that he is kind to you).

HENRY   Well. He invited me to Easter.

SIMON   Oh?

HENRY   With him and Twyla.

[SIMON *experiences a tiny, imperceptible heartbreak.*]

SIMON   . . . You should go.

HENRY   Apparently she makes a very good lamb.

SIMON   You should. You should go.

HENRY   Who cares.

SIMON   You need to start doing things without me.

HENRY   Oh, shut up.

SIMON   You do.

HENRY   All this was before Jonny drew his gun on me.

SIMON   What?

HENRY   Jonny drew his gun on me.

SIMON   Is that a euphemism?

HENRY   No. Jonny drew his gun on me. And I no longer work there. At the House for Dead White Men.

SIMON   . . . What are you talking about?

HENRY   I got fired.

SIMON   You did not.

HENRY   I did.

SIMON   You did not!

HENRY   Yes, I did.

SIMON   . . . Don't fuck with me.

HENRY   I'm not. I touched the Rembrandt.

SIMON   (Why does everything sound like code?)

HENRY   I touched the Rembrandt in room thirty-nine. *Aristotle with a Bust of Homer*. Painted by one of the greatest painters our civilization has ever known. The subject of which is two of the greatest thinkers our civilization has ever known.

And I touched it!

Specifically the Golden Chain of Being (that Aristotle is wearing)—

[HENRY *holds up his middle and pointer fingers.*]

I touched it.

[SIMON *just sits there, stunned.* HENRY *disappears into the memory of it.*]

It was . . . surprisingly—*spiky*.
The paint.
Slashes of ochre
and black
and white
and red.
I suddenly thought—
Art is such a *slight* thing.

It's a trick.
The closer you get, it recedes, like a shadow.
It *lives*, it *glows*, and then you touch it and it's not really there.
Or it's *all* there—Rembrandt. Homer.
I touched *it all*. . . .
Well, specifically *three* of us touched it—myself, this girl Madeline, and Dodger.
We counted to three, and we touched it.

SIMON   . . . What the fuck's a dodger?

HENRY   He's a new guard. Or—well—who knows if they'll keep him on—
but they might—give him another chance. . . . I hope so, he's a sweet lad. (A
sweet lad, God I sound old.) I *felt* old, watching them exchange phone
numbers, arguing about where to meet for dinner, their faces like wet
paint. . . .

[*Like it's beautiful.*]

I felt *ancient.*

SIMON   [*Dreamily, from a faraway place.*] It's as if I'm on a great ship. I'm
honestly not sure if I'm dreaming this conversation. . . .

HENRY   I know! I already feel it wasn't real or something. . . . Look at my
hand—it looks so LARGE. . . .

[*The sight of his large hand triggers the memory.*]

I remember my dad reading in the paper that this Rembrandt had been
purchased for $2.3 million—and this was 1961, mind you!—and he turned
to me, I was all of *five*, and he said,

[*Ala gruff dad.*]

"Come on, Hank, we're going to see what the hell is worth $2.3 million." And
he dragged me to the exhibit. We stood in front of it, his brow furrowed, the
callouses on his hand. . . . There was something about the way he stood
there—staring—as if he felt *separate*—as if it was some great thing that
would always be just beyond his reach. . . .

I never asked him what he thought of it, the painting.
If he liked it.
If it pleased him.
(I'd like to think it did—that somehow he was—touched by it.)
I regret that actually.
Terribly.

It's just a slight thing—canvas, paint—and yet it contains—what?
Worlds. Truths.

[*As he speaks he is also seeing his beautiful* SIMON.]

I stood there today, and I thought,
There is only *one* of this—in *all of time.*
I touched that fragility
and my heart just . . .

[*Sometime in the last few minutes* SIMON *has closed his eyes. He is very still.*]

HENRY   My love? Are you there?

[SIMON *doesn't answer. We can hear his breath drawing gently in and out.*]

I want you to know.
You've been
a wonderful
partner.
You have.
I have failed you so terribly.
So terribly.
But I am here now.
I'm here.

[HENRY *puts his hand on* SIMON's *head, just like Aristotle with a Bust of Homer. They sit like that for a tender moment. Then blackout.*]

———————————

KING LIZ

by
Fernanda Coppel

Photograph by Paul Gregory Schlott

Production History

King Liz had its world premiere at Second Stage Uptown, at the McGinn/ Cazale Theatre, in July 2015.

Second Stage Artistic Staff

ARTISTIC DIRECTOR   Carole Rothman
EXECUTIVE DIRECTOR   Casey Reitz
ASSOCIATE ARTISTIC DIRECTOR   Christopher Burney

Cast

MR. CANDY   Michael Cullen
FREDDIE LUNA   Jeremie Harris
COACH JONES   Russel G. Jones
BARBARA FLOWERS   Caroline Lagerfelt
GABBY FUENTES   Irene Sofia Lucio
LIZ RICO   Karen Pittman

Creative Team

DIRECTOR   Lisa Peterson
SCENIC DESIGN   Dane Laffrey
COSTUME DESIGN   Jessica Pabst
LIGHTING DESIGN   Tyler Micoleau
SOUND DESIGN   Darron L. West
FIGHT DIRECTOR   Corey Pierno
PRODUCTION STAGE MANAGER   Lori Ann Zepp
STAGE MANAGER   Alisa Zeljeznjak

Biography

Fernanda Coppel is a playwright and screenwriter. Her play King Liz received its world premiere at Second Stage Theatre in an acclaimed, extended run in the summer of 2015. King Liz was recently sold to Showtime and is being developed into a half-hour comedy-drama. Fernanda recently wrote on From Dusk Til Dawn for Robert Rodriguez and the El Rey network and is currently writing for Shonda Rhimes's How to Get Away with Murder on ABC. Her professional New York debut, Chimichangas and Zoloft, premiered at the Atlantic Theater Company in 2012 and is published by Samuel French. Fernanda's work has been developed at New York Theatre Workshop, Pregones Theater,

INTAR Theatre, the Juilliard School, the Lark Development Center, the Flea, the Old Vic (London), Naked Angels, Rattlestick Playwrights Theater, and the Sundance Institute. Fernanda is a member of the MCC Playwrights' Coalition and was a member of the Old Vic's US/UK TS Eliot Exchange Program. Her work has won the Asuncion Queer Latino Festival at Pregones Theater, the 2012 HOLA Award for Outstanding Achievement in Playwriting, and the 2012 Helen Merrill Award. She was a three-year Lila Acheson Wallace Playwriting Fellow at the Juilliard School and received her MFA in dramatic writing from New York University. Fernanda's additional television credits include *The Bridge* on FX.

Characters

LIZ RICO, 40s, African American, a powerful sports agent, scares men.
GABBY FUENTES, 30s, Latina, Liz's assistant, a disgruntled over achiever.
MR. CANDY, 60s, the CEO of a top sports agency, self-starter, liberal when
    it's convenient.
FREDDIE LUNA, 19 years old. Afro-Latino. Star basketball player. Naive.
    Defensive. A diamond in the rough.
COACH JONES, 50s. African American. Coach of the New York Knicks,
    terrified of getting fired.
BARBARA FLOWERS, 50s. A world-renowned journalist with a prime-time
    investigative TV show.

Setting

New York City

Time

2015

ACT ONE
There's Always a List

[*Early morning in a large corner office. The walls are covered with pictures of NBA players in fancy frames. A snazzy couch, a mini-bar, and a mahogany desk. The place looks peaceful until . . .*]

[GABBY FUENTES *sprints into the room. She's dressed in business professional attire, she carries high heels in one hand and a large coffee in the other. The phone rings, GABBY doesn't answer, she runs around the room turning on all the lights and pouring the coffee into a coffee cup on the desk. The phone stops ringing, silence.* GABBY *freezes.*]

GABBY   SHIT!

[*The phone rings again.* GABBY *lets out a sigh of relief, she fiddles with the computer on the desk as she answers the phone.*]

GABBY   Good morn— . . . Yes, yup, boss. Affirmative. Operation Morning Pump Up in effect.

[*She hangs up the phone and puts on her high heels. She fixes her hair and applies lip gloss, quickly.* GABBY *pulls an iPad from her purse and clicks something on the computer. She puts on sunglass.* GABBY *sprints to the door.*]

[*A hip-hop beat plays loudly from the computer.*]

[LIZ RICO, *dressed in a suit, heels, and a gorgeous/elegant coat, enters.* LIZ *confidently dances around the office as she removes her coat and sips her coffee.*]

[GABBY *acts as her DJ/hype man, as she controls the music from her iPad (*GABBY *uses the DJ app to scratch the record, it sounds like music you would hear at a club.) This is routine for them, a choreographed ritual to get* LIZ *pumped for another day of business. The music stops abruptly.*]

[LIZ *sits at her desk.* GABBY *quickly removes her sunglasses, puts away the iPad and heads to her desk. She hands* LIZ *a stack of folders and a newspaper.*]

[*It's business as usual. It's as if their morning pump-up routine never happened.*]

[LIZ *checks her e-mail as she speaks.*]

LIZ   What is this? Oh no. No, cancel this meeting with Sullivan. I don't have time for that.

GABBY   Sullivan wanted some advice about a client. We've rescheduled him five times within the past month.

LIZ   Sullivan was begging me for a promotion, now Sullivan's just going to have to put on his big boy pants and figure it the fuck out.

GABBY   Okay. Random House called, they want to know how your book is coming along.

LIZ   Tell them it's fan-fucking-tastic.

GABBY   Got it.

LIZ   And don't forget to mention that if they keep hounding me about it I will call Simon and Schuster up. I will, I'll sell them the fucking rights to my future bestselling fucking book. Got it?

GABBY   Yes, Liz.

LIZ   People, get out of my way. I feel like making some fucking money today.

[*A beat.*]

[*Both work quietly at their desks.* GABBY *hesitates to speak, then finally musters up enough courage.*]

GABBY   Liz?

LIZ   Gabby?

GABBY   Can we, perhaps, talk about my . . .

[LIZ *knows what she's referring to but she plays dumb.*]

Last week you said we'd talk about it. Remember?

LIZ   Next week.

GABBY   My landlord raised my rent and I'm the only person I know with an MBA who's about to be homeless.

LIZ   Pencil it in. Too busy today, hun.

GABBY   I . . .

LIZ   The sooner you schedule the talk, the sooner we can get to it.

[LIZ *goes back to reading her e-mails.*]

Can you get me floor seats for the Nets playoff game? I want to sit next to Deron William's wife. In fact, seat me in the wife section. It's poaching season.

GABBY   Yes. I'm on it, Liz.

[GABBY *sits at her desk. Defeated.*]

LIZ   Is my lunch set with Phil Jackson?

GABBY   Yes. 12:30, car's coming at noon.

LIZ   Where's the Buddhist turd taking me this time?

GABBY   Jean Georges, do you want me to come and take notes?
LIZ   Nope. He's going to be begging for some trade intel. He's desperate, it won't be pretty.

GABBY   Okay. Well, do you mind if I take an extra ten minutes for lunch today? I have to run to the post office.

LIZ   Absolutely not. Gabby you're very whinny today. Stop it.

[GABBY *quietly types away at her computer. A beat.*]

[LIZ *reading her computer screen.*]

I hate this picture of myself, schedule another round of head shots for next week and a facial before that. Charge it to the company card.

Gabby   Got it, Liz.

Liz   What about Coach Donovan's OKC contract?

Gabby   I took the liberty of reviewing it myself, it looks pretty good.

[Liz *looks up at* Gabby *for the first time since she's been in the office.*]

Liz   The Liberty . . .

Gabby   I've been here for five years. I've seen thousands of contracts glide over my desk. I figured it was time.

Liz   Do you know how long I was Mr. Candy's assistant, Gabby? Seven years. Do you know what that's like?

Gabby   I will know in two years.

Liz   DO NOT touch the contracts unless your name is Liz Rico. Got it?

Gabby   Yes, Liz.

Liz   Everyone has to pay their dues. How many times do I have to tell you?

Gabby   Five times a day for the past five years.

Liz   I'll say it another 5 million times until you get it through that stubborn head.

Gabby   But why? I feel ready.

Liz   Because "It's good to be king."

Gabby   King? Why? Can't I just ask / you . . .

Liz   Now, now. You'll know when you're king. Many, many years from now. And don't you dare forget about my facial.

[Gabby*'s fuming. She sits at her desk and angrily types away at her computer. We hear a computer alert sound.* Gabby *jumps up.*]

Gabby   Five Oh. Five Oh.

[Liz *fixes her hair.*]

Liz   What's his ETA?

Gabby   Less than one minute.

[Gabby *scrambles to clean up her desk, she spritzes* Liz *with perfume then runs to the door with a note pad, ready for . . .*]

[*Enter* Mr. Candy, *dressed in an expensive suit, hair slicked back. He enters with purpose and promptly ignores* Gabby.]

Good morning, Mr. Candy. Nice suit, sir. Did you have a good weekend?

Mr. Candy   Liz, you read the news this morning? There's some good stuff on the Web.

Liz   Maybe I did and maybe I didn't.

Mr. Candy   My top agent doesn't the surf the Net?

Liz   I'm very busy, Candy, why don't you give me the Cliff Notes?

Mr. Candy   Well, Bleacher Report and ESPN.com had some exquisite top-ten lists. In fact, I popped a woody reading them and I usually require assistance in that department.

Liz   I'll have Gabby look into it. Mr. Candy, now if you'll please excuse me. Gabby can schedule a lunch for us this week to catch up.

Mr. Candy   Not acceptable. I need to speak with you now.

Liz   You don't pop in on any of the other agents here.

Mr. Candy   Oh, am I inconveniencing you? I'm here to give you a big tip.

Liz   It's the playoffs and the draft is just around the corner. I've got a lot on my plate here so . . .

Mr. Candy   I'll have to keep all this in mind the next time you need a favor.

Liz   Listen, I've been getting calls all month from CAA. They want me and they want me bad. What are you going to do about it?

Mr. Candy   You don't want to go over there. CAA's like fucking purgatory, the underworld, and you're a star, babe.

Liz   They're offering me a great package, Candy.

Mr. Candy   You can't leave me, we've got history here. Twenty-five years and counting, that doesn't mean anything to you?

Gabby   Twenty-two years, sir.

[Mr. Candy *and* Liz *ignore* Gabby.]

Mr. Candy   Twenty-five years is a long fucking time, Lizzy. I named my first daughter after you.

Liz   Her name's Cynthia.

Mr. Candy   Her middle name is Elizabeth.

Gabby   It's Cynthia Jane Candy, sir.

Mr. Candy   Well, I wish her name was Liz. In fact, I'll make some calls and change her name to Liz if that's what it takes.

Liz   Ya, sure you will. What's the tip?

Mr. Candy   High school guard out of Brooklyn. Athletic freak. He's got a jump shot as pure as the Holy Grail. He's got the flashy passing of Chris Paul and is as quick as Derrick Rose off the dribble. A dynamic dunker. Ball-handling capabilities of old-school Isaiah Thomas. AND THEN, on top of all that, he's got a nice little step-back three that's un-guardable. We gotta sign him. We gotta sign him now.

Liz   High school kid? Please. I've got better things to do.

Mr. Candy   Well, that's the thing, he goes to a shitty school down in Red Hook. He's been held back a bunch. He's a 19-year-old high school senior. Just barely graduated.

Gabby   Technically he's eligible, he should have graduated last year. We can fudge the details and make it look like he's been out of high school for a year.

Mr. Candy   I saved you the good stuff. He's half Hispanic too, they're hot right now in the press. Mom's illegal or something, had to go back to South America. Kid's been in and out of foster homes and group homes.

Liz   Quite a sob story, Candy. I'm sure this one's gonna be a lot of work.

Mr. Candy   You know how to play the game.

Liz   Why don't you sign him?

Mr. Candy   I'm not taking on any more clients.

Liz   Since when?

Mr. Candy   A couple of months. Mrs. Candy won't allow it.

Liz   Since when do you listen to your wife?

Mr. Candy   There comes a time in every man's life when you're not as quick as you used to be. Your balls droop to your ankles and the R word starts to come into your periphery.

Liz   R-word?

Mr. Candy   Don't make me say it out loud, Liz. In fact, let's just call it an extended leave of absence in Florida.

Liz   I see. Is this a new revelation?

Mr. Candy   I was in with Phil Stern this morning. He seemed to know before the official announcement.

[Liz *looks to* Gabby. Gabby *types away at her desk and avoids eye contact.*]

Liz   [*Pissed.*] Oh, he did, did he? Good old Phil Stern knew about this.

Mr. Candy   Don't you worry about him. I'd rather leave the company to you.

LIZ   Can I get that in writing? Gabby, a pen and paper, please.

MR. CANDY   Well, it's not that easy. The board has to come to an agreement about who will take over and Phil's at the top of their list. You're both the best agents we've got.

LIZ   I started at this agency when it was just you and me working out of your garage. I've helped build these walls, not Phil Stern.

MR. CANDY   Look, the board is aware of your commitment to this company. Trust me.

LIZ   That's not good enough for me.

MR. CANDY   You're a partner and you run the whole NBA division of the top sports agency in the country. That isn't enough?

LIZ   What's the real reason behind the board's hesitance?

MR. CANDY   There is the intimidation factor. It's not the first time I've had to talk to you about your people skills.

LIZ   Are you kidding me?

MR. CANDY   If you just smiled more. Made more of an effort to be cordial to people, I think it would make a difference.

LIZ   This company is 95 percent men and men are scared of me. How is that my problem?

MR. CANDY   Phil Stern keeps great relationships with all the board members.

LIZ   If by "good relationships" you mean Titty Tuesdays down at Penthouse Executive Club, then I can't compete with that.

MR. CANDY   Maybe you will put the board members at ease if . . .

LIZ   If . . .

MR. CANDY   Well, this Red Hook kid is going to be a big, big star.

LIZ   How do you know that?

MR. CANDY   You could use a home run, Liz. Something that reminds the board of why you are an asset to the agency and why you deserve to be CEO. This kid's coming at the right time.

LIZ   My 22-year career at the Candy Agency is a home run.

MR. CANDY   Imagine, this kid goes early in the draft, gets a Nike deal, a Gatorade commercial, and wins a couple games, yadda, yadda. You make this talented kid a star within the next year and Phil Stern will be reporting to you by next season's draft.

[*A beat.* LIZ *thinks on it.*]

Liz   What's this kid's name?

[**Gabby** *keeps typing at her computer and doesn't look up, just responds.*]

Gabby   Federico Luna. Goes by Freddie. Venezuelan mother, African American father who died of a gunshot wound to the head by a gang member when Freddie was four. He's the oldest of five. All foster kids that barely see each other because they were placed with different families all over the country.

Mr. Candy   Sign him.

Liz   I've got a full plate, Candy.

Gabby   I can schedule something for this week. I've already got his address, phone number, and Facebook profile pulled up on my computer.

[*They ignore* **Gabby**.]

Liz   Why me, Candy? Besides impressing the board, why me in particular.

Mr. Candy   You have a similar background.

Liz   You want me to represent him because we both are from the projects?

Mr. Candy   Maybe you can connect with the kid on that level. And he's been in trouble with the law.

Liz   He has a record? How bad are we talking?

Gabby   I've got it right here.

Mr. Candy   Before you look at his files, just remember, he's a young man with a lot of potential. And we can't lose him to Jeff Schwartz or Leon Rose for Christ's sake.

Liz   What were the charges?

Gabby   Assault, battery. Spent some time in juvie.

[**Gabby** *hands* **Liz** *a file.*]

Mr. Candy   Sign this kid and work your magic, Liz.

Liz   This is a tough one, Candy.

Mr. Candy   Oh, come on. You're Liz-fucking-Rico. Where's the song and dance? You're my best fucking showman. Or would you prefer I ask Phil Stern to get this job done?

Liz   Stern? Stern's from Maine. His idea of the projects is anything below 14th Street.

Mr. Candy   I'm keeping the board members hot on you, Liz, don't let me down, kiddo.

[**Mr. Candy** *exits.*]

[LIZ *sits at her desk and goes over the file. She takes out two pictures, they're graphic.*]

GABBY   These are the victims.

LIZ   That kid lost his eye?

GABBY   Yup and he paralyzed that other boy. Allegedly.

[*A beat.*]

[LIZ *takes a deep breath and lets it out.*]

[GABBY *brings her another file.*]

Here are his high schools stats.

[LIZ *opens it and reads.*]

LIZ   Fuck.

GABBY   I know.

LIZ   Fuckety freaking fuck.

GABBY   It gets even better.

LIZ   Fucking fucker.

GABBY   The second coming.

LIZ   These can't be right. These are LeBron James's stats right?

GABBY   Nope, it's Freddie Luna.

LIZ   Are you *positive* that these are correct?

GABBY   I triple checked them with the scouts and the school just now. They are 100 percent accurate.

LIZ   Cancel everything I have today. We're going hunting.

[*Lights out.*]

Lunch

[*A diner.*]

[LIZ *sits in a booth going over notes.* GABBY *enters with hand sanitizer and a rag, she squirts the sanitizer all over the table top and cleans.*]

LIZ   Let's hear it.

GABBY   What?

LIZ   I know you, Gabby.

GABBY   Know me?

LIZ   You're cleaning the table with contempt. Every wipe is a "Fuck you, Liz, I could do this ten times better."

GABBY   That's not it at all. I just wouldn't have brought a potential client here.

LIZ   Oh, really? Where would you have scheduled the meeting?

GABBY   The Four Seasons. The office. I could think of ten better places.

LIZ   We are meeting him here because we want to come off as down to earth. Trust me. This kid will respond to that more than the Four Seasons.

GABBY   Whatever you say.

LIZ   You want my job. I know it. That's why I hired you.

GABBY   [*Scrubs harder.*] I'm a tad overqualified for this position, but I wanted to learn from the best. So. I'm still here.

LIZ   I sleep with one eye open. You have keys to my penthouse, and one of these nights, I just know you're going to sneak in and stab me to death with a letter opener.

GABBY   I'm not sure how to respond to that. I'll be waiting outside for you.

[LIZ *opens her mouth as* GABBY *sprays some Binaca in it.*]

Good luck.

[GABBY *begins to exit.*]

LIZ   . . . Wait.

GABBY   Yes?

LIZ   I'll let you sit at the table with us.

GABBY   *Really?*

LIZ   If you promise to not speak.

GABBY   You won't hear a peep. I swear to God.

LIZ   In fact, I need you to stop breathing. I basically need you to do your best impersonation of a cadaver. Can you do that?

GABBY   [*Giddy.*] Cadaver. Dead. Got it, Liz.

[GABBY *sits next to* LIZ *and watches her excitedly.*]

LIZ   Don't do that.

GABBY   Sorry.

[GABBY *looks out the window and hums to herself. She excitedly taps her fingers on the table.*]

LIZ   Do you need Ritalin or something?

GABBY   My first time.

LIZ   You've got to treat every deal as if it were your last. You never know when someone's going to pull the rug from under you.

GABBY   You've got this, Liz.

[LIZ *doesn't know how to take a compliment. She gives* GABBY *a half smile and continues to pore over the files.*]

[*Enter* FREDDIE LUNA, *handsome and athletic.*]

LIZ   Mr. Freddie Luna?

FREDDIE   'Sup.

[LIZ *and* GABBY *stand to great him.* LIZ *extends her hand,* FREDDIE *doesn't shake it. He gives her a high five.*]

LIZ   It's a pleasure to meet you, Freddie.

FREDDIE   They got cheeseburgers at this place? The lady on the phone said we'd have cheeseburgers and that you'd be paying.

GABBY   The cheeseburgers are the best in the city, get a double on us. With bacon.

LIZ   This is my assistant, Gabby. She's not allowed to speak. Have a seat, please.

[*They sit.* GABBY *fights for positioning in the booth,* LIZ *shoves her to the side and gives her a dirty look.*]

You're a little shrimpier than in the pictures.

FREDDIE   You're a little older-looking than your pictures.

LIZ   So you've heard of me.

FREDDIE   Ya. Of course.

LIZ   Good things I hope.

FREDDIE   Jeff Schwartz says that you'll eat the testicles off a newborn.

LIZ   Jeff has a very, very small penis.

FREDDIE   Word?

LIZ   Really, it looks like an elevator button. Don't ask how I know that.

FREDDIE   He also said you're a good agent.

GABBY   Uhm, she's the best.

[LIZ *stares* GABBY *down again.* GABBY *mouths "sorry."*]

FREDDIE I'm the best player to come outta Red Hook since Carmelo. So, what's your pitch?

LIZ Pitch?

FREDDIE I've been on a couple of these so far, lady. You're not impressing me.

LIZ Oh?

FREDDIE People are saying that I'll go in the top ten in the draft. People are saying that I've got major endorsements coming my way. I'm kind of a big deal.

LIZ And so humble.

FREDDIE Humility doesn't make the Benjamins, you feel me?

LIZ You're very ambitious. You ready to put in the work?

FREDDIE I won the state championship, two years in a row. I'm rated number one in the country. That sound like I'm fucking lazy?

LIZ It sounds like you're talented, but that only gets you so far. A lot of promising players make it to the NBA and drop off the face of the earth. They aren't interested in listening to their coach, putting in the work, or winning. They just wanna get paid, you feel me? Ever heard of Lenny Cooke?

FREDDIE Lenny who?

LIZ Exactly. That could be you in five years, boy.

FREDDIE I doubt it.

LIZ This business is a graveyard of talented promising players. It can happen to anyone, even you, Freddie.

FREDDIE Why did you ask me here? What can you do for me?

LIZ This is the reality of your situation. Can you deal? That's the industry you're stepping into. Can. You. Deal.

FREDDIE The other agents didn't say this shit.

LIZ I'm not like other agents. I'm really fucking good at my job, look at my client roster. Kevin Love, Carmelo Anthony, Russell Westbrook, Anthony Davis, James Harden. I take talented young guys and I make them international superstars, that's my legacy.

FREDDIE Jeff Schwartz said I could be the next Jordan.

LIZ Jeff Schwartz says that to every motherfucker he meets. His client list is also chock-full of old geezers. Paul Pierce, Ray Allen, Kobe Bryant, they are all on their way out.

Freddie   Alright, I'm gonna be real with you, I've got some obligations.

Liz   You have kids? Gabby?

[**Gabby** *shrugs nervously and checks her notes.*]

Freddie   No, I've got two sisters and two brothers, all younger. We've been in foster care but I want to make enough money so that we can all live together. My mom's in Venezuela struggling to make ends meet. I need to buy her a nice house.

Liz   That's a lot to put on a boy's shoulders.

Freddie   I'm a man. Who the fuck do you think you are?

Liz   You're a boy but the day you put on that NBA jersey, they'll judge you like a man. The day you sign your first NBA contract you'll kiss your youth good-bye. Are you ready for that?

Freddie   Yup.

Liz   Do you party? Do you do drugs?

Freddie   Why the fuck do you care?

Liz   I'm making an investment. I need to know. Do you do drugs?

Freddie   I don't have to answer that.

Liz   Two words. Len Bias.

Freddie   Those aren't two words, that's a name.

Liz   You know the story?

Freddie   Am I even getting my fucking cheeseburger? Or was that a lie.

Liz   Gifted athlete from Maryland who was drafted to the Celtics in the first round, second pick overall in 1986, died two days later of a drug overdose.

Freddie   Ya so.

Liz   He really could have been the next Michael Jordan, he was that good. The potential was limitless. Now he's just another statistic. Another stereotype.

Freddie   That won't happen to me.

Liz   You don't just stand for Freddie Luna. You carry a whole community on your shoulders. The press is going to be merciless. The second you fuck up, it fucks it up for all of us. Is your back strong enough to hoist us up? You tell me.

Freddie   This is bullshit. You're bullshit.

Liz   I'm being 100 percent real right now. The honest truth.

Freddie   What can you do for me? The other agents offered me cash upfront to sign with them. One even showed up with a 20-million-dollar Adidas contract, ready for me to sign. What about you?

Gabby   That's completely unethical.

Liz   I'm not going to offer you a cent, Freddie.

Freddie   What's in it for me?

Liz   The truth. Straight up. I won't sugar-coat it. Trust me, the truth is something that's extinct in this business. In this world.

Freddie   The truth, that's it . . . this meeting is a complete waste of time. Seriously. Who the fuck do you think you are?

Liz   Let me tell you a little something about who I am.

Freddie   I don't want to hear anymore of your crap / . . .

Liz   My mom died of cancer when I was three because my father couldn't afford her treatment, so when I got a full scholarship to Yale my goal was to grow up to be someone who could pay to kill cancer.

Now, I've got a penthouse on the Upper West Side overlooking Central Park, my neighbors are Steven Spielberg and Oprah Winfrey, and a house in the Hamptons next door to Commissioner Adam Silver. Within the last three years, my current client roster has collectively made over 900 million dollars. I've been the only woman on the *Forbes* most powerful sports agent list three times and *Time* magazine most influential list twice. Nobody can stop me. No one. Not even God.

Gabby   Oh my God, I have /goose bumps. . . .

Liz   What I can offer you as an agent isn't anything you can buy. It's my marrow, it's the tenacity that led me to this table.

I will fight for you to be successful the way I fought for myself to make it in this world that doesn't want people like us to succeed. I make that promise to you in exchange for a commitment. I need you to promise that you will stay out of trouble.

Freddie   You saw my files.

Liz   Hey, shit happens, right?

Freddie   I didn't do it. I was on the wrong street at the wrong time.

Liz   That happens when you're hanging with the wrong crowd.

Freddie   Don't talk to me like that.

LIZ   Like what?

FREDDIE   Like I don't know shit. I know shit, or else we wouldn't be here meeting.

LIZ   Point taken.

FREDDIE   Is my past going to be a problem? Is it going to come up again?

LIZ   You can't allow your past to define you. That's the bottom line. My job is to ensure that your past informs where you want to go. Straight to the top. I want you to be one of those success stories. From Red Hook to the Upper West Side. Shit, I grew up in the projects too and now look at me.

FREDDIE   Nah, really?

LIZ   I grew up on mayonnaise sandwiches and sugar water, but I worked my ass off to get out. And look at me now. Baby, I run shit.

FREDDIE   I've worked hard too. I wake up at 4 a.m. every morning so I can do conditioning before school. Then after practice I stay on the court 'till 8 p.m. to shoot around with my coach.

Then I play pick-up games around the neighborhood until 11 p.m. That's my schedule six days a week.

LIZ   That's the kind of dedication I'm talking about. I'm here to help you with the business side of things. Freddie, I've been an agent for a very long time and if there's one thing I've learned it's that white people don't want us, they want our money.

FREDDIE   Meaning?

LIZ   Corporations don't want to hire people like us, they usually have to by law. But they want our money. They need our money so they can continue running the world.

FREDDIE   How are you gonna help keep me in business? When I leave Red Hook, I'm not trying to go back.

LIZ   That's my specialty. I will keep you relevant. We'll create a public persona for you and keep re-creating that persona throughout your career. I've got you. Buy your one-way ticket out of this place and join me in Manhattan.

[*A beat.*]

[FREDDIE's *starting to be persuaded.*]

FREDDIE   You think I'll go in the top ten?

LIZ   I will ensure that for you, Freddie. I've already called the Knicks and they've expressed a lot of interest.

FREDDIE   They did?

LIZ   I deal with the Knicks all the time. They're good people. I can get you there.

FREDDIE   Empty promises.

LIZ   It's not empty. Have you ever Googled me?

FREDDIE   You are a very cocky chick.

LIZ   Call me a chick again and I'll let you sign with Jeff Schwartz and make the biggest mistake of your life.

[*A beat.*]

[FREDDIE *laughs it off. This lady is the real deal.*]

FREDDIE   You really gonna get me on the Knicks in the first round?

LIZ   Try me. Are you going to listen and keep putting in the work?

[LIZ *extends her hand to* FREDDIE.]

FREDDIE   Try me.

[*They shake on it.*]

GABBY   Waiter? Cheeseburgers, we need a couple cheeseburgers over here *stat.*

[*Lights out.*]

The Draft, Baby

[*The office, it's messier than before.* LIZ *and* GABBY *sit by the TV, the NBA draft is on. They look exhausted and have paperwork surrounding them.*]

[GABBY *works on a laptop and wears a phone head set.*]

[LIZ *wears a Bluetooth and sips on a Red Bull.*]

[*They are both on their respective phone calls.*]

LIZ	GABBY
You're playing me, Marc. Why the fuck . . . Cold feet? This kid is the second coming. I'm telling you. His field goal percentage. His defense. He can even shoot the three. He's unique. Fuck you, Marc. Just fuck you	Billy King, Liz is on the other line but she'd really like to speak with you. Can you hold? Please Hold. I know it's a busy day but I assure you that it's worth your while to hold. Who is she on

[LIZ *hangs up the phone on Marc.*]   with? I shouldn't /

. . . who do you have?   Say . . . Take a wild guess.

Who do you have? WHO DO   That's a great guess.
YOU HAVE?

[LIZ *snaps wildly at* GABBY. *She's off her call but* GABBY'*s still on the line and wasn't aware that* LIZ *was speaking to her.*]

LIZ   Marc's off. Who do you have?

GABBY   [*Covers her receiver.*] Are you talking to me?

LIZ   Yes, De Niro. Who the fuck do you have on the phone? It's draft day, pay attention.

GABBY   The Nets.

LIZ   Transfer him over. NOW.

GABBY   [*To the phone.*] I have Liz Rico, Mr. King.

LIZ   Billy. Big Willy. How are the kids? Oh good. You know I love you, right? Whose my Bill-ster? Who? . . . You heard about the Mavs? . . . No, I think Marc is such a dick wad. I . . . I've been meaning to call you. I want to screw the Mavs. I mean, who likes Dallas? Freddie's from Brooklyn. *He wants* to stay home. I've got your back, Billy. When have I lied to you? When?

[GABBY *waves* LIZ *down.*]

GABBY   Knicks. I have the Knicks call coming.

[LIZ *does a giddy dance and mimes for* GABBY *to give her one minute.* GABBY *answers the call.*]

Liz Rico's office. Yes, Mr. Mills. Please hold.

LIZ   Billy. I gotta call you back. But don't let me down. Remember our good times at the draft in '99. No, I wasn't that drunk, Billy. I remember every word. Yes, babe. Okay. You stay strong over there. We wanna go with you. Talk soon. Bye.

[LIZ *hangs up the call and takes the next call.*]

Steve. Steve-o. My Stevie Wonderful. You know Freddie wants to stay local. He's a Brooklyn kid who grew up watching Patrick Ewing and John Starks. He wants to be a Knick.

He has a poster of Melo in his locker. . . . Nope. Fuck the Mavs. No, we wanna do business with *you.* Just *you.*

[LIZ *high fives* GABBY. GABBY *turns up the TV. The Commissioner of the NBA speaks.*]

Commissioner   The Los Angeles Lakers have selected Anthony Miller from UCLA as their first round pick.

Liz   You need a superstar guard, Steve. You also need a miracle. I know. I hear you . . . well, look at your TV screen because Miller's a Laker now. Yup. I know . . .

[*We hear the crowd go wild.*]

Gabby   [*To* Liz.] Knicks are next.

Liz   Would I lie to you? Would I? . . . okay, so I've lied to you but this kid is different. . . . I realize that, but he's matured since then . . . I assure you. He's a harmless kid, Steve. I'd bet my life on it.

[Gabby's *phone rings.*]

Gabby   [*To* Liz.] I have Billy on the line.

[Liz *mimes to* Gabby *that she needs to stall Jim.* Liz *mouths "5 minutes."*]

Liz   Steve, this would be the biggest mistake of your life. I mean, how will you be able to look your kids in the eye after this. Freddie Luna will be the next Kobe Bryant, the next Chris Paul. I'll let you go then. It's up to you. But I've got the Nets on the other line, Steve. They want him bad, so it's up to you. When Luna scores the game-winning dunk and the Nets sweep you this season, I won't be saying I told you so, I'll just be sipping Cristal and cashing the checks. Buh-Bye.

Gabby   Good evening, Mr. King. You sound a little sick, do you have a cold? . . . Liz will be with you in five short minutes. How's your wife doing? . . . I'm not at liberty to tell you who Liz is speaking with. . . . I'm aware of that. . . . Liz is not playing the field, sir. She's very honest about her client's intention to sign with the Nets. I assure you. . . .

[Gabby *waves to* Liz, *mimes that* Liz *NEEDS to take this call NOW.*]

[Liz *waves for* Gabby *to transfer the call.*]

Liz   Billy. I missed you. . . . Whoa, whoa. What's with the tone? No, I was not on the other line with Steve. I'm committed to you. Freddie Luna wants to be a Net. . . . Are you gonna fuck me over? Your pick is coming up, Billy, put your money where your mouth is.

Gabby   Knicks have one more minute.

[Liz *gives* Gabby *a thumbs-up.*]

Liz   Make the right decision, Billy. Listen to your heart.

[*Sings.*]

Listen to you heart. Shhhh . . . just, what does your heart say? . . . Okay,
okay . . . how about your gut? Is that telling you anything different? . . . Okay,
you should go with your gut here, Billy.

GABBY They are announcing it.

LIZ I've gotta get going, Billy. . . . No, it's not because of the Knicks pick. . . .
I've gotta go to the bathroom. . . . I have lady needs, alright? Jesus. Talk to
you in five. Pick wisely. Bye.

[GABBY *turns up the TV. The NBA Commissioner appears again.*]

COMMISSIONER The New York Knicks have selected Federico Luna from
Red Hook High School.

[*The crowd on the television goes wild.*]

[GABBY *and* LIZ *let out a sigh of relief. They are too exhausted to be excited.*
LIZ *takes out her Bluetooth and kicks off her heels. She plops her feet on the
couch.*]

GABBY Martini?

LIZ Whiskey on the rocks. This one was a real ball buster.

[GABBY's *phone rings.*]

GABBY Nets are on the line.

LIZ Don't answer, that needy bastard needs a shrink, *not* me.

GABBY You played him, Liz.

LIZ You have to come at all these deals from a place of yes. When the
offers come in, then you can be picky. Until then it's "YES. YES. YES."

[GABBY *pours two whiskeys. They clink glasses.*]

GABBY To Freddie Luna.

LIZ To *us.*

[*They both take sips.* MR. CANDY *enters with a bottle of champagne. He pops
the cork.*MR. CANDY *sings "For she's a jolly good fellow. For she's a jolly good
fellow. For she's a jolly good fellow, which nobody can deny."*]

Candy, you have a lovely singing voice.

MR. CANDY WE DID IT, KIDDO!

GABBY We?

MR. CANDY Get us a couple glasses, would you? Uh . . .

LIZ Gabby.

MR. CANDY Gabby, yes. The nice crystal glasses in my office.

[Gabby *exits. Disgruntled.*]

You did it again.

Liz   Are you surprised? I've been doing it for 22 years.

Mr. Candy   Can't we sit and enjoy the fruits of our labor for one minute?

Liz   Okay. Alright.

[*They sit quietly. Not much to say.* Mr. Candy *looks around her office.*]

Mr. Candy   I like what you've done with the place.

Liz   I've been in this office for ten years.

Mr. Candy   Why don't you have any African art up on the walls? Berry in accounting has this great African art up, he's really proud of it.

Liz   Just because Berry and I are both black doesn't mean that we are going to decorate our office the same way.

Mr. Candy   I know. I know. I'm just saying. Be proud of your heritage. It's unique and exotic.

Liz   Do you have white artists plastered all over your walls?

Mr. Candy   Not specifically, no.

Liz   You're not proud of your heritage?

Mr. Candy   Don't get defensive. You're always getting so defensive. That's my biggest criticism of you after all these years.

Liz   Uh-huh.

Mr. Candy   Be proud of your heritage. Be proud of your past.

Liz   That's not the issue.

Mr. Candy   I'm just so proud of you. I've seen you work so hard. . . . Can I confess something to you, Liz? Do you mind?

Liz   Yes, but try your hardest not to be offensive.

Mr. Candy   Well, ever since your father passed away, I've felt like your father figure. Like your father passed the reigns onto me.

Liz   But you have your own children that you never see.

Mr. Candy   I've been looking out for you, it's an instinct. And secretly I've been hoping you would find a nice man to marry who could take care of you. So I wouldn't have to worry about you so much.

Liz   I can take care of myself, did that ever occur to you?

Mr. Candy   I know you can, but as a father, you want the best for your daughters. Safety. Good man by her side.

Liz You're not my father, Mr. Candy. You're my boss. It's a very different type of relationship.

Mr. Candy I feel comfortable with you, Lizzie. Think of it as a compliment.

Liz Lucky me.

Mr. Candy Listen, the board is going bananas over the Luna kid. They couldn't be happier with the good publicity. My assistant caught Phil Stern masturbating while crying in the men's room. You're in the lead, my dear.

Liz Are you surprised?

Mr. Candy You going to miss me around here?

Liz Kind of, I guess.

Mr. Candy You guess?

Liz I'm sure you'll be around.

Mr. Candy Nope. I'll be out of your hair forever.

Liz You'll be calling me every five minutes.

Mr. Candy No, no. I'm leaving the place in good hands. I'll back off.

[Gabby *returns with two champagne glasses as* Mr. Candy *gets up to leave.*]

Catch you later, my little supernova.

[Mr. Candy *exits.*]

Gabby What did I miss?

Liz Pour it. One for you too.

[Gabby *pours the champagne and they toast.*]

To all the motherfuckers who want a piece of you when you're on top.

Gabby Like Mr. Candy?

Liz You remember this, Gabby. You remember how hard we worked and how fast someone else pranced in here to take all the credit.

[Liz *downs her champagne.* Gabby *watches her.*]

[*Lights out.*]

Welcome to the Pros, Now Fuck Off

[*An office.* Freddie Luna *and* Liz *sit.* Freddie's *nervous, he keeps fidgeting.* Liz *checks e-mails.*]

[Freddie *starts to beat box. He starts to dance along to the beat. He gets into it.*]

[Liz *slaps* Freddie *upside the head.*]

Liz   Grow the fuck up.

Freddie   I'm grown.

Liz   Sit up straight. Stop moving around in your chair. You look like a lizard on coke.

Freddie   Coach Jones is someone I really look up to, I wanna make a good impression.

Liz   Tuck in your shirt and don't say anything stupid.

Freddie   When I was little my mom would sing to me when I was scared.

Liz   No fucking way, buddy.

Freddie   She would sing in Spanish. It really calms me down.

Liz   Take a Xanax like a mature person.

Freddie   I just wanna do a good job. This is the only way I know how.

[Liz *makes a call on her cell.*]

Liz   Get in here.

[Gabby *enters before* Liz *can hang up the phone.*]

Gabby   Did I forget something? I'm so sorry if I forgot something. I swear I triple-checked all the arrangements last night and again this morning.

Liz   Shut up and sing something.

Gabby   Excuse me?

Liz   Sing in Spanish, for Freddie.

Gabby   Uh.

Liz   Name a song, Freddie.

Gabby   This is kind of racist, Liz.

Freddie   I don't know the names of the songs. I was little.

Liz   Sing whatever you want, do it.

Gabby   [*Hesitantly sings J. Lo song.*] "I luh you, Papi? I luh-luh you / Papi."

Liz   Something traditional!

[Gabby *thinks, then it hits her.*]

Gabby   [*Sings.*] De la Sierra Morena, cielito lindo, vienen bajando,

Freddie   Oh snap, I know this song. I love this shit.

Gabby   Sing it with me, Liz.

Freddie   Yes! Come on, Liz. We're all nervous.

Liz   I don't speak Spanish.

GABBY   But I got your Rosetta Stone for Christmas?

LIZ   Oops.

FREDDIE   How can you not speak Spanish? Get Leon Rose on the phone. He speaks it fluently.

LIZ   You're killing me, kid. Killing me.

[GABBY *and* FREDDIE *sing together.* FREDDIE's *smiling and enjoying himself.* LIZ *works on her phone.*]

GABBY AND FREDDIE   Un par de ojitos negros, cielito lindo, de contrabando.

GABBY   Why don't you come in on the chorus, Liz?

LIZ   Why don't you look for another job, Gabby?

[FREDDIE *takes out his phone and pretends to dial.*]

FREDDIE   Hello? CAA? Ya, I need to speak with Leon Rose, please?

[LIZ *groans and puts her phone down. She half-heartedly hums along.*]

GABBY AND FREDDIE   Ay, ay, ay, ay, Canta y no llores, Porque cantando se alegran, cielito lindo, los corazones.

LIZ   Alright. Okay. Alright. This isn't therapy, kid. Gabby? Meet you outside.

GABBY   Sure.

[GABBY *smiles and exits.*]

FREDDIE   She's the best.

LIZ   I'm the best. She's my assistant.

FREDDIE   Jealous?

LIZ   Did Gabby get you here? Or did I?

FREDDIE   I've been thinking a lot about you, Liz.

LIZ   You have?

FREDDIE   Why the fuck would anyone want to be an agent? It's the fucking worst job in the universe.

LIZ   Yep. It's pretty bad.

FREDDIE   I mean, you don't really do anything and you take 4 percent of my money. What the fuck do you even do all day?

LIZ   I do a lot, kid.

FREDDIE   Like what?

Liz I ensured this deal. The Knicks deal? Twenty million for three years. I got you a shitload of money.

Freddie Ya but how?

Liz Let's put it this way: I do all the things that nobody else wants to do. I lie, cheat, and steal for my clients. I make sure they're rich.

Freddie So you just woke up one day and said to yourself, "I want to be an agent."

Liz I was a basketball player, played for Yale back in the day.

Freddie What position?

Liz Point guard. Had a mean crossover.

Freddie Seriously.

Liz To this day I'm convinced that Allen Iverson stole my moves. He was six or seven years old when we won the NCAA championship and it was nationally televised. I know that ass wipe stole my game.

Freddie You're fucking nuts, Liz. I love it.

[Coach Jones *enters. He's dressed in a track suit and chews gum profusely.*]

Coach Jones Liz.

Liz Coach, good to be doing business with you.

Coach Jones Always a pleasure.

[Coach Jones *hugs* Liz *warmly.*]

Liz Is that an iPhone 6 in your pocket or are you happy to see me, Coach?

Coach Jones Maybe a little of both.

Liz Allow me to introduce you to this future hall of famer. Federico Luna.

[Freddie *extends his hand to* Coach Jones, *they shake hands.*]

Freddie It's a real honor, sir.

Coach Jones Call me Coach.

Freddie Coach, I . . . I've read all your books. I think you're one of the greatest coaches of all time. I can't believe you are my coach. I . . . I'm your best player.

Liz He's a little nervous.

Coach Jones Do you want some water, kid?

Freddie I meant to say, you will make me a better player.

Coach Jones Right. Good.

LIZ   We are thrilled to be with this franchise, Coach.

COACH JONES   I see that. I feel it. Liz, you mind letting us talk? Man to man here. I mean, you won't be around the majority of the season. I'd like to get to know Freddie one on one.

LIZ   Okay. Sure. I'll be waiting outside if you need me, okay, Freddie?

[LIZ *opens the door to leave, we hear her scream for* GABBY.]

LIZ   GABBYYYYY? GAAAABY?

[LIZ *exits.*]

[*A beat.*]

[COACH JONES *stares at* FREDDIE *intensely. It's searing.* FREDDIE *feels warm/nervous, he grins at him.*]

FREDDIE   Coach Jones, holy shit. I can't believe you're my coach, sir.

COACH JONES   You better. This is all very real, son

FREDDIE   I didn't mean it like that. I just really look up to you, Coach.

COACH JONES   Uh-huh. Okay. You have some great stats, Luna.

FREDDIE   I'm ready to play, Coach, I'm locked in.

COACH JONES   You averaged a triple double every game last season. Two-time state champ. That's all pretty good . . . for high school.

[*A beat.* FREDDIE *doesn't know how to respond.*]

There's a big difference between playing against a bunch of teenagers and playing against professional athletes. Do you think you're ready? Or do you just need the money? That happens a lot nowadays.

FREDDIE   I'm ready to play, that's all you need to know.

COACH JONES   Uh-huh. Uh-huh. What about your criminal record? Those assault charges. That something I need to worry about?

FREDDIE   I was at the wrong place at the wrong time, sir.

COACH JONES   But I heard you have a temper. I heard that it's possible that you actually beat the shit out of those kids.

FREDDIE   I'm telling you the facts. The truth. I'm a lot of things but I'm not a liar.

COACH JONES   Answer the question, do you have a temper? Do I need to worry about technical fouls here?

FREDDIE   I mean, I get passionate, sir. I'm not going to lie.

COACH JONES   Latrell Sprewell passionate? Another Ron Artest?

FREDDIE   I just like to win. That a bad thing, Coach?

COACH JONES   When do you turn 20?

FREDDIE   January.

COACH JONES   Capricorn.

FREDDIE   Hm?

COACH JONES   Astrology.

FREDDIE   That matter?

COACH JONES   Just trying to get a sense of you. I don't normally like Capricorns.

FREDDIE   I don't even know what that means, sir.

[*A beat.*]

[COACH *continues to stare at* FREDDIE.]

COACH JONES   I'm going to be honest with you. I didn't want to draft you.

FREDDIE   Oh?

COACH JONES   I wanted us to draft Anthony Miller. He's led UCLA to the Final Four, twice, he's poised, mature *and* he has great stats.

FREDDIE   Anthony Miller?

COACH JONES   But fuck me. Last year our record was the laughing stock of the league and I don't have a say within this doomed organization.

FREDDIE   Word? You seem powerful, sir.

COACH JONES   Listen. If Anthony Miller was here we'd have a shot at winning some games this year. But the higher-ups just want us to sell tickets and entertain a bunch of beer-drinking assholes with hot dogs sticking out of their dick-sucking lips. Instead of a championship contender, they drafted me a fucking baby. I'm not a coach. I'm a babysitter.

FREDDIE   I . . . uh.

COACH JONES   I'm gonna make this really easy for you, okay?

FREDDIE   Okay, ya.

COACH JONES   Show up. Don't do anything stupid. Don't make me look bad. I like my job, I've been here for a couple of years and the front office has stuck with me. The second we start losing again, the second some baby throws a tantrum on the bench, then my ass is out on the street. So don't fuck up or I will kill you. Got it?

FREDDIE   I got it, sir.

COACH JONES   Glad we had this chat. See you in practice.

[COACH JONES *shakes* FREDDIE*'s hand. Meeting's over as far as he's concerned.*]

FREDDIE   That's it?

COACH JONES   Oh, sorry, did you want me to roll out the fucking red carpet, you little shit?

FREDDIE   No, sir, I just wanted a little direction. My goal is to start.

COACH JONES   Start?

FREDDIE   I'll work hard. I'll do whatever you say, Coach. I just want to start.

COACH JONES   So I start you, then what?

FREDDIE   I'd be eternally grateful.

[COACH JONES *puts his head in his hands, lets out a deep sigh. This kid doesn't get it.*]

COACH JONES   It's not about you, idiot.

FREDDIE   Okay?

COACH JONES   Get out of my office, you fucking baby.

FREDDIE   Okay. Uh, thanks, Coach.

COACH JONES   Welcome to the pros. Get out.

[FREDDIE *exits, his dignity is barely intact.*]

[COACH JONES *works at his desk quietly for a beat.*]

[LIZ *enters without knocking.*]

LIZ   What did you say to that boy?

COACH JONES   Mom's back.

[LIZ *shuts* COACH JONES*'s door and rolls up her sleeves.*]

LIZ   You're sitting on a winning lottery ticket. You're not going to cash it in because you wanted Anthony fucking Miller?

COACH JONES   That kid is not a winning lottery ticket, he's a publicity stunt.

LIZ   He has natural talent, sure it's raw but you're a coach. You're supposed to help him grow. He could be the biggest success story of your sad-ass career, Jones.

COACH JONES   I feel like we are looking at one of those 3-D posters. You see a whole landscape there, a Utopia. I see a wasteland, honey. Just the way it goes.

Liz   Do not bench him, Jones. I repeat, do not bench this kid.

Coach Jones   I will until he shows me something in practice.

Liz   You sorry sack of shit.

Coach Jones   I love it when you talk dirty.

Liz   Your ego's getting in the way.

Coach Jones   It's not my ego. It's child support, it's alimony. I can't afford to lose my fucking job right now. I just can't.

Liz   You need to give this kid a chance.

Coach Jones   Why? 'Cuz you want the endorsements? 'Cuz you want the publicity? I worked my ass off to get this position. I assisted ten teams, paid my fucking dues. Now this kid is gonna have to do the same. Shit, even Kobe Bryant came off the bench his rookie year.

Liz   Coach Jones, you have the opportunity to mold your own Kobe or Kevin Garnett or LeBron James.

Coach Jones   So what you're saying is, I should just roll up my sleeves, put in the work so you can cash the checks.

Liz   I'm saying it will benefit you.

Coach Jones   You and I both know that if anything goes wrong the coach is the first to go.

Liz   Do you want to be an average employed coach? Or do you want to be a heroic hall of famer?

Coach Jones   What the fuck do you think, Liz?

Liz   Good coaches have good records and then they fall off the face of the earth. Great coaches, they make an impact, they touch people. They put themselves on the line. Did your ex-wife chop your balls off? Or were you born a eunuch?

Coach Jones   You've been pushing me around for years, but this time it's not gonna work. I'm absolutely right about that kid. You won't pressure me into thinking differently.

Liz   I'm crying for you. On the inside, I'm a river of tears. Poor you. Your boss drafted you a young athletic guard with promise. I mean, this kid is 19, he's got zero miles on the speedometer. You're looking at 14 years in this league. That's so many championships. That's so many MVP awards. That's so many Coach of the Year awards.

Coach Jones   . . . I'll see.

LIZ   Sure. Sure.

COACH JONES   He's gotta do well in training camp

LIZ   Of course.

COACH JONES   And he's gotta listen to every word I say.

LIZ   I love it when you assert whatever shred of ego you have even after you've realized that I'm completely right. It's cute.

[LIZ *exits.* COACH JONES *throws a pen at the door.*]

COACH JONES   Fucking bitch!

[*Lights out.*]

This Fool

[LIZ*'s office, weeks later.*]

[LIZ *has her shoes off and dribbles a basketball nervously. She skillfully bounces the ball between her legs.*]

[GABBY *enters quickly, she's on her cell phone.*]

LIZ   Is he here? Is he?

[GABBY *waves her off, she's trying to hear the person on the phone.*]

Is that him? I will end him if he doesn't get up here.

GABBY   He brought an entourage, they are causing a raucous at security.

LIZ   That insignificant spec of feces.

GABBY   I'll get him up here alone. Take a deep breath.

[GABBY *exits.* LIZ *continues dribbling.*]

LIZ   Deep breath . . . I love my job. I love my job. My clients are immature prepubescent morons *but* I love my job. I love my job.

[GABBY *re-enters with* FREDDIE, *he's cussing* GABBY *out. He's fuming.*]

FREDDIE   THIS IS BULLSHIT. MOTHERFUCKING BULLSHIT.

GABBY   Shhh, this is a place of business.

FREDDIE   My boys are down there getting harassed by security. You hear me? Huh? You hear me, you dumb bitch?

[*A fearful* GABBY *walks to her desk.* LIZ *approaches a heated* FREDDIE, *she gets in his face. She's not scared of him.*]

LIZ   You're the dumbest bitch around here as far as I'm concerned.

FREDDIE   Fuck you, don't call me a bitch.

Liz   Sit down, boy. And SHUT UP.

Freddie   I'll stand.

[Liz *grabs* Freddie *by the ear and forces him to sit on her couch.*]

Liz   Sit your ass down.

Freddie   Ouch. Ouch.

Liz   Where were you today? Peter Roth from Puma waited for an hour and a half for you.

Freddie   Puma sucks, I prefer Nike.

Liz   Oh, so Puma isn't your preference. That's it. Did you get that, Gabby?

[Gabby *nods and rolls her eyes.*]

So the 70 million dollars you cost me today, was that also not your preference?

Freddie   Oops.

Liz   This is fucking business, Freddie. Don't fuck with me and my legacy.

Freddie   I got held up with my boys.

Liz   Peter from Puma flew in from Germany to meet with you.

Freddie   Fine, I'll meet with him.

Gabby   Peter didn't want to reschedule, the meeting's canceled for good.

Freddie   Shut up, bitch. No one's talking to you until you let my boys upstairs.

Liz   You call her or any female a bitch in my presence again and I will whoop your ass all the way back to the projects. Got it?

Freddie   Ya.

Liz   Ya, what?

Freddie   Yes, ma'am.

Liz   Now, what the fuck is really going on.

Freddie   Nothing.

Liz   I could have a 70-million-dollar contract on my desk right now, but I don't. I need an explanation.

Freddie   I was hanging with my boys, we went shopping on 34th street.

Liz   Who was paying?

Freddie   Look, I'm sorry I missed the meeting.

Liz   Do your boys know what you did today?

FREDDIE   They don't care.

LIZ   Do you care?

FREDDIE   I guess.

LIZ   If you don't care, then what the fuck am I doing here? I'm putting in the work.

FREDDIE   And I'm not?

LIZ   You gotta show up for yourself. At the end of the day when you rest your pretty little head down on your pillow, you have to be able to tell yourself that you tried your best that day. Can you say that about today?

FREDDIE   . . . Guess not.

LIZ   Nope. You did a shitty job. You get an F in life today.

FREDDIE   I'm a great player and I work hard on the court. My boys know it's true.

LIZ   You know what I think?

FREDDIE   I don't give a / fuck.

LIZ   You're scared shitless and your boys only feed into your insecurities.

FREDDIE   Maybe. Maybe.

LIZ   Quit acting like a moody teenager.

FREDDIE   Things are changing fast, Liz, I'm getting recognized on the street all the time. This morning I had my first paparazzi experience.

LIZ   Get used to it, it's part of their business.

FREDDIE   I was walking around Midtown. Usually, I blended in with the packs of tourists and business dudes but today this hot girl stopped me and started shouting, "You're a Knick! Can we take a selfie?" I was like, "With me? Sure, okay." Then another guy was like "Yo, Freddie Luna, you're gonna lead the Knicks to a championship." Pretty soon a sea of fans crowded around me wanting my autograph. I felt like I was LeBron James strutting around Cleveland, like I was Michael Jordan swagadelically walking around Chicago, like I was Kobe Bryant striding around L.A. I'm *the guy* and this is *my city* now. It was like a dream until this fat asshole with a camera ran up. He stuck a super-bright light in my face and started asking me questions about my case. The crowd started leaving. Some fans started looking at me like I was a criminal. The paparazzi guy just kept naming shit off my rap sheet, asking me what it's like in Juvie. He even asked me if I dropped the soap.

LIZ   What did you say?

FREDDIE   I just kept walking but he was bothering me, "Freddie, are you aware that the victims have started a Boycott Freddie Luna Facebook page?"

LIZ   Bullshit, once you start winning everyone will get amnesia. That's the way it goes.

FREDDIE   I told you, I didn't hurt those guys / I was. . . .

LIZ   Shh. I don't wanna know. I don't need to know.

FREDDIE   You've gotta believe me.

LIZ   It doesn't matter what I think, Freddie.

FREDDIE   It matters to *me*. If you want me to trust you, you've gotta believe me.

LIZ   I don't know what I think.

FREDDIE   I wouldn't hurt anyone like that. Swear to God. And I'm no snitch either. I took the fall like a man. Shit, where I come from that's a noble thing to do for a friend.

LIZ   What did your friend do for you?

FREDDIE   He doesn't have to do anything, it's called loyalty.

LIZ   Where's my loyalty? You made my look really bad today, Freddie. Where's my loyalty?

FREDDIE   Say it.

LIZ   Okay, fine. I believe you. Alright? Now don't ever tarnish my good name again? *Got it?*

FREDDIE   Say it like you mean it.

LIZ   Don't give me a line reading, boy.

FREDDIE   Seriously. Say it for real.

LIZ   Freddie, I believe that you are an innocent man.

[*A beat.*]

[FREDDIE *grabs* LIZ's *hand and squeezes it tightly. He puts her hand over his heart and holds it there for a moment.*]

FREDDIE   Thank you, Liz. Thank you so much.

[*A beat.*]

[LIZ *is moved by* FREDDIE's *sincerity, he just wanted someone to believe him.*]

[*Lights out.*]

Buzzer Beater

[*Weeks later. LIZ's office, late night. LIZ and GABBY work side by side in her office. The basketball game is on TV. The Knicks vs. the Heat.*]

LIZ   Nike call back?

GABBY   Nope.

LIZ   Gatorade?

GABBY   Nope.

LIZ   Subway?

GABBY   Nope.

LIZ   Trojan condoms?

GABBY   No, none called. For the millionth time.

[*A beat, they work quietly.*]

You think Peter Roth from Puma spread the word about Freddie's accountability issue?

LIZ   Don't ask me stupid questions, Gabby. Just put some bourbon in your coffee and keep working.

GABBY   He's a good player and he has star quality.

LIZ   He's playing shitty and he pissed an important person off.

GABBY   He's a rookie.

LIZ   Well, in tonight's game he's gotten dunked on by the whole Heat organization. Pat Riley could suit up and dunk on his ass.

GABBY   What should we do?

LIZ   Just sit and wait. The kid's just nervous. It happens.

[*GABBY watches the game for a moment, Dwyane Wade dunks on FREDDIE.*]

[*GABBY and LIZ respond as if they've just witnessed a car crash.*]

GABBY AND LIZ   Oh shit. That's gotta hurt.

NBA ANNOUNCER   Wow! That's some vintage Dwyane Wade stuffing it down Luna's throat. Welcome to the NBA, kid. And the Heat are up by two with 6.8 seconds left in the fourth. Knicks have the ball.

GABBY   It's a close game. They could come back. The Knicks will pull through and win this game, right?

LIZ   Off the record?

GABBY   Ya, just between us.

LIZ   Not a chance in hell.

GABBY   So how do we get endorsements?

LIZ   Call the WME talent department. Maybe we can get him a famous girlfriend?

GABBY   Who?

LIZ   Someone cute and young. Someone on TV, like an edgy cable show.

GABBY   I don't have time to watch TV.

LIZ   Google it.

[LIZ *and* GABBY *watch the game.*]

NBA ANNOUNCER   Galloway will inbound the ball. Anthony's double teamed. Hardaway's being hounded by his man. Calderon's fighting to get free, Knicks need to get the ball in fast. Nobody's open, except . . . the rookie's open? Luna, the rookie's wide open. Luna gets the inbound pass.

[LIZ *and* GABBY *jump up.*]

LIZ   HOLY CRAP!

GABBY   Get it, Freddie!

LIZ   DON'T FUCK THIS UP.

GABBY   SHOOT! SHOOT!

NBA ANNOUNCER   Luna dribbles out. Bosh and Wade come to help. Luna pump fakes and shoots the three and . . . IT'S GOOD! KNICKS BEAT THE HEAT. THE ROOKIE WINS THE GAME. LUNA WINS THE GAME in an incredible shot right over Dwyane Wade!

LIZ   HOLY SHIT / HOLY SHIT.

[LIZ *and* GABBY *are screaming, they hug each other while jumping up and down. The office phone begins to ring.*]

[LIZ's *cell phone begins to ring.*]

[GABBY's *cell phone begins to ring.*]

[*Lights out.*]

Big Shot

[*A press conference.* COACH JONES *is answering a question from a reporter. He's giddy.*]

COACH JONES   . . . game was a close one. But we really came out and competed. I mean, the Heat are a talented team and we really gave them a hard time on the defensive end. Bosh struggled, Wade struggled, and now that James went home they have no one to bail them out offensively

[*The press laughs.*]

But on a serious note, I'm very proud of our guys. Very proud.

REPORTER   Did you draw up that last play for the rookie, Luna?

COACH JONES   The last play was not drawn up for Freddie. But he was open and he made the shot.

REPORTER   If he had missed the shot, would there have been consequences?

COACH JONES   I'd rather not answer that.

REPORTER   It's common sense, if a rookie doesn't listen to his coach it's usually off with his head.

COACH JONES   I wanna keep it positive, this win really boosted our confidence. Freddie's an ambitious young player with a lot of talent. He's proved to me tonight that he can handle the pressure.

REPORTER   Do you think Luna will get Rookie of the Year?

COACH JONES   I hope so. I'd love that for him.

[FREDDIE *enters with* LIZ. *They are glowing.*]

Liz?

LIZ   [*Beaming.*] Great game, Coach! Everyone, I present to you future Rookie of the Year Freddie Luna.

[*The press clap for* FREDDIE *as does* COACH JONES. FREDDIE *loves the attention.*]

FREDDIE   Thanks, Coach. Thanks, Liz.

COACH JONES   The day we drafted this kid was a great day for this franchise. Have a seat, son. The man of the hour, folks.

[FREDDIE *and* LIZ *sit.*]

Freddie's overbearing agent will be joining us.

[LIZ *rolls her eyes, the media laugh.*]

FREDDIE   She's the best.

LIZ   That's Liz Rico. R-I-C-O.

REPORTER   Freddie, great shot. How do you feel?

FREDDIE   Yo, I'm just happy it went in.

[*The media and* COACH JONES *laugh.*]

Liz   He's being modest. Talk them through it, Freddie.

Freddie   For real, though, I wanted the ball. I knew I could do it. And I did.

Reporter   That's a lot of confidence for someone with a rough start to your rookie season. Averaging 2.2 points a game and one rebound. How were you able to bounce back?

Freddie   Don't know, I just got the opportunity tonight to prove myself and I, uh . . . I look forward to proving myself in the future.

Reporter   Coach: do you think Luna will be your clutch player from now on? Has he earned that spot?

Coach Jones   He takes the credit tonight, and as for the future, he just needs to keep up the good work.

Reporter   Freddie: How did it feel to shoot over a future Hall of Famer and three-time NBA champion Dwyane Wade.

Freddie   To be honest, I loved it. I want to be the best, so—

Reporter   Freddie: there are some reports going around about your past. Do you care to respond to that?

Liz   No comment.

Coach Jones   We just wanna talk about the game.

Freddie   What kind of stuff?

Reporter   Your criminal record.

Freddie   Oh. I mean, that's not something we gotta talk about, right?

Liz   Right. Next question?

Reporter   There are reports that two of the victims you assaulted were in the crowd tonight.

[**Coach Jones** *tries to deflect the question.* **Freddie**'s *rage begins to bubble.*]

Coach Jones   A lot of people come to the games, there is no way to confirm that.

Reporter   We've confirmed their tickets and seats. They've been yelling obscenities at Freddie, hoping he will play poorly.

Liz   Madison Square Garden is one of the loudest stadiums in the league. He can't hear all the conversations going on. He's focused on the game.

Reporter   Freddie, do you hear them? They have a group that's been yelling and tonight they threw trash at you.

Freddie   I didn't do shit, man.

Liz   Calm down.

Reporter   So you do hear them.

Freddie   Fuck them.

Liz   Freddie.

Freddie   Those motherfuckers wanna waste their money on tickets just to fuck with my head. They can do that, but I didn't hurt those guys.

Coach Jones   (*To* Freddie.) Relax.

Reporter   You were convicted and served time, right?

Freddie   I won the game, doesn't that mean anything to you people?

Liz   Coach? Let's wrap this up.

Coach Jones   Good idea. That's all for tonight, folks, thanks.

[Coach Jones *and* Liz *start to stand, they try to get* Freddie *to leave.*]

Reporter   We confirmed all this with the New York State courts.

[Freddie, *still seated, slams his hand on the table.*]

Freddie   Man, I said I didn't want to talk about this.

Liz   You don't have to.

Freddie   I'm fucking past that shit, Liz.

Reporter   He answered the question.

Coach Jones   Look, this is his first postgame interview. Cut him a break.

Reporter   Freddie, can you confirm that you assaulted those boys and served time for the crimes you committed?

Liz   Get your ass up.

[Coach Jones *tries to get* Freddie *out of his chair.* Freddie *pushes* Coach Jones *off of him.* Coach Jones *doesn't budge, he continues helping* Freddie *out of his chair.*]

Freddie   FUCK You. FUCK ALL OF YOU. I'M A KNICK.

Coach Jones   Quiet, let's get going.

Liz   This press conference is officially *over*.

Freddie   I'M A MOTHERFUCKING KNICK NOW, OKAY?

Liz   Good night everyone.

Reporter   FREDDIE! FREDDIE, one more question!

[Freddie *pushes* Coach Jones *harder. This time* Coach Jones *flies backwards.* Freddie *stands to see if* Coach Jones *is okay.*]

[Liz *tries to block* Freddie *from the press, but the cameras start to flash wildly.*]

Freddie   LOOK WHAT YOU MADE ME DO. I shouldn't have to deal with this shit anymore. YOU HEAR ME?

[*Lights out.*]

End of Act One

ACT TWO
Grounded

[*A nice hotel room. We hear the shower running. It turns off.*]

[Freddie Luna *emerges from a steamy bathroom. He's got a towel wrapped around his waist.*]

[*He stands in front of a mirror looking at himself.*]

[*A beat. He has no idea who he is. He takes a deep breath and lets it out.*]

Freddie   [*To himself.*] Come on now. Man up. You got this.

[Freddie *walks over to the bed. He sits for a moment, then turns on the TV. He changes channels for a moment, we hear different shows in the background. ESPN's Sports Center theme song starts to play.* Freddie *watches as we hear the announcers.*]

TV Announcer   Top story tonight is Freddie Luna. The rookie guard for the Knicks is causing quite a stir around the league. During last night's press conference he pushed his coach to the ground. Bobby, I gotta tell you, some guys. they just aren't ready for the NBA. It's not just about skill. It's not just about talent. It's really about maturity. This kid's behaving like a thug with a criminal past. But he's a professional athlete, he needs to grow up. . . .

Freddie   Man, you don't know me.

[Freddie *turns off the TV, he's furious. He paces the room in his towel.*]

[*A beat. He takes a deep breath and tries to calm himself. That doesn't work. He goes to the bed and punches the shit out of some pillows.*]

[*He stops. He feels a little bit better. He goes to the closet and slides open the door.*]

[Liz Rico *pops out.* Freddie *jumps.*]

Freddie   HOLY / FUCK.

Liz   I know this is weird.

Freddie   SHIT. HOLY SHIT / THIS IS BULLSHIT.

Liz   Drastic times call for drastic measures.

Freddie   How long have you been in my hotel room?

Liz   I need to talk to you.

Freddie   Who let you in here? What the fuck is wrong with you?

Liz   It's not important.

Freddie   Are you a stalker or an agent?

Liz   Tomato, *tomahto*. I needed to speak with you in private.

Freddie   Then hit me up like a normal person.

Liz   You're not answering my calls, Freddie. I thought we had a trust between us.

Freddie   Trust my ass, everywhere I look someone's bashing me.

Liz   That's not my fault.

Freddie   What the fuck are you doing about it?

Liz   We need to work together on this.

Freddie   This fucking sucks and I'm fuckin' ragin', Liz.

Liz   At me? What did I do to piss you off?

Freddie   Everyone's fucking laughing at me.

Liz   You made a mistake.

Freddie   Those reporters were trying to start shit with me.

Liz   You're supposed to say, "No comment."

Freddie   I had never been in a situation like that, Liz. They're calling me a thug. I just lost my fucking temper, it was an honest mistake.

Liz   It's a business. Press needs to make money too. They make this a bigger deal than it really is to pay their mortgage.

Freddie   I'm not that guy. Everywhere I look I see my face but I don't recognize him.

Liz   You've gotta trust me.

Freddie   All of a sudden everyone's turning to me for money. I've got long-lost cousins calling me. "Primo, spot me a couple thousand." Or "What's good, fam, can you pay my rent this month?" Everyone wants a piece. Why should I trust you?

Liz   What year were you born?

FREDDIE   1995.

LIZ   Fuck. That was a terrible year. I lost Karl Malone to CAA and got my car stolen.

FREDDIE   Way to cheer me up, Liz.

LIZ   Back in 1995 life was very different. Biggie was still alive. We barely had cell phones, they weighed ten pounds and never had good reception. The Internet was new and nobody trusted it. Fax machines and beepers were in. I wore shoulder pads for Christ sake.

FREDDIE   What's your point?

LIZ   When you're in 1995 you think that life will always be that way. You think that's the end all be all, but then you wakeup to your iPhone ring tone and your flat-screen TV and its 2015. Everything is different. 1995 is a distant past. You'll probably laugh about this when you're my age from your spaceship or whatever the fuck you will drive in the future.

FREDDIE   You really wore shoulder pads?

LIZ   I rocked those motherfuckers like I invented them.

[FREDDIE *grabs a photograph from his desk. It rests on top of a stack of papers. He hands the picture to* LIZ.]

LIZ   Nice house.

FREDDIE   I bought it for my mom, just like I said I would.

LIZ   Funny, I also bought my dad a house when I got my first big check.

FREDDIE   Where's your dad's house?

LIZ   Long Island. He didn't believe it was his. He refused to go inside until I showed him the contract.

FREDDIE   Does he still live there?

LIZ   He's dead.

FREDDIE   Word? What happened to him?

LIZ   You don't want to know.

FREDDIE   I do.

LIZ   He threw in the towel, let's leave it at that. I had just been promoted to an agent, it was my first week. I threw myself into my work, I vowed to never give up, no matter how hard life gets. The day my father died was the day that I was born. Life tests us, Freddie, this is your test.

FREDDIE   What if I fail?

LIZ   Don't make it an option. Failure is not an option.

FREDDIE   My mom's really proud of me. This house I bought comes with a pool, two-car garage, even hired my mom a maid. Her whole life she's been breaking her back to clean up other people's messes. Now she's got someone to do that for her, so she can chill. . . . I don't want to lose this. Please help me. Please.

LIZ   First things first. You need to be on your best behavior. Monastic shit. Give me your phone.

FREDDIE   What?

[LIZ *gets up and searches the room. She finds the phone and grabs it before he can.*]

That's my personal business, don't look at that.

[LIZ *goes through his texts.*]

LIZ   Okay, any woman who texts you a coochie shot is not someone you need to be talking to right now.

FREDDIE   I'm a man. I've got needs.

LIZ   It's called porn, Freddie. You'll live.

FREDDIE   I need physical contact, Liz. I need the release.

LIZ   Release into your own hand, buddy. I don't want to Google you tomorrow and find a dick pic on TMZ. You feel me?

FREDDIE   Fuck . . . this is gonna be tough.

LIZ   Your image needs a makeover.

FREDDIE   Maybe I can be a bad boy, like Bill Laimbeer.

LIZ   Honey, if Bill Laimbeer looked like us, they would have kicked his ass out onto the streets.

FREDDIE   . . . Did I fuck it up, Liz? Honestly.

[*A beat.* FREDDIE'*s dreams are slipping away from him.*]

LIZ   Lucky for you, I'm a PR god. I represented Dennis Rodman during the "Bad as I wanna be" era. If I can keep him afloat through his dress-wearing, head-butting, Madonna-fucking days, I can certainly manage this.

FREDDIE   Dennis Rodman won five NBA championships, was a two-time All Star, two-time Defensive Player of the Year, *and* was a seven-time NBA rebounding champ.

LIZ   Yes, I'm aware.

FREDDIE   I just started my career. I've barely played enough minutes to get good stats.

[LIZ *paces. This is going to be a tough one. She picks up the phone.*]

LIZ   Hi, can I get a whiskey neat and a . . .

[LIZ *motions to* FREDDIE.]

FREDDIE   Can I have some milk, please?

[*A beat,* LIZ *looks at* FREDDIE *for a moment. She sees a child inside a man's body.*]

What?

LIZ   Nothing.

[LIZ *continues ordering on the phone.*]

So one whiskey neat and a milk.

FREDDIE   With chocolate.

LIZ   Make that a chocolate milk.

[LIZ *hangs up the phone.*]

FREDDIE   It helps me calm my nerves.

LIZ   You can trust me, buddy. My clients mean everything to me, my clients are my legacy.

FREDDIE   I don't want to be remembered this way.

LIZ   You won't. I'm gonna get you a really classy interview with Barbara Flowers. A prime-time special report.

FREDDIE   More interviews? I don't know, Liz.

LIZ   This one will be under my control.

FREDDIE   You can't control those reporters, they're crazy.

LIZ   Barbara and I go way back. She's Mr. Candy's cousin.

FREDDIE   You trust her?

LIZ   The interview will be scripted. Barbara will stick to the script. I'll get Coach Jones on board. It will be great.

FREDDIE   What am I gonna say?

LIZ   We will go over it in detail over the next couple of days. You'll be completely prepared.

FREDDIE   You really think this is gonna work?

LIZ   I'll get you out of this mess, I promise. I'll protect you.

FREDDIE   Thanks, Liz. You know, they were wrong about you.

LIZ   I don't really care what people think of me.

FREDDIE   Good, because everyone I know is intimidated by you.

LIZ   And you?

FREDDIE   Nah, I feel like I know you deep down inside. You're a nice lady when no one is looking.

[*Lights out.*]

Wine and Dine

[*An elegant restaurant.* COACH JONES *sits at a table, he's wearing a suit and tie.* LIZ *enters, she's wearing a sexy dress.*]

LIZ   Waiting long?

COACH JONES   Ten minutes.

[LIZ *sits.*]

LIZ   You ordered me a martini?

COACH JONES   Did you want something else?

LIZ   It's fine.

COACH JONES   Good. Good.

[*A beat.*]

[LIZ *looks over her menu.*]

LIZ   What are you getting?

COACH JONES   You're paying?

LIZ   The company is.

COACH JONES   Lobster.

LIZ   Still cheap, I see.

COACH JONES   And I'm ordering a bottle of Cristal for the table.

LIZ   Ya, fine, whatever. Get two. So . . . what do you want?

COACH JONES   Can't we have a friendly dinner?

LIZ   I'm not friendly, you know that.

COACH JONES   But you're in the people business.

LIZ   I fucking hate people. They never know what they want. They just want to bother you with their indecision. People lie to you. People shit on you. People love you when you have something they want. In my spare time I prefer solitude. I look forward to it.

COACH JONES   Solitude?

LIZ   I had a cat, Mr. Kitty, but I gave it away. I need to be completely alone for a certain number of hours of the day, or else I will lose my shit. Where's the waiter? I'm starving.

[LIZ *looks for the waiter.*]

COACH JONES   I'm extending my friendship here.

LIZ   I stopped believing in friendship when I got rich.

COACH JONES   That's a sad thought.

LIZ   Eat or get eaten. It's my world. I'm not complaining.

COACH JONES   Fine, don't be my friend. I don't care.

LIZ   Typical.

COACH JONES   What?

LIZ   You think you're the center of the fucking universe. Well, not mine, maybe someone else's but not mine.

COACH JONES   It's like I'm eating dinner with a block of ice.

LIZ   Poor baby.

COACH JONES   Fuck you, Liz.

LIZ   For that I'm making you pay for the drinks.

COACH JONES   Let's just talk about Luna. What's the plan?

LIZ   Barbara Flowers. We do a special about where he's from. Show clips of the Red Hook projects and Flowers will ask Luna questions about his past. He apologizes, a couple tears would be nice, and then *bam*, we're back in business.

COACH JONES   It's as easy as that.

LIZ   Yup.

COACH JONES   I hate to say it, but . . .

LIZ   Then don't say it.

COACH JONES   I told you so.

LIZ   That's all you wanted, isn't it. You have nothing better to do than make me feel small.

COACH JONES   I love being right, Liz. You know that.

LIZ   There's a lot on the line with this kid. Candy will leave me his company *if* Luna makes it big.

COACH JONES   What are you doing with your life?

LIZ   Excuse me? You want to pay for your fucking lobster, son?

COACH JONES   Candy tells you to jump, you jump. Candy tells you to play puppet master with this poor innocent kid and you have your hand up his ass. Making him say whatever. This kid isn't ready.

LIZ   What if you're wrong?

COACH JONES   You're not in the trenches every day. You're not on the court, in the locker room. I know Luna. He's got a lot of growing up to do.

LIZ   You've been wrong before.

COACH JONES   You want your name on some office door and in the process you're going to destroy someone's life.

LIZ   What the fuck do you know?

COACH JONES   I know you. Last month you went on a drunken rant about leaving Mr. Candy high and dry but you woke up hungover and took it all back. Said you didn't mean it.

LIZ   You're a disgruntled little coach. You have absolutely no power within that organization. You're aching to shit on someone and I'm the closest person around. You're a pathetic man.

[*A beat.*]

[LIZ *drinks her martini.* COACH JONES *finishes his cocktail. Liquid courage.*]

COACH JONES   I want you to sit on my face, so I can make you come so hard that your screams could shatter a glass window.

[*A beat. Sexual tension.*]

LIZ   I thought we said that last time would be the *last*.

COACH JONES   You've got me chocolate pussy-whipped. Marry me?

LIZ   You're just lonely.

COACH JONES   I'm not. I have options.

LIZ   You're just plain stupid then.

COACH JONES   I can't stop thinking about the last time. It was a half marathon of fucking, my back still hurts but I can't stop smiling. I'm wondering if we can give it another go.

LIZ   I'm not promising anything.

COACH JONES   You can't tell me that you didn't have a great time. You were making animal sounds.

LIZ   I'm not confirming or denying it. We're talking about the present here.

COACH JONES   We could make a good team off the court.

LIZ   I've been down this road several times with other men, Jones. It never works out.

COACH JONES   I'm not like other men.

LIZ   Because you're a bottom?

COACH JONES   Because I know you. Like *really* know you. Professionally and personally. For years.

LIZ   It never works out, so I stopped trying. I'm married to my clients.

COACH JONES   That's very disappointing.

LIZ   Last year I made the *Forbes* Top 50 Most Powerful Women in the Country list. That's enough for me.

COACH JONES   You can have both.

LIZ   No one can have both.

COACH JONES   I'm successful and I'm very understanding.

LIZ   You are now. But the 7th time in a row that I have to fly out on your birthday for a client. The 15th time I cancel our anniversary dinner, the understanding will melt away. I'm operating at a high level, Bill. It's not fair to anyone.

COACH JONES   You've never even been married.

LIZ   Yesterday was my work anniversary, 23 years at the Candy Agency, so I decided to celebrate. I worked until 7 p.m., which is early for me. Then I went home and had three tins of gold Imperial Caviar with crackers and a bottle of Johnnie Walker Blue for dinner. I was naked in my penthouse with floor to ceiling windows. I turned off my phone and watched the sun creep behind Jersey. The orange and pink streaks of heaven that peek out from behind the majestic Manhattan skyline. And it hit me, I just plain forgot to have children and a husband. I didn't mind it at all.

COACH JONES   I don't want you to be alone. I care about you.

LIZ   I want to be alone. I want to run shit, babe. Power's not something you share.

[*A beat. This is not the response that* COACH *was hoping for.*]

COACH JONES   You're a phenomenal woman. I just wanted to take care of you, is all. I think I can do that.

LIZ   That's my kryptonite, Coach.

COACH JONES   I see.

[*A beat.* COACH JONES *sinks his head into his menu. He's sulking, this wasn't the way this dinner was supposed to go.*]

[LIZ *sips on her martini and watches him.*]

LIZ   Ready to order?

COACH JONES   I'm not so hungry anymore. Maybe just drinks and dessert.

LIZ   Oh, okay.

COACH JONES   . . .

LIZ   Want to come over tonight? For old time's sake? I have more caviar in the fridge. No strings attached, I'll just ride you like a rodeo. Sound fun?

COACH JONES   Maybe we should just stick to business.

LIZ   Sure. Fine.

[COACH JONES *and* LIZ *stare into their menus.*]

[*Lights out.*]

Barbara Flowers Special Report

[*A studio set.*]

[BARBARA FLOWERS, FREDDIE, COACH JONES, *and* LIZ *sit in front of a film crew.*]

[BARBARA *speaks out to the audience.*]

BARBARA FLOWERS   Good evening, I'm Barbara Flowers and tonight we have a special report on NBA superstar rookie Freddie Luna. Luna's antics are a hot topic of discussion across the country. Last week he lost his temper during a postgame press conference and attacked his coach. Freddie's past doesn't help his image, he's from the rough neighborhood of Red Hook, Brooklyn, and at 19 has already spent a lengthy amount of time in a juvenile detention center. Is Freddie actually the thug he's recently been labeled by the media or is he a glimmer of hope for the struggling Knicks franchise? This evening, we sit down with Freddie, his coach Bill Jones, and his agent Liz Rico to find out who the real Freddie Luna is.

[*Cue the theme song.*]

Welcome, everyone.

FREDDIE   Thank you for having me, Barbara, I'm a huge fan.

BARBARA FLOWERS   Freddie, if there was anything you could say to your fans right now, anything at all, what would it be?

FREDDIE   I'd like to apologize for my behavior. There are no excuses for my actions. I'm sorry to the fans and to the Knicks organization.

COACH JONES   Barbara, Freddie's a great kid. He's extremely talented with lots of potential, but potential must be cultivated. There are lots of organizations out there who want talent without helping shape it. The New York Knicks are not one of them.

BARBARA FLOWERS   So, Freddie, what consequences will you face because of your actions?

FREDDIE   I've been fined by the league and I've been benched for three games. I just want to play basketball. It's been my dream since I was a little boy. I've learned from my mistakes and just want to move forward.

BARBARA FLOWERS   Liz, you signed Freddie from a Red Hook high school basketball team and got him a multimillion-dollar contract with the New York Knicks. Why Freddie?

LIZ   That's a great question, Barbara, and I love your suit.

BARBARA FLOWERS   Oh, thank you.

LIZ   Freddie Luna's story is tragic, his father was murdered when Freddie was four. His mother was deported to Venezuela. Freddie has been in and out of foster care. He spent his teens sharing a two-bedroom apartment in the projects with ten other people. He's lost many friends to gang violence and drugs. But when I met this young man, his fortitude and ambition really struck me. I thought, this kid's really going to make it.

BARBARA FLOWERS   Were you aware of Freddie's criminal record?

LIZ   I was, Barbara. But everyone deserves a second chance, especially people like Freddie who are born into difficult circumstances. In today's world these young men of color don't even get a first chance. Trayvon Martin, Michael Brown, and Tamir Rice deserved the opportunity to make mistakes, they deserved a fair shot at life. If Freddie was of another race you wouldn't think twice about this.

BARBARA FLOWERS   So it's racism?

COACH JONES   I think that Liz is referring to the negative press that's been coming out recently. Freddie's been called several names, including a "thug," a "criminal," etcetera. What happened between Freddie and I didn't warrant these allegations. The media took what happened and ran with it.

BARBARA FLOWERS   How does this make you feel, Freddie?

FREDDIE   I'm not gonna lie. I'm upset about it.

[*A beat.*]

[LIZ RICO *is overjoyed by* FREDDIE's *emotional honesty but tries her best to hide it.*]

LIZ   Do you need a tissue, Freddie?

[COACH JONES *gives* LIZ *a nudge to stop taking pleasure in this boy's pain.*]

COACH JONES   You okay, kid?

FREDDIE   I just want a chance to prove to everyone what I can do. It's a dream come true to put on that NBA jersey. A couple of months ago I had posters hanging in my locker of my teammates and now they are my friends. It's crazy. I don't want it to end because of my temper. I'm truly sorry.

BARBARA FLOWERS   Freddie, reports state that the two boys whom you allegedly assaulted have been coming to your Knicks games in protest. They've rallied outside of Madison Square Garden pleading that you be taken off the team because of your alleged crime. Are you aware of this?

LIZ   He doesn't have to speak about this. You don't have to answer that Freddie.

FREDDIE   It's okay. I haven't seen them but I've heard about them.

BARBARA FLOWERS   You claim you're innocent but served six months in a youth detention center for brutally assaulting Ronald Smith and Peter Jordan. One of whom you left in a wheelchair for life.

FREDDIE   I'm innocent. I did someone else's time.

BARBARA FLOWERS   You're covering for someone else? Are you familiar with the legal terms accessory or accomplice? Depending upon the degree of your participation in the assault, you would still be at fault.

FREDDIE   Barbara, where I come from, nobody likes a snitch. I'm better off serving my time and keeping my mouth shut.

BARBARA FLOWERS   So the person who hurt those boys, left one without an eye and the other paralyzed for life, that person is still out there roaming the streets?

FREDDIE   Yes.

BARBARA FLOWERS   And you know the identity of this person but won't tell authorities?

LIZ   He's not going to go any further with this, Barbara.

BARBARA FLOWERS   Let him respond, Liz. It's just a question.

COACH JONES   The league doesn't want him speaking on this subject.

FREDDIE   Hold up. Barbara, I didn't hurt those guys. I'm innocent. I want everyone watching to know that.

BARBARA FLOWERS   Freddie, you are an accessory or possible accomplice to assault and battery. According to the law, you are by no means innocent.

FREDDIE   You can't say that. What the fuck.

COACH JONES   [*To* FREDDIE.] Calm down.

BARBARA FLOWERS   I have a law degree and this is my show, I can say anything I damn well please.

FREDDIE   Liz? She's not sticking to the script.

LIZ   Alright, I'm pulling him.

BARBARA FLOWERS   Liz, you're being touchy. Come on.

LIZ   Freddie, take off your mic.

COACH JONES   [*To* LIZ.] Don't let them use this footage.

BARBARA FLOWERS   Wait, Freddie, let's discuss your mother. She was deported in 2009, what are your thoughts on immigration law in this country?

LIZ   This interview is over. Mics off, cameras off, let's go.

[FREDDIE *and* COACH JONES *stand and start to remove their mics.*]

BARBARA FLOWERS   Freddie, we reached your mother, Susana Flores Luna. She gave us a quote. It's in Spanish / but we've translated . . .

FREDDIE   You told my mom about this? Are you fucking serious?

LIZ   What the fuck? This is below the belt, Barbara, this is low.

BARBARA FLOWERS   Susana said, "It's my fault. I did the best I could but I wish I had been a better mother. I let my son down."

[FREDDIE *lunges at* BARBARA.]

FREDDIE   That's my family, you white devil bitch!

BARBARA FLOWERS   Calm him down!

[LIZ *tries to hold* FREDDIE *back, but he's lost his shit.*]

FREDDIE   My family's all I got! Don't fuck with them!

LIZ   No. / Stop the cameras!

BARBARA FLOWERS   Security! / Security!

COACH JONES   FREDDIE / stop!

[BARBARA *hides behind* COACH JONES, *who shields her from* FREDDIE's *rage.*]

FREDDIE   Leave my family alone! You hear me?!

[*Lights out.*]

Shitty Shit

[LIZ's *office.* GABBY *and* LIZ *are on their respective phone calls.*]

LIZ   I don't care about her ratings, she screwed me . . . that wasn't the agreement. If Barbara presses charges on Freddie, then I'll press charges on her . . . breach of contract. . . . It was a verbal agreement between me and that lying whore. . . . Don't tell her I said that. . . . I don't give a shit about her ratings. She can shove them up her skinny little ass. . . .

[GABBY *waves at* LIZ.]

GABBY   I've got Kevin Love on the phone.

LIZ   [*Whispers to* GABBY.] I'll call him back.

GABBY   He's called five times within 48 hours. I think he really needs to talk.

LIZ   I'll call him back.

GABBY   [*Into the phone.*] Kevin, she's not available. . . . I'm so sorry. I know. I know.

LIZ   [*Into phone.*] You there? I want action, not your apologies. Just do it.

[LIZ *hangs up the phone.*]

Do you want lunch? I haven't seen you eat in 48 hours.

LIZ   Get me a tuna melt and an attorney.

GABBY   Who exactly?

LIZ   Some hot shot civil rights attorney. I don't care how young or old they are. We need the best.

GABBY   Okay.

LIZ   Make sure Freddie makes it to practice today.

GABBY   You want me to call him a car?

LIZ   Yes, call him my car. Make Luis get out of the car and drag him by the ear to practice.

GABBY   Got it.

LIZ   Has Barbara called back?

GABBY   Nope.

LIZ   What an asshole. Call her again.

GABBY   I don't think I should.

LIZ   I don't care what you think.

GABBY   Between Freddie's calls and your calls, I think Barbara's pretty fed up.

LIZ   Does it look like I give a fuck? Does it?

GABBY   You were subpoenaed this morning. She is putting a restraining order on you and Freddie.

LIZ   Cunty. Cunt face. Send it to Candy's attorney. Get him on the line, please.

GABBY   There are some other people looking for you.

LIZ   Who?

GABBY   You've got a ton of messages, Liz.

LIZ   Okay, shoot.

GABBY   Kevin Love. He sounds pissed.

LIZ   He'll survive.

GABBY   Carmelo called yesterday and you never returned his call. James Harden called about the new Taco Bell commercials. And Anthony Davis has texted you seven times asking about his Gatorade deal.

LIZ   Okay. Fine. Get Candy's attorney on the line.

GABBY   What should I say to the others?

LIZ   They can wait. All of them. Tell them to wait.

GABBY   Every time they call, they get bitchier and bitchier.

LIZ   Get tougher skin, Gabby.

GABBY   Love said that CAA has been calling him nonstop.

LIZ   Oh, please. Love isn't leaving.

GABBY   How do you know?

LIZ   He loves me. No pun intended.

GABBY   You won't call him back.

LIZ   I will, later. I'll get to it. You have to prioritize.

GABBY   Kevin's a huge client. He's not a priority all of a sudden?

LIZ   Are you married to him or something?

GABBY   No, I'm just asking about your strategy. Trying to learn and observe. Isn't every client relationship supposed to be a priority?

LIZ   I don't like your tone.

GABBY   I have no tone, I'm just asking you a question.

LIZ   Keep the attitude at a minimum and get me a stiff drink.

GABBY   Do you want me to dial Kevin or Carmelo or Anthony Davis?

LIZ   Did I ask for that?

GABBY   No, but . . .

LIZ   Do what I ask of you. It's not that hard of a job.

[GABBY *nods. She goes to the mini-bar and pours* LIZ *a drink.*]

[*A beeping alert is heard from* GABBY's *computer.*]

What is that?

GABBY   Five oh, five oh.

[LIZ *panics.*]

LIZ   SHIT. ETA?

GABBY   Less than one min/ute.

[MR. CANDY *enters.*]

MR. CANDY   Liz? A word?

LIZ   Yes, Mr. Candy.

MR. CANDY   May I sit.

LIZ   Of course. Gabby? Get him a drink?

MR. CANDY   No thanks.

LIZ   How can I help you?

MR. CANDY   How can I help *you*?

LIZ   Everything's great. Just peachy.

MR. CANDY   Have you lost your mind? This Luna kid's a sinking ship.

LIZ   Why did you beg me to sign him?

MR. CANDY   Liz, I just came from a board conference call about you and how much you fucked this up. Phil Stern is twerking in the lunch room, all hell's breakin' loose, my dear.

LIZ   The board is "intimidated" by me. They don't want me running the company. You said it yourself.

MR. CANDY   We want you to drop Luna.

LIZ   What?

MR. CANDY   The board's down my throat. Barbara Flowers is up my ass. Everyone wants blood.

Liz   I've been through worse situations with clients. I can get him out of this.

Mr. Candy   You're in over your head.

Liz   I'm not.

Mr. Candy   I've gotten calls from Kevin Love, Carmelo Anthony and James Harden. They're complaining about your lack of attentiveness lately.

Liz   I see.

[Liz *smells a rat. She makes eye contact with* Gabby.]

[Gabby *avoids her gaze.*]

Mr. Candy   I figure that you drop Luna and you get back to normal.

Liz   Kick him when he's down.

Mr. Candy   You're not yourself.

Liz   In what sense?

Mr. Candy   Distracted by the kid. He's one name on an elite client list that you've built over several years.

Liz   He's in trouble. I'm trying to get him out of it.

Mr. Candy   It's not worth it.

Liz   I see something in him.

Mr. Candy   I miss the old Liz Rico. Get her back here.

Liz   I'm still Liz.

Mr. Candy   We have history. A long and rich past full of good memories. I hate to tarnish two decades of success over one lousy kid out of Red Hook.

Liz   . . .

Mr. Candy   Your hesitance is unnerving.

Liz   I'm just not sure about this.

Mr. Candy   This is a no-brainer, Liz. Come on. You're the best in the business, this is an easy choice.

Liz   Normally this would be a no-brainer but I feel responsible for this kid.

Mr. Candy   You need to think of yourself. Of the agency. Not Luna. He's on his own.

Liz   Yes. Right.

Mr. Candy   Just call him up and apologize profusely. Tell him to get a good therapist and another agent.

Liz   Okay.

MR. CANDY   Gabby? Can you get Luna on the phone, please?

GABBY   Yes, Mr. Candy.

MR. CANDY   Let's get this over with.

[*A beat.* GABBY *dials.*]

LIZ   . . . Wait.

MR. CANDY   Wait?

LIZ   I . . .

MR. CANDY   What's the big deal? It's just one kid.

LIZ   He's in trouble.

MR. CANDY   What do you care?

LIZ   . . . I don't know.

MR. CANDY   Liz, you look like hell. You're tired because you've been putting in the effort. I appreciate it, don't get me wrong. But you're wasting your time at this point.

LIZ   What if you're wrong?

MR. CANDY   Guys like Luna are a dime a dozen. Freddie baffles me. He's got loads of talent and a great agent. Why does he want to fuck it up for himself?

LIZ   He's not doing it on purpose. He just doesn't know any better.

MR. CANDY   And what are you supposed to do about that? Play Mommy?

LIZ   No. I've never wanted kids.

MR. CANDY   Then drop Luna. It's a five-minute phone call. Do it and get it done.

LIZ   Let me do it on my own terms. In my own time.

MR. CANDY   No.

LIZ   Why are you pushing?

MR. CANDY   Pull it together. I've offered to leave my entire company to you, don't make me question my decision.

[*A beat.*]

LIZ   [*Firm.*] I'll do it on my own terms. In my own time.

MR. CANDY   It better get done. Today. I'm not fucking around, Elizabeth.

[MR. CANDY *exits.* LIZ *sits back in her chair. What to do?*]

GABBY   Do you want me to get Luna on the phone?

Liz . . .

Gabby LIZ?

Liz . . .

Gabby You should eat something. Then we can call Luna. Okay? Let me get you that tuna melt, stat.

Liz Go home, Gabby.

Gabby What? Why?

Liz Take the rest of the day off.

Gabby Am I in trouble?

Liz No.

Gabby Good, because I haven't done anything wrong.

Liz Are you talking to Candy behind my back?

Gabby No.

Liz Whose side do you think you're on?

Gabby Liz, I'm grateful for everything you've taught me but it's time I branch out on my own.

Liz You think you're ready for that?

Gabby Yes. Absolutely.

Liz Do what you want. If Candy's offering you a promotion for ratting me out, you should take it but be prepared for the consequences.

Gabby Candy did offer me a job.

Liz What did you give him in return?

Gabby What are you offering me? I need the job. I need the money.

Liz Integrity. You stick with the people who helped you when you were nothing.

Gabby Integrity?

Liz Yes.

Gabby I've watched you be deceitful and dirty for the past five years. Freddie Luna? You've ruined his life so that you could get ahead. Your sense of "integrity" is fucked up.

[Gabby *exits in a blind rage.*]

Liz [*Yells after her.*] Go cry to Mr. Candy. He'll dry your tears.

[*A beat.*]

[Liz *sits at her desk quietly. Perhaps some of what* Gabby *said resonated with her.*]

[Liz *picks up her desk phone and dials a number.*]

[*SPLIT STAGE:* Freddie Luna's *wearing workout clothes. He's walking home post-practice. His phone rings, he answers.*]

Freddie. It's Liz.

Freddie   What's up, Liz? I'm walking into practice.

Liz   Listen, kid. I'm gonna make this quick and painless.

Freddie   What's going on?

Liz   I can't be your agent anymore.

Freddie   Oh.

Liz   Don't worry about the Barbara Flowers thing. The agency will cover your legal expense. You can call me anytime to check in, I just can't advise you professionally anymore.

Freddie   Why? Are you mad at me?

Liz   No, not at all, Freddie. This is strictly about business.

Freddie   Uh . . .

Liz   Hello? Are you there? Do you understand what I'm saying.

Freddie   I understand, yes.

Liz   Okay, good.

Freddie   I don't know what I'm supposed to say.

Liz   You'll be fine. You keep playing and get your temper under control. Okay? You'll be good.

Freddie   So this is about the Barbara Flowers interview?

Liz   The company's just going in a different direction right now. The market dictates where we will go and there's been a shift. It happens.

Freddie   Okay . . .

Liz   Take care, okay, Freddie?

Freddie   Ya whatever.

[Freddie *hangs up on* Liz. Liz *gets up and pours herself a drink. She tries to take a sip but can't. She throws the glass of whiskey across the room. The glass shatters.*]

[*Lights out.*]

Get It Gurl

[MR. CANDY *stands at a podium in a board room with a glass of champagne. He speaks directly to the audience as if they are the company/investors.* MR. CANDY *taps the champagne glass with a spoon to get everyone's attention.*]

MR. CANDY   Good afternoon, everyone. I'll make this quick since we all have business to attend to. With a heavy heart, I announce my retirement from the Candy Agency. I assure you that I'll be leaving you all in good hands. The best. Ladies and gentlemen, I introduce to you your fearless new leader: Elizabeth Rico, CEO of the Candy Agency.

[*We hear clapping as* LIZ *enters, she gives* MR. CANDY *a hug.*]

LIZ   Thank you, Mr. Candy.

MR. CANDY   You're very welcome.

LIZ   I've known Mr. Candy for a long, long time now.

MR. CANDY   Don't give away my age, dear.

LIZ   I know what he looked like before the grays, before he was married, it's been a pleasure, sir. I feel like we've grown up together.

MR. CANDY   The pleasure's been mine. I'll let you address your team.

[MR. CANDY *takes a step back and let's* LIZ *take center stage.*]

LIZ   [*To the group.*] I'm honored that Mr. Candy has allowed me the opportunity to run this magnificent sports agency. I started working for Mr. Candy when I was 21 years old. A recent Yale graduate, I had the ambition and drive to make something of myself. Mr. Candy invested in me when I was a diamond in the rough, a girl from the projects with a dream, and he taught me how to identify that tenacity and potential in my clients. Here at the Candy Agency, we pride ourselves on our client relationships. We want to grow with our clients. We want to find those diamonds in the rough and nurture them into success. We want to invest in young athletes, that's what the Candy Agency /stands for. . . .

[GABBY *rushes in and interrupts* LIZ *mid-speech.* GABBY *whispers something into* LIZ's *ear.* LIZ *receives shocking news and tries her best to hide it.*]

You'll have to excuse me. A family emergency has just . . . I have to excuse myself. I'm very sorry.

[LIZ *exits abruptly.* GABBY *quickly follows.*]

[*Lights out.*]

Guilt

[*A hospital waiting room.* COACH JONES *is on the phone.*]

COACH JONES   No comment and stop calling, have some fucking decency.

[COACH JONES *hangs up his cell phone as* LIZ *enters in a rush.*]

LIZ   Can I see him? Where is he?

COACH JONES   The league suspended him for a year and the Knicks terminated his contract. He took it pretty hard.

LIZ   I heard.

COACH JONES   I guess his well-being isn't your concern anymore because he isn't a client.

LIZ   It was a business decision.

COACH JONES   Save the bullshit for the office, Liz.

LIZ   I think we can do without the insults, alright, Bill?

COACH JONES   I was on my way to kick him out of the Knicks' housing and I saw him there on the pavement. He fucking jumped.

LIZ   When can I see him?

COACH JONES   He's in surgery now but he was asking for you before they put him under.

LIZ   What did he say?

COACH JONES   Mostly gibberish. He should be dead.

LIZ   I can't fucking believe this. I just can't.

COACH JONES   I couldn't get a hold of his mother.

LIZ   I had Gabby call before I left the office. She already knew about it from the news. There's a media shit storm outside.

COACH JONES   And he left a note for you.

LIZ   For me?

COACH JONES   It's addressed to you. I thought you might want to read it.

[COACH JONES *hands* LIZ *the suicide note. She reads it to herself, then reads out loud.*]

LIZ   "Liz, I'm your legacy." . . . Motherfucker. . . . He's such an asshole. I can't even . . .

COACH JONES   Freddie's not in the right state of mind.

Liz I can see the headlines now, "CEO Leads Ex-Client to Suicide." 23 motherfucking years mean nothing because of this. Funny how that works out.

Coach Jones This will blow over, this is about Freddie, not you.

Liz This will ruin me.

Coach Jones Liz, I know we've had our ups and downs, but trust me Freddie's decision isn't a reflection of you, get over yourself.

Liz Oh, fuck you, who are you? Mr. Perfect?

Coach Jones Look, we're both human and this is a complicated business. You always say, "You can't mix the personal with the business."

Liz I broke my own rule.

[*The cap that* Liz *uses to keep her emotions hidden has burst off,* Liz *tries to hide her tears from* Coach Jones.]

[*He tries to embrace her. She pushes him away.*]

Bill. I think I just need a minute.

Coach Jones I'm not leaving.

Liz Just a fucking minute. I just don't understand it, Bill. I could have given up a million times but I never did. I don't understand.

Coach Jones Freddie's not built like you are. You're invincible.

Liz I'm not.

Coach Jones You're the strongest person I know.

Liz I've been scared all this time. Terrified.

Coach Jones You don't act like it.

Liz I've been trying to cram myself into this box for years . . . but that's just not me. . . . It's not me. . . .

[*Lights out.*]

Equity, Bitch

[*A couple weeks later.*]

[Liz'*s office, which is now* Gabby'*s office. It's redecorated and has* Gabby'*s diplomas hanging from the walls.*]

[Gabby *sits behind her desk, she's on the phone. Mid-conversation.*]

Gabby Marc. Marc? Marc. MARC. His stats say it all. He's up in rebounds and steals. He's a role player. Marc. I don't care if you don't like his wife, just pay him what he's worth! I'm going to give you 24 hours to counter Miami's offer.

[LIZ *enters.*]

[GABBY *waves her over to have a seat.*]

GABBY   Marc, if not, we are walking. Marc? Marc. Do you . . . do you hear. . . . Got it? He's excited about Miami but he'd rather play for you. . . . Okay, good. Bye.

[GABBY *hangs up the phone.*]

Coño, hijo de la gran . . .

LIZ   Marc Cuban?

GABBY   How the fuck did you ever get a word in with that guy?

LIZ   Just tell him how great he is, he loves that. All the owners have different ways of running their teams. What are you gonna do?

GABBY   Strangle him.

LIZ   You'll be okay, just remember to be firm. Stand your ground.

GABBY   I know, Liz. I know. So? What's going on?

LIZ   This is a little odd, isn't it?

GABBY   "It's good to be king," Liz.

LIZ   Cute. I'm happy the office went to someone like you. I don't think I said this enough when you worked for me, Gabby, but you're as good as gold. Truly.

[*A beat.* GABBY'S *taken back by the compliment. She grows skeptical of* LIZ.]

GABBY   That's uncharacteristically nice of you.

LIZ   I mean it.

GABBY   I still don't get it. You had it all and you just walked away. I'm still waiting for you to bust down my door wanting your office back.

LIZ   I had a change of heart. That's why I'm here actually. I'm going to start my own agency.

GABBY   Uh . . . okay. . . .

LIZ   We're going to be small at first.

GABBY   Well, ya, I mean, you have no clients.

LIZ   But I will.

GABBY   Who? They all stayed at the Candy Agency, either with me or Mr. Candy.

LIZ Honey, I let you have those clients. That was a gift.

GABBY Okay, here we go.

LIZ I'm not here to argue.

GABBY Fine. You have a clientless new agency. Congrats. I wish you the best.

LIZ You wish me the best. Don't play dumb with me, you know what comes next.

GABBY What is it?

LIZ You're not going to make this easy for me, are you.

GABBY Nope, not one bit.

[LIZ *laughs.*]

If you're doing what I think you're doing, I would appreciate a formal offer. I mean, if that's why you are here.

LIZ Gabby, I'm here because I want you to come work for my company. It's a big decision, I know that. But take some time to think / about it.

GABBY I want health insurance.

LIZ Done.

GABBY A signing bonus.

LIZ Sure.

GABBY Really?

LIZ I'm serious.

GABBY I want . . . equity.

LIZ You'll have it.

GABBY WHAT? REALLY?

LIZ Yes.

GABBY Bullshit, you hate sharing. You're going to give me shares of your brand-new company just because I asked you for them?

LIZ I'll do whatever it takes.

GABBY I'm very happy here, Liz. I have a great relationship with Mr. Candy. I've been promoted, given a hefty raise and am on track to make partner.

LIZ You'd have to give those things up, but I will do everything in my power to ensure that we are successful.

GABBY You can't "ensure" anything in this business.

LIZ   It's called faith. I hired you five years ago when you were twenty pounds heavier and your speaking voice was as loud as a whisper. I miss that girl, I had faith in her.

GABBY   We are at very different places in our lives. It's a big risk for me.

LIZ   Whatever you're feeling deep down inside, that's what you should do. I can't tell you what that is.

[*A beat.* GABBY *thinks about it.*]

GABBY   I'm going to stay here, Liz. I'm very sorry.

[*A beat.*]

[LIZ *takes this in, she's disappointed but she hides it.*]

LIZ   Don't you dare be sorry. You've made a decision and as a woman I respect that.

GABBY   Liz, I owe a lot to you, really.

LIZ   No, Gabby. You're family to me, I'm just . . . I'm not good at letting people know.

[LIZ *exits.*]

[*A beat.* GABBY *exhales and looks around the office she's worked so hard to get.*]

[*Lights out.*]

Crossroad

[*A hospital room. The bed's empty and unmade.* FREDDIE LUNA *sits in a wheelchair and stares out a window. Both of his legs have casts on them, as does his arm, but he is now conscious.*]

[LIZ *enters, she's surprised to see him out of bed.*]

LIZ   Hey. Feeling / better?

FREDDIE   What the fuck are you doing here?

LIZ   You asked for me before your first surgery. It took me awhile to get here.

FREDDIE   Fine. You showed up. Good job. Now get the fuck out.

LIZ   No.

FREDDIE   You're not my friend. You're not my agent. You're nothing to me.

LIZ   Why would you do this to yourself?

FREDDIE   I'll call security on your ass.

LIZ   You're in the psych ward, babe. They're not gonna listen to you.

[FREDDIE *turns his face in the opposite direction of* LIZ. *He's upset with her but also ashamed of himself.*]

Look, you don't know this yet but life's a long journey full of peaks and valleys.

FREDDIE Spare me the speech.

LIZ Trust me, Freddie, life's about so much more than basketball.

FREDDIE Not to you.

LIZ I've chosen to live a very focused life. You've got your whole life ahead of you. You can choose to live it however you want.

FREDDIE I've got no place to go except back to the projects. I'd rather kill myself than show my face in Red Hook again. My mom's really disappointed in me. You promised me that you wouldn't let this happen.

LIZ You can be angry with me. But don't be angry with the world, Freddie, trust me. Anger's like putting cement shoes on and trying to run down Canal Street to catch the bus. It won't get you anywhere.

FREDDIE You talk a lot of game but I think you forgot who you are and where you came from / Liz.

LIZ Just stop.

FREDDIE I heard about Mr. Candy leaving the agency to you if I made it big. You used me.

LIZ Freddie. This is about you. I'm worried about you.

FREDDIE You weren't worried about me before when you dropped me over the phone. Over the phone. Like I was nothing to you.

LIZ I have to live with my mistakes. You have to live with yours. Are you going to be a victim or are you going to be a survivor?

FREDDIE I tried, Liz. I fucking tried so hard and it lead me here.

LIZ The world's a shitty place. It wasn't built for people like us to be kings.

FREDDIE No, it wasn't.

LIZ We have the power to change that. Did you know? We've been blessed with a second shot at life, how are you going to use it? Are you going to sit here and rot away? Or are you going to learn from this and give it another go.

FREDDIE What do you want from me?

LIZ I told you, you asked for me so I came.

FREDDIE Why? You could have blown me off. I know you, you don't do anything unless it benefits you. What's in it for you?

Liz   Nothing. Absolutely nothing.

[Liz *reaches for* Freddie's *hand.* Freddie *opens up to her. He let's it all out, his depression, his lack of confidence, his fears, his anger, his loneliness.*]

[Liz *embraces* Freddie. Freddie's *sobs grow louder, deeper, he's realized how shitty life can be but he's made a friend to help him bear it.*]

[*Lights out.*]

———————

LOST GIRLS

by

John Pollono

Photograph by José Element

Dedicated to Jenny

Production History

New York premiere produced by MCC at the Lucille Lortel Theatre, October 21–December 4, 2015.

Cast

GIRL   Lizzy DeClement
PENNY   Meghann Fahy
BOY   Josh Green
LINDA   Tasha Lawrence
LOU   Ebon Moss-Bachrach
MAGGIE   Piper Perabo

Creative Team

DIRECTOR   Jo Bonney
SCENIC DESIGN   Richard Hoover
COSTUME DESIGN   Theresa Squire
LIGHTING DESIGN   Lap Chi Chu
SOUND DESIGN & ORIGINAL MUSIC   Daniel Kluger

Biography

A writer and actor from New England, John Pollono co-founded the award-winning Rogue Machine Theatre Company in Los Angeles, which has produced several of his full-length plays and one-acts. At RMT, he is the co-producer of the hit underground storytelling series Rant and Rave. His play *Small Engine Repair*, which he wrote and starred in at RMT, swept the 2011–2012 Los Angeles Theater Awards, winning Best Production, Best Playwriting, and Best Ensemble at the Ovations, LA Weekly, Garlands, and LADCC. MCC Theater produced it with director Jo Bonney in NYC in fall 2013 and produced *Lost Girls* as well in 2015.

Setting

Manchester, New Hampshire. Mid December. Present day.

Scene 1

[*A very modest apartment home with a couch, a TV, some chairs, and the corner of the kitchen, with a kitchen table and four chairs. Quaint, clean but nothing flashy. It's the type of living space that feels warm and inviting but exudes compromise and budget. There are some basic Christmas decorations set up—some figures, a small tree, some colored lights (unplugged). Through the windows we see a nonstop barrage of snow slamming against the glass. The radio plays classic rock which is interrupted by this:*]

RADIO DJ   [*Thick New England Accent.*] . . . Londonderry, Hudson schools, all closing early . . . once again, winter storm warning still in full effect . . . the Nor'easter continues to pound all of New England . . . low pressure over the Carolinas have moved inland, insuring that these blizzard-like conditions will continue into tomorrow morning. . . . Manchester may see twenty-six inches by sunup. . . . People, if you don't need to be on the roads, don't drive. Wicked wet snow out there, temp's gonna drop and roads will ice right up.Let the plows do their job and only drive if you really gotta. Once again, record-setting accumulation throughout New England. This is the real thing. . . . You're listening to WGIR FM. Stay safe out there. . . .

[*As the DJ talks, a woman enters. This is* MAGGIE LEFEBVRE, *in her mid-thirties. She is pretty but has had a hard life and there is perma-worry etched on her face. Her hair is still reminiscent of bygone fashion. Her makeup is nice; she wears tasteful but inexpensive clothes and a name tag as she is a saleswoman at Bloomingdale's Outlet Store in Merrimack, New Hampshire. She moves about, in a rush, as in her life she is always ten minutes behind, collects her purse, her keys, puts her cold coffee in the microwave and hits it. She gathers her coat, her gloves. Microwave bings and she takes out coffee, screws on the lid, turns off the radio, and then walks out the front door and steps outside and locks the door.*]

[*After a moment, the door unlocks and she comes in (dusting of snow on her shoulders), puts all her shit down.*]

MAGGIE   Goddamn motherfucking sonofagoddamn cunt!

[*She collects herself. Sloughs off her coat.*]

Dammit dammit dammit! Motherfucker. Goddammit!

[*She yells up the stairway.*]

MA! WAKE UP!

LINDA   [*Offstage.*] What?!

MAGGIE   I NEED YA!

LINDA   [*Offstage.*] What are you yelling for!

MAGGIE   Come down here, okay? Somebody—it's an emergency, just get dressed and come down.

Linda [*Offstage.*] What happened?

Maggie A crime was committed. Okay?

Linda [*Offstage.*] Holy shit. Seriously! I'm coming!

[**Maggie** *dials the cell phone.*]

Maggie Leonard, hey, it's Maggie. Listen, I know I'm already late but . . . just relax, listen to me . . . my car was stolen. I don't know, some cocksucker wanted a 2002 Honda Accord, and they took it. I know you don't like that word, but I'm a little stressed at the moment and—I know, I know.

[**Linda** *walks in. She has on a nightgown and a sweatshirt.*]

Linda Somebody hurt? Is it Erica?

Maggie No, Jesus. Don't even say that.

[*Into phone.*]

Look, you're the first call I made, okay? Even before the cops. I understand the position yer in but who's even shopping the outlets in this weather?

Linda What's the crime, for God's sake?

Maggie [*Into phone.*] No, you can't. . . . I need the shift. I already spent my paycheck. I gotta jump off and call the cops. I'll get a ride and be there in like an hour. Fine, half hour.

[*She hangs up.*]

FUCK! FUCK! FUCK! Somebody stole my car.

Linda The Honda?

Maggie I got another car I don't know about?

Linda Wha'd'ya faggot boss say?

Maggie He's being all right about it. Listen, lotta people are gay these days, Ma, you gotta have an open mind. And I told you, I don't want talk like that around Erica.

Linda She's not even here. Where the hell is she anyway?

Maggie School.

Linda This early?

Maggie This is what we do on weekdays, Ma. She's at school before I'm outta the shower and she's eating lunch before you're even fucking awake. Can't believe the buses ran today. Jesus. Okay, I gotta call the cops now.

[**Maggie** *dials the phone.*]

[*Into phone.*]

Hello? Sure, I'll hold.

LINDA   How many parking tickets ya got?

MAGGIE   Won't tow 'til ya get five.

LINDA   Pissing snow out there.

MAGGIE   You think what? The snow disintegrated it?

LINDA   I don't know . . . this is terrible, though.

MAGGIE   No shit.

LINDA   What are we going to do? This is . . . I mean . . . really bad timing, tragic even. I feel like you've been violated. Like this is a kind of rape or—

MAGGIE   I don't need this right now.

[*Into phone.*]

Hi, yeah, my car was stolen. My name is Maggie Lefebvre. Ya, you know my husband . . . my ex-husband . . . Lou Lefebvre. . . . No, you didn't meet me at a party, that was his new wife. . . .

LINDA   You can't get fired, Maggie. Ya behind on mortgage payments.

MAGGIE   [*To* LINDA.] Just shut the fuck up for a second.

[*Into phone.*]

Last night sometime, parked it at like seven when I got home from work. PM. I didn't see broken glass, but it snowed and the plows mighta covered it.

LINDA   Well, why'd you wake me up if you just want me to shut up? You know how I am, I talk all the fucking time. If you didn't want me to talk, why'd you wake me up?

MAGGIE   [*Into phone.*] I'm at 835 Kearsarge, Unit C. Okay. Thanks, I'll have the VIN and all that shit ready.

[*She hangs up.*]

LINDA   What'd they say?

MAGGIE   They said have a cup of coffee and relax, they'll send over a prowler. Like I can fucking relax right now.

LINDA   I can make coffee.

MAGGIE   Who knows what my deductible is. Five hundred bucks maybe? I don't have five hundred bucks.

LINDA   Who has five hundred bucks lying around in this economy?

MAGGIE   Goddamn thieves. I hope they crash into a tree and burn alive.

LINDA   Where's the coffee beans?

MAGGIE   In the freezer. Erica says it keeps the beans better.

LINDA   Does it work?

MAGGIE   I tell her it does, but I'm not so sure. Shit. You know, when I talked to that dispatcher, I shouldn't have mentioned that I was, you know, Lou's wife—ex-wife. I don't know why . . .

LINDA   What's the big deal? It's true.

MAGGIE   They're gonna call him, I know it.

LINDA   Okay. Maybe take a cab, lemme take care of the car?

MAGGIE   That'd be what? Thirty bucks? You know what this month's cushion is? Twenty-three bucks. I'm a pizza an' a six-pack away from bouncing the fuckin' electric bill.

[*Her phone rings.*]

[*Looking at caller ID.*]

Speak of the devil.

[*Answers it.*]

Hello? Yeah, I don't know. Just . . . out front. Look, you don't gotta . . . I got it handled, okay? I'm a big girl here. Bye.

[*She hangs up. Tries to pull herself together.*]

LINDA   That was Lou?

MAGGIE   Who else it gonna be?

LINDA   Call somebody and get a ride.

MAGGIE   Everybody's at work.

LINDA   Ya can't piss off ya boss, Mags. Look, I know you're not gonna like this but you could call you-know-who. . . . He works nights.

MAGGIE   I don't care if he pulled up in a Snowcat with a working fucking Jacuzzi. I'm done with that prick.

LINDA   He wasn't *that* bad.

MAGGIE   Guess I got higher standards than you. Anyway, I gotta wait for the prowler to come, take my details. I got a lotta shit to do before I can go sell winter coats at Bloomingdale's fucking Outlet Store.

LINDA   Maybe I call insurance for you.

MAGGIE   You gotta have the fucking police report number, Ma!

LINDA   Stop yelling at me! It's gonna be okay. Just relax, it's a friggin' ten-year-old car.

MAGGIE   I got no car, I got no job. I got no job, I got no way ta pay bills, you, me, Erica—we're all out on the street.

[MAGGIE's *cell phone rings again.*]

[*Into phone.*]

What? Look, I got it under control, I don't need you. . . . I can tell you're already driving, Lou. I can hear the wind and the radio. Fine, come over. But don't act like you were waiting for permission.

[*She hangs up.*]

Says he wants to fill out the report himself, make sure it gets done right.Like I'm an idiot or something.

LINDA   He bringing the new girl?

MAGGIE   She's not new, Ma. They been married two years.

LINDA   She's, like, wicked religious, huh?

MAGGIE   She's a boring fuckin' retard is what she is. Jesus Christ. I look like shit.

LINDA   You look nice.

MAGGIE   No I don't, I look like shit. I haven't been eating good, haven't been to Curves in months.

LINDA   I think you look pretty good considering . . .

MAGGIE   What do you mean "considering"?

LINDA   I mean you look very nice for a gal who hasn't been going to the gym, just got up for work, found out her car was stolen, and she's probably gonna lose her job.

[LINDA *plugs in the Christmas lights.*]

MAGGIE   Ma, look at your goddamn, your nightgown is stuck, I can see your ass.

LINDA   Sorry.

MAGGIE   You was wearing that yesterday.

LINDA   I'm behind on laundry.

MAGGIE   Go in my room, put on something of mine, and I'll wash that later.

LINDA   Hold on, listen ta me. I'm serious. All this, it's fixable, okay? Ain't nobody's life at stake here. We'll work it out.

MAGGIE   [*Deep breath.*] Yah. Ya right, ya right.

[*A knock at the door.*]

LINDA   Jesus, that was quick.

MAGGIE   Mr. Punctual has arrived. Go.

[LINDA *scurries out.* MAGGIE *takes one last look in the mirror, opens the door.*]

[LOU *is in his mid-thirties. He's well groomed but a little square, an off-duty NH State Trooper. His wife,* PENNY, *is younger, in her twenties, sweet-looking, from Ohio.*]

LOU   Hey-O. How we doing?

MAGGIE   What were you, like, two blocks away?

LOU   Pretty much, actually.

PENNY   Hi, Maggie. It's Penny.

MAGGIE   Ya, I remembah. Stop standing in the doorway. Come on in.

LOU   You doing okay, Mags? How we doing?

MAGGIE   I'm fine. Just pissed off is all. You didn't need to come over and do police work on your day off.

PENNY   I had an appointment up the street.

MAGGIE   In this weather?

LOU   It's like a two month wait to see this guy, so we kicked in the four-wheel drive and said hell with common sense.

PENNY   But they called and cancelled on account of this storm.

LOU   Right as we're pullin' into the parking lot. Can ya believe it?

PENNY   They lost power and all.

LOU   Then, as I'm turning around, dispatch hits me up about ya car. So it really worked out well.

MAGGIE   Glad my grand theft auto was convenient for you.

PENNY   He didn't mean it that way, Maggie.

LOU   It's okay, Pen . . .

[LOU *takes out his clipboard and starts filling out the stolen vehicle report.*]
I'll just take the report and get out of your hair. So they stole the Honda?

MAGGIE   I didn't check my other cars, but, yeah, I think that's the one.

LOU   Okay. Look, I know you're freaking out.

MAGGIE   I'm not freaking out.

LOU   Okay, fine, you're not.

MAGGIE   Just pissed off.

PENNY   Theft can feel like a real violation.

MAGGIE   It's just a fucking car.

LOU   So where's, uh . . . what's his butt?

MAGGIE   He's done. Erica didn't tell you?

LOU   No, she didn't mention that. I'm glad, he was a Chowdahead, that guy.

MAGGIE   You never even met him.

LOU   No, but Erica said he was always teasing her.

MAGGIE   Why you think I ended it? None of your fucking business anyway.

LOU   I know, I just . . .

[LINDA *comes back in. She's now wearing* MAGGIE's *bathrobe.*]

You didn't need to get all dressed up for me.

LINDA   Hey, Lou. You're looking fat.

LOU   You know why, Linda? Because I've been eating a lot.

LINDA   All them donuts at Dunkies, look at you, walking fucking cliché. This the new girl?

LOU   You mean my wife?

PENNY   We met last year. At Erica's piano recital.

LINDA   Yeah, yeah. I remember. You spilled tonic all over my bag.

PENNY   I still feel awful about that.

LINDA   I'm over it. So, Mr. Supercop, you gonna personally find these cocksuckers who stole my daughter's car or what?

LOU   Well, I'm gonna do my best. I'm not on patrol anym[ore]—

LINDA   That's right, you're a Statie now. I forgot. Went from walking the beat, solving actual crimes, to becoming a glorified traffic light. Let me ask you somethin'. You ever feel guilty fuckin' over regular citizens with that gay-ass radar gun of yours?

PENNY   Oh my.

LOU   It's okay, Pen. This is just how she communicates. Speed kills, Linda.

LINDA   Right. Plus state's gotta quota and pot holes don't fix themselves.

Lou You taking online courses on city public works infrastructure or something?

Linda Fucking Lou here. Hey, you tell your fellow Statie bitches they find the guy that stole my daughter's car, they break his face with their Maglight for me. I'll cook 'em a turkey.

Lou I'll put that in the report.

Maggie Aren't you gonna call it in?

Lou Already did. Pulled the vin offa copy of the title in my dash.

Penny Weird they stole it the middle of a snowstorm, right?

Lou Sometimes scumbags use a storm for cover. Who the hell knows. Honda Accord very easy vehicle to sell on the black market.

Linda Lou, let me ask you something. Why would a cop go to a dealership and buy one of the most stolen car in existence? To me that's, like, beyond fuckin' idiotic but . . .

Lou I wanted the Mustang.

Maggie Mustang's no car you got a kid. Consumer Reports gave the Honda Accord very high safety ratings. Anyway, ten years later, I'm still driving the same goddamn car.

Linda He got a newer model.

Lou See that, Linda. That's the line I'm not gonna let you cross.

Linda Oh, Lou, we're just getting warmed up.

Maggie Okay, Ma. Enough.

Lou You have anything of value in the vehicle?

Maggie Just CDs and shit. Maybe some returns in the trunk. Don't matter, I don't have coverage for incidentals.

Penny Yeah, they never pay that stuff out anyway. I had my car stolen once in Cleveland, took my entire Beanie Baby collection. Never saw a cent.

Linda That's a harrowing story.

Maggie Fuck. I had Erica's Christmas present in the trunk.

Linda What was it?

Maggie A fucking iPhone. Jesus Christ. Took me a year to . . .

Lou You got her the iPhone? We got her the iPhone too.

Penny Lou.

MAGGIE   Yeah, well, good thing. Now, more than ever, we can illustrate that her mom is a giant losah.

LINDA   You're not a losah.

MAGGIE   I shouldn't have left it in there but I didn't want her to see it. She's so goddamn nosy—

LINDA   Who knew it'd get stolen?

LOU   You know what, Linda? I will personally bury my Maglight in this asshole's forehead we catch him.

MAGGIE   You know, I gotta call her.

LOU   Why?

MAGGIE   I'm supposed to pick her up today.

[MAGGIE *dials her cell.*]

LOU   We don't need to bother her in school.

MAGGIE   I don't want her to worry I don't show up.

LOU   I'll pick her up.

MAGGIE   Right to voicemail. We can have her paged.

LOU   Do not.

MAGGIE   First Wednesday every month is Dunkies day. It's our thing. I pick her up after piano lessons and we go to Dunkins. We sit there, drink our coffee, eat fucking cinnamon rolls, and talk. Well, I do most a the talking and she plays with her phone, but still. Fact that she sits there with me is glorious. And it's our tradition, you understand?

LOU   So you pick up the tradition next week. By then we'll have you squared away, rental or whatever.

MAGGIE   Drive me to the school right now.

LINDA   You gotta go to work, hon.

LOU   We can drop ya off at work ya want.

MAGGIE   I wanna see my daughter face-to-face and explain our family car was stolen. That was her car too. She was learnin' how to drive in it.

LOU   Let's not distract her. She has that language arts exam today.

MAGGIE   That was last week.

LOU   Okay, maybe I'm thinking of Espagnol.

MAGGIE   She got a B+ in Espagnol. You don't know the fuck you're talking about.

LOU   Take it easy.

PENNY   She's just upset, hon.

MAGGIE   Pardon me. We're just not used to this whole "involved father" routine. It's still in the break-in phase, feels weird.

LOU   You don't get to talk to me that way, Mags.

PENNY   We're all very emotional right now.

LOU   Of course I'm emotional, I love my daughter!

MAGGIE   I'm not saying ya don't!

LINDA   Hey, assholes, settle down here! I'm on the phone.

[*Into phone.*]

This is Linda Dolman, my granddaughter is Erica Lefebvre. She's in the tenth grade. Can you have her paged or whatever, we have a family crisis here.I understand you may close soon from the storm, that's very interesting and I'm glad you told me. Okay, sure, take all the time you want. I'll just sit here doing my nails.

[*To the room.*]

Fucking public schools, they'll hire an orangutan they got no criminal record.

[*Into phone.*]

Hello? You sure? Oh my God. Ya . . .

LOU   What?

LINDA   You absolutely positive? You absolutely one hundred percent—

MAGGIE   WHAT?

LINDA   Okay, thanks.

[*Hangs up phone.*]

Okay . . . everybody take a deep breath. Now what I'm about to tell ya is gonna be . . .

MAGGIE   This ain't your fucking moment onstage, Ma!

LINDA   Erica didn't show up for school today.

MAGGIE   [*Like a punch to her gut.*] Fuck.

PENNY   Erica stole the car?

LOU   Oh shit . . .

[*That hangs in the air for a beat.*]

[MAGGIE *looks out the window at the storm.*]

Scene 2

Budget motel somewhere in Connecticut. Night.

[*A clean but simple motel room with one double bed. The door opens and a sixteen-year-old* GIRL *walks in. Even at sixteen, she has a world-weary edge to her, which is reflected in her attitude and choice of clothing. She puts her small suitcase down and takes a few steps in, brushing snow off of her shoulders. Behind her, a* BOY *her age enters. He's a young jock, sweet-faced and clean cut. He's wearing a damp varsity letter jacket, hoodie, and a Red Sox hat.*]

GIRL   You said you could drive in the snow. You fucking lied.

BOY   I didn't lie. I've been driving in snow since I was ten years old. But you can't drive if you can't see.

GIRL   God, you're such a pussy.

BOY   You gotta see. No matter how good a driver you are.

GIRL   I'm gonna be a whole day late. He's throwing a kegger for me and I won't even fucking be there.

BOY   Sorry.

GIRL   I hate the snow. It's cold and it serves no purpose.

BOY   What about skiing?

GIRL   The fact that rich assholes enjoy something so cold and useless only makes me hate both snow and rich people even more.

BOY   Oh. All right.

GIRL   Can we just not talk for a few minutes?

BOY   Sure. So that restaurant across the street. What's it called? McSorley's? Bet they have great fries.

GIRL   What did I just say, dude?

BOY   I thought you didn't want to talk about snow.

GIRL   I was issuing a general let's not talk policy. Not a specific no snow talk policy.

BOY   Oh. Sorry. Again.

GIRL   Go. Get fries if you want them. I don't give a shit. Bars are open until like 2 a.m. here.

BOY   Aren't you hungry?

GIRL   I'm a teenage girl living in a society where I'm constantly barraged with unrealistic expectations. I've never not been hungry.

Boy   Yeah, I love eating.

Girl   You're not a very good listener, are you?

Boy   I'll just sleep on the floor, I guess.

Girl   No fucking shit. I didn't mean . . .

[*She walks into the bathroom.*]

[*The* Boy *picks up the house phone and listens to the dial tone. She comes back in and catches him.*]

Are you calling somebody?

Boy   What?

Girl   Are you calling your mother?

Boy   No.

Girl   Pull it together, dude. It's almost midnight, everybody's asleep.

Boy   I'm excited. I've never even been out of New England before.

Girl   Connecticut is part of New England, dumbass.

Boy   You know what I mean, this isn't the real New England. Man, I wonder when palm trees will start. Maybe like Virginia? I bet it's Virginia. Do you think it's Virginia?

Girl   I give zero fucks where palm trees live.

Boy   Check this out. Water glasses. With paper hats on them. Are these for us to keep?

Girl   Why do you need them?

Boy   I don't, I just . . . I could give them to my mom when I get back. As like a "I'm sorry" present. She wakes up and reads that note, she's gonna go apeshit. She's gonna like shoot me in the nut sack with an Uzi. And you think I'm joking but she really does have an Uzi. And a Glock-17 and a thirty ought six.

Girl   Is she like a hunter?

Boy   She loves animals. The guns are for people.

Girl   I hate people.

Boy   So what did your friends say when you told them you were running off?

Girl   I only told Wilma.

Boy   Wilma with the droopy eye?

Girl   You know another Wilma in our school? Anyway, she said, "Send me a postcard if you don't die."

Boy   What kind of shit is that to say? Why would you die?

Girl   You wouldn't. She's just . . . she's morbid. That's why we're friends.

Boy   I didn't tell anybody.

Girl   Why?

Boy   To make it more of an adventure.

Girl   It is a fucking adventure, isn't it? We almost made it three hours south of Manchester.

Boy   So this guy I'm driving you to in Florida . . .

Girl   Yeah?

Boy   He's like a fisherman?

Girl   I think he's the captain or something. They make a lot of money on his boat, though, especially if they catch a bluefin tuna. Bluefin worth its weight in gold to the Japanese, you know. Anyway, he has a place right near the ocean.

Boy   That must be awesome.

Girl   Better than fucking Manch-Vegas, right?

Boy   How old is he?

Girl   Not that old.

Boy   Like how old, though?

Girl   Like . . . thirty-nine, I think.

Boy   Jesus Christ. That's like . . . wow. That's not as old as my mom but it's, like, in the ballpark.

Girl   So?

Boy   And you two banged already?

Girl   So?

Boy   Isn't that illegal because of your age?

Girl   Drinking beers and smoking doobs is illegal but you've done both.

Boy   I don't drink or smoke, but I see your point.

Girl   Did you, like, take classes on being a pussy or you a natural?

Boy   I'm not judging ya. My oldest sister is thirty.

Girl   And you fuck her?

Boy   What? Hell no. That's not my point. Gross. My point is that I understand that you can have, like, a relationship with someone old. Because me and my sister, we watch movies and go sledding, and hiking . . .

Girl   Sledding? That's so gay. You know what? You're, like, way younger than her. You're totally a mistake.

Boy   They told me I was planned.

Girl   They lied. Your dad totally gave one thrust too many and he nutted all up in there and was like, "Oh shit, Nancy, got some baby batter up in there. Hope we don't got another brat to feed."

Boy   Her name's not Nancy.

Girl   I'm just messing with you. My mom was a teenager when she had me. I'm a total mistake too.

Boy   Really?

Girl   Yup. I basically fucked up her whole life. So now she makes it her hobby to fuck up my life. Because she doesn't have one.

Boy   Maybe she'll call my mother, and both our mothers will put out a bounty on our asses.

Girl   Dude, relax.

Boy   I still . . . I just can't believe I'm doing this.

Girl   Can you stop saying that?

Boy   Yeah. But I can't believe I'm doing this.

Girl   Why not?

Boy   Because I'm an athlete.

Girl   What the fuck does that mean?

Boy   Means I take care of myself and, you know, I have a future.

Girl   So why'd you say yes?

Boy   For the money this old dude's gonna give me for driving you down. Why else?

Girl   Because you were bored and this is the most exciting thing to ever happen to you.

Boy   I wasn't bored.

Girl   Sure you were. You know why?

Boy   Why?

Girl   Because you're boring.

BOY   I'm not boring.

GIRL   Let's break it down, Sporto. Your life is boring, your friends are boring, your hair, your clothes, even your fuckin' dog. All boring, boring, boring.

BOY   My dog is not boring.

GIRL   I went over your house once in the second grade and I met your shitty dog. He just fucking sat there and farted.

BOY   Not Falcor's fault he has digestion issues. He's a rescue.

GIRL   Sticking up for your old-ass dog is wicked boring too.

BOY   Oh yeah? Is getting into college prep classes boring? Is lettering in varsity baseball my freshman year boring? Is winning an academic award for my paper on conflicts in the Middle East boring?

GIRL   Hmmm. . . . Hat-trick yes.

BOY   So why'd you ask me to help you drive down there?

GIRL   Because you're so boring I knew you'd say yes!

BOY   Stop calling me boring. It's pissing me off.

GIRL   Sorry. Did you say something? I just, like, nodded off there for a second.

BOY   Okay. Well, at least I don't stick some old dude's dick inside me and try to act like it's not totally fucked up and depressing.

GIRL   Yeah. You got that on me.

BOY   I do.

GIRL   You do.

BOY   I know.

GIRL   That's what I just said.

[*The* GIRL *starts putting her coat on.*]

BOY   Where are you going? Hey! I'm sorry, wait!

[*He takes her arm in his hand.*]

GIRL   Don't touch me! Don't you ever fucking TOUCH ME!

[*She pushes him hard against the wall and hits him savagely a few times in the shoulder and chest—her outburst is ugly and scary. This girl has demons. Against his better judgment, he grabs his jacket and follows her out.*]

BOY   Wait! Don't run away! I'm sorry!

Scene 3

[*In the kitchen,* MAGGIE *is pacing, smoking, and on her cell.* PENNY *sits nearby, praying.*]

MAGGIE   You lemme know she calls or anything. Don't you worry if she's in trouble, that's not your concern, darling. Buh-bye.

[MAGGIE *hangs up, looks outside at that terrible storm.*]

Goddammit. Why today?

[*She turns to see what* PENNY'*s doing.*]

What the hell are ya doing?

PENNY   [*Finishes praying.*] Oh. I'm, uh, asking God to protect Erica and help guide her home safely.

MAGGIE   Ya see the snow out there? I'd say he ain't listening.

PENNY   He's always listening.

[*Beat, changing subject.*]

Any luck?

MAGGIE   Nobody knows where she is. Called all her close friends. All three of 'em.

PENNY   I was the same way.

MAGGIE   Yeah?

PENNY   I was, like, a really sensitive kid too. I lived in this town in Ohio called Steubenville until I was twelve.

MAGGIE   Okay.

PENNY   My dad was a pastor at the Crossroads Christian Church and he died when we were pretty young, so we didn't have a lot of, you know, amenities. I had three older brothers, but . . . old steel town, not a lot of options.

MAGGIE   Sure.

PENNY   My oldest brother, Eddie, he died when he was seventeen. Drunk driving. Mom said enough's enough, we're gonna figure out how to leave this town.

MAGGIE   [*Yelling to other room.*] Ma, you almost done in there?

PENNY   She found an article on the Marcellus Shale, how they're pulling clean natural gas right outta the ground under our feet. She went to night school, got a degree in petroleum administration. Got a good job and moved us all to Cleveland, into a real house. Had my own room. Two rabbits. Joined the swim team.

MAGGIE   Why you're telling me this shit right now?

PENNY   Just so you, like, know I didn't make many friends outside of church. Like Erica.

I mean, she doesn't got to church regularly, but . . . I can relate. Kids are mean at that age if you don't, you know, wear the same clothes or listen to the same music. Especially when you move schools. You know what I mean?

MAGGIE   I don't actually, I've lived in this fucking town since I was a fetus. You and me, Penny? We ain't ever gonna be friends.

PENNY   Oh. Okay. Sorry.

[LINDA *enters.*]

LINDA   Bunch of her clothes are gone, hon. Duffel bag too.

MAGGIE   Fuck

LINDA   I don't know how we didn't hear her doing all that, sneaky little bitch.

MAGGIE   Her being a female got nothing to do with this.

LINDA   Fine. Sneaky little asshole. Jeezum.

[LINDA *places a cup in front of* MAGGIE.]

MAGGIE   I told you I don't want a fucking cup! Why you gotta give me a cup anyway?

LINDA   Everything I do, you yell at me. I didn't steal your goddamn car and run off in the middle of a snowstorm.

MAGGIE   We don't know she ran off.

LINDA   Of course she ran off. You did this exact same shit, snowstorm and everything. Had me worried sick. This is what teenage girls are wired to do.

PENNY   I never did, actually.

LINDA   See? It's abnormal not to.

MAGGIE   I fuckin' pray Erica makes better decisions than I did at her age.

LINDA   Ah, what are you gonna do? Truth is, we're supposed to have babies at fifteen or whatever. That age, baby spits right outta there. But nowadays, society's so complicated, women waitin' until they're fuckin' forty. Gotta pump their vaginas full of chemicals and do headstands to get knocked up.

Then they hire a fleet of fuckin' hippies to build a pool in their living room, light candles around it, and chant for three days, 'til somebody sticks in the ceremonial salad spoons.

Maggie   What the fuck you talking about?

Linda   I'm saying times have changed and teenage girls' bodies ain't caught up yet.

Maggie   What about teenage boys?

Linda   You can't put the blame on boys. Nature made 'em hunters. They're wired to stick their dicks into everything. Shampoo bottles, sheep, hollowed-out pumpkins, don't matter. Up to girls to tell 'em what's what.

Maggie   So it's all Erica's fault she gets in trouble?

Linda   Girls got more at stake is all I'm saying.

Maggie   You ever think, maybe a girl oughta be able to grow up, make a mistake or two, without the world chewing her up and fuckin' spittin' her out, huh?

Linda   Oh, enough already with the liberal bullshit, Mags. Let's agree to disagree.

[Lou *enters from outside, hanging up his cell.*]

Lou   Okay, no luck yet.

Maggie   My car?

Lou   Is still in the system. Not as stolen, I don't want nobody overreacting, but somebody, one of the boys, they see her, they call me instantly. Also checked her credit cards. She hasn't used any of them.

Maggie   What cardzzz? She has a card. A Discover card. But it's like a debit card, I put money on it. Different thing.

Lou   She has another card.

Maggie   No she doesn't.

Lou   I got her a Chase card.

Maggie   Why the fuck you not tell me that?

Lou   That's my job now?

Maggie   Well, she should have told me.

Lou   Yeah, she shoulda.

Maggie   Like I'd fucking use it or something? Gotta hide it from me?

Penny   Nobody thought that, Maggie. It was just a misunderstanding.

LOU   Relax.

MAGGIE   Relax? How's that? Because here's the reality. Either she ran off and is, like, halfway to California by now—

LOU   She can't charge anything without us knowing about it.

MAGGIE   She knows her dad is a cop, she's not a fucking moron. She's got a workaround, I guarantee it. So either she crashed into a tree . . .

LOU   Hey.

MAGGIE   Or some creep has her hog-tied in a fucking basement somewhere and . . .

LOU   None of that happened. Contain yourself.

MAGGIE   That's ripe. You of all people telling me not to go off the deep end.

LINDA   This ain't nobody's fault, hon.

MAGGIE   Always somebody's fault.

LINDA   What? Me again?

PENNY   It's nobody's fault. She's going to be fine.

LINDA   It's society's fault. Fucking social media and whatnot. Not me.

MAGGIE   You guys exhaust me.

LINDA   How could it be my fault? I mean, I made mistakes, who doesn't? I was goddamned sixteen years old I had a baby. Carried her around in a backpack while I waited tables. But she turned out pretty good.

MAGGIE   Yeah, I had it easy.

LINDA   What's that mean?

LOU   Linda, just let it go, would ya?

MAGGIE   I don't need your help no more, Lou, thank you very much.

LINDA   I did the best I could with you.

MAGGIE   Well, I'm glad I didn't have to see second best.

LOU   Maybe now's not the right time to open up a can of fucking worms.

MAGGIE   Stay the fuck outta this.

LINDA   What worms?

MAGGIE   Forget it.

LINDA   I wanna know what fuckin' worms.

MAGGIE   Okay, Ma! Ya really wanna talk about all the shit I went through growing up?

LINDA   Ya know, I don't wanna talk about this right now.

MAGGIE   [*To* LOU.] Lou, did you track her cell phone?

LOU   It's turned off at the moment. But as soon as she makes a call . . .

LINDA   At least you got iPhones and technology and shit. Back in my day, your kid took off, you just sat there on the couch, opened a box a wine, and waited all night. Worry chewing its way outta ya belly. Way harder for a single mom back in the day.

PENNY   Women making great strides these days because of the precedents your generation set.

LINDA   I can't tell if you're being sarcastic.

PENNY   Oh, I don't really "do" sarcasm.

LINDA   Oh, well then . . . thank you. But you know who had it worse of all?

[LOU *tries to motion* PENNY *not to encourage her.*]

PENNY   Who?

LINDA   Maggie's grandmother.

LOU   Oh boy.

LINDA   Fifteen she had me. Fifteen goddamn years old. Her mother grabbed her by the hair and threw her out into the street. And that was a rough transition, going from a warm house full of French Canadians out to backwards-ass 1960s Rhode Island. Whole world a mess. Civil rights. War. Assassinations. Not a lot of soft places to land for a fifteen-year-old with a belly full of baby those days. But she endured. We both did.

PENNY   She must have been an amazing woman.

LINDA   She was kind of a bitch, actually. But who can blame her. Women hadda be extra tough in those days.

PENNY   I'm sure.

LINDA   If it had been today, way modern teenagers think, I'd a been pushed out in the woods in the middle of January. They'd find this pink little frozen blob with leaves stuck to it, thawing out in the spring. And then what? None of us be here right now. Put that in your pipe and smoke it. You come from tough goddamn stock, my dear. Women with hearts of iron.

MAGGIE   More like iron skulls.

LINDA   Every generation we get better.

MAGGIE   How you figure that?

Linda   My ma was fifteen, I was sixteen, you seventeen.

Maggie   In another ten generations we'll be at the median age of the rest of the fucking nation?

Lou   She's not pregnant, she's too smart for that.

Maggie   Smart girls get pregnant just the same as dumb ones.

Penny   You're scared. But you have to make a choice not to go to that dark place.

Maggie   I exist in that dark place.

Lou   Erica's gonna walk through that door any minute. And you and me, we're gonna sit her down and give her hell. Okay?

Maggie   You better not make me the bad guy here.

Lou   I won't.

Maggie   I don't need Drunken Fists of Glory Lou in here, but I need some backup. . . .

Lou   Stop stabbing me in the back, Maggie.

Maggie   How is it a back stab when I'm saying it clear-eyed and right to your face? Listen, all your precious feelings aside, it's that mushy snow out there. The temp drops like they say it's gonna, the roads are gonna be a sheets of ice.

Lou   Mags, I told you . . . don't go there, okay?

Linda   Regarding that pregnancy thing. It's not like she even has a boyfriend, you know? I didn't finish high school, but I know you need a set of balls to scramble them eggs. I know that much at least.

Penny   Lou?

Maggie   Lou, what?

Penny   He has something to tell you.

Lou   Okay. Listen. Calm down first. Put your hands on the table and relax, okay?

Maggie   I'm about five seconds from clawing somebody's fucking lips off.

Lou   Erica has a boyfriend.

Maggie   No, she doesn't.

Lou   She does. She told me.

Maggie   She didn't tell you.

Lou   How do you know?

MAGGIE   Because she would have told me.

LOU   She woulda told you she told me?

MAGGIE   No, dumb fuck. She would have told me she had a boyfriend.

LOU   I didn't know you didn't know. She just . . . look, I heard her on the phone and I could tell it was a guy, okay. I sat her down and she denied it. She denied it for like an hour. But then Penny found a—

PENNY   This isn't going to be easy to hear.

MAGGIE   Just say it then!

PENNY   I found a condom in the laundry.

MAGGIE   Like a used one?

PENNY   No, in a package, but . . .

MAGGIE   Maybe it wasn't hers.

PENNY   We don't use those, Maggie.

MAGGIE   TM-fucking-I.

LINDA   At least she's using protection. That's evolution right there.

LOU   You want to keep discussing this or you need a breather? Because I did. Penny told me about the condom, I felt like our little girl was a piece of china that had just slipped through my fingers and shattered on the concrete floor.

PENNY   He cried in my arms for like half an hour.

LOU   They don't need to know that.

MAGGIE   Who is this guy?

LOU   I don't know. I got her to say yes, there's a guy. Then she clammed up. You know how she is.

MAGGIE   You let her get away with everything. Make me be the asshole every time.

LOU   She wouldn't talk to Penny either.

MAGGIE   She shoulda talked to me. Her mother. Not Virgin fuckin' Mary here.

PENNY   You have a right to be upset. But not at me, Maggie. I have never, for one second, pushed my beliefs on Erica. That is not my place. I told her to talk to you.

MAGGIE   Wait, what beliefs?

LOU   Let's not—

PENNY   Abstinence.

MAGGIE   You really were a virgin ya got married?

LOU   That ain't none of your business.

PENNY   It's okay, Lou. Yes. I was.

LINDA   So only flava you ever tried was . . . fucking Lou here?

[MAGGIE's *very rattled by this revelation.*]

MAGGIE   Ma, enough.

LINDA   Sorry, it's like meeting a unicorn or something.

MAGGIE   When was this you talked to Erica about him?

LOU   Last week.

MAGGIE   Okay, dumbass. Pull her cell phone records. Find out this guy's number, call the piece of shit.

PENNY   Can you do that, Lou?

LOU   Yeah, I actually can. Cell phone's under my plan. Good idea.

MAGGIE   I should be the cop. Somebody get me a fucking donut.

[LOU *dials his cell phone.*]

Where you going?

LOU   I'm stepping outside to make the call.

PENNY   Why not talk in here?

LOU   Because I don't need three batshit women clawing into my every fucking word, okay?

MAGGIE   Go then!

LINDA   Go!

PENNY   Go!

Scene 4

[*The motel door slams open and the* GIRL *rushes the* BOY *back inside. He has a bloody rag pressed up against his nose, containing a gusher. She slams and locks the door, closes the drapes.*]

BOY   Did we lose him?

[*They dart over and look out the downstage window.*]

GIRL   He was too shit-faced to run very fast. Oh God. We gotta keep it down, okay? He could be right outside.

BOY Okay.

GIRL Lemme see.

[*He removes the towel. His nose and lip busted up.*]

Jesus.

BOY Am I still handsome?

[*A rough man's voice erupts somewhere offstage, dangerously close.*]

OFFSTAGE VOICE (JERRY) Boy! Where are you, ya fucking Red Sox faggot! We ain't done talking about this! Not by a fucking long shot!

[*They turn out the lights and hide from the window.*]

GIRL Look, I didn't need you doing that for me.

BOY He was being inappropriate.

GIRL You can't hit a man every time he acts inappropriate. You'll be hitting men all day.

BOY Not true. I would never be that way to a girl.

GIRL It's no big deal.

BOY It should be a big deal.

GIRL It's not like I asked him to grab on me. He bought me a beer so I laughed at his joke. I didn't ask him to stick his hand between my legs. Jesus.

[*She rushes into the bathroom, gets a damp towel, and comes back to clean him up.*]

BOY I didn't mean that you wanted him to do that. But assholes like that sense that you are, like, not going to start World War Three if they try to paw all over you. And they act inappropriate. You need to know you're worth more than that.

GIRL You only say that because you don't really know me.

BOY We've known each other since second grade.

GIRL Yeah? What do you know?

BOY That you're, like, really cool and smart and funny. And kinda mean but in a sweet way.

GIRL The old days I was like that, I guess.

BOY What old days? You're sixteen!

[JERRY *offstage, closer.*]

OFFSTAGE VOICE (JERRY) I know you're in one of these rooms, asshole! You and your little bitch!

[*We hear* JERRY *slamming on a door, getting closer.*]

GIRL   Listen, dipshit. You gotta be careful. Old dudes have those old dude muscles.

BOY   He totally sucker punched me.

GIRL   Well, you did call him a pedophile.

BOY   At least it's not broken

GIRL   What, you're an expert on boxing now?

BOY   Not the first time I've been cracked in the nose.

GIRL   By who?

BOY   My dad.

GIRL   Your dad? Seriously?

BOY   He used to drink a lot and go fucking ballistic. But he doesn't any more. Now he goes to meetings, smokes all the time, and reads the Bible. At least I hit him once.

GIRL   Your dad?

BOY   No, I'd never hit my dad. Even when he beat on me, I knew that it would really hurt his feelings to hit him back. I'm talking about the guy who wants to kill me.

GIRL   Speaking of sucker punch, you totally split his scalp open with that ginger-ale bottle. Bet he's gonna need stitches.

BOY   You think?

GIRL   Yeah.

BOY   Awesome.

JERRY   [*Offstage, even closer, smashing things outside—bottles, banging doors, etc.*] I'm gonna kick your goddamn teeth in, you little prick! Come on out, fucking pussy!

[*They spot the table nearby and drag it to barricade against the front door.*]

BOY   Maybe we should call the cops.

GIRL   We're runaways, dumbass!

BOY   It's only been, like, four hours. I bet nobody's even noticed.

GIRL   I promised Marty.

BOY   Who?

GIRL   My boyfriend.

Boy   Right. Him.

Girl   What?

Boy   Nothing.

Girl   He loves me.

Boy   Love doesn't ask a teenager to drive three thousand miles to meet him.

Girl   What the fuck do you know about it?

Boy   I know plenty.

Girl   You've never even had a girlfriend.

Boy   So. I've been in love.

Girl   With who?

Boy   My parents, my sisters, my dog, my Nana.

Girl   That's not the same kind of love. This is romantic love.

Boy   Well, I know that too, I just . . .

Girl   What? Nothing. What?

Boy   You really want to hear what I'm gonna say?

Girl   No. Yes.

Boy   Ever since the second grade, when I look at you, I feel like I'm chewing on electric cables.

Girl   What?

Boy   I'm in love with you. That's why I dropped everything to drive you to Florida. Even though my mother's gonna shoot my nut sack with an Uzi.

Girl   You don't love me.

Boy   You're the most amazin' person I've ever met.

[*A banging at the door makes them jump.*]

Offstage Voice (Jerry)   I know you're in there, kid! I see blood in the snow here! Open the fuck up! Ya hear me! OPEN IT!

Girl   Why you gotta fuck with me like this?

Boy   Because it's the truth.

Offstage Voice (Jerry)   OPEN THE FUCKING DOOR!

Boy   Let's jump out the window.

Girl   He'll catch us.

[*She stands at the door and slams her fists defiantly against it.*]

Listen close, you dumb Connecticut hillbilly fuck! We're both sixteen years old and you got attempted statutory rape in one hand and assault of a minor in the other! So you better get outta here before I call the cops, got me?

[*The* BOY *joins her, banging beside her.*]

BOY   Yeah! Got us?

GIRL   We're not messing around here! We're young and crazy and we will fucking destroy you! Got me! JERRY!

OFFSTAGE VOICE (JERRY)   Fine, fuck you both. I hope your boyfriend bleeds all over the floor, cunt!

[*The* GIRL *turns back to the* BOY.]

BOY   You saved me.

[*She kisses him. Gently. When she pulls away:*]

GIRL   Are you crying?

BOY   Yeah. I am.

[*She kisses him again.*]

Scene 5

[MAGGIE *is pacing, chain-smoking.* PENNY *sits at the table with* LINDA. LOU's *on the phone, furious. It's late afternoon, the sunlight is waning.*]

LOU   [*Into phone.*] This is Lou Lefebvre with the New Hampshire State Police . . . again. Okay, guy. Listen up. I don't get a call back in the next five minutes, I'm gonna find out where you live and I'm gonna knock on the door, and when you answer I'm gonna punch you in the kidneys until you leak blood out your asshole, you got me? And if you got my daughter in any kind of trouble, I'm kicking every fucking tooth outta that miserable cunt of a mouth you got. You understand me? We're worried sick about our daughter here. Be a man and call me the fuck back! Please!

[*He hangs up the phone.*]

MAGGIE   Ya sounded real professional there, Lou.

LOU   He got the fuckin' point.

PENNY   Hon, you gotta relax.

LOU   I'm fine. I just . . . need some air.

PENNY   You sure?

LOU   Gimme one of those fucking cigarettes.

[MAGGIE *hands him one. He takes her lighter.*]

PENNY   You're going to smoke?

LOU   How could you tell?

PENNY   I'm going outside with you.

LOU   I need some fucking air by my-fucking-self!

PENNY   It's not good for you.

LOU   Don't worry, end of my life, when I'm lying in a hospital bed and I die fifteen minutes ahead of schedule, you can remind me of my fucking indiscretion here today, okay?

[LOU *steps outside, slamming the door.*]

PENNY   He never smokes around me. Or curses like that.

MAGGIE   Almost like he's a different person around you.

PENNY   What's that mean?

LINDA   Come on, Mags.

PENNY   Like it or not, I'm part of Erica's life. I think we ought to make an effort to get along.

MAGGIE   You don't know me very well. I'm expending a massive effort.

PENNY   Look. I get it. I'm the new wife. I'd like to think I'd be different, but who knows. But here's the thing. By the time I met Lou he had been single for a good two years. If it wasn't me, it would have been someone else. That being said, I'm glad it was me. Because I love him.

MAGGIE   You got about the worst fuckin' timing I've ever seen.

PENNY   With all the adversity we face as women, there's no reason, as different as we may be, we have to be at each other like this.

MAGGIE   You're right. Let's go get fuckin' mani-pedis.

PENNY   I know we'll never be friends, Maggie. But we can be civil. You have a daughter and I have a step-daughter who is in the middle of some serious life business and we should all make the decision to be on the same team. Especially around the holidays, which are tough on everyone.

MAGGIE   Life is so much easier when you're an idiot.

[PENNY *takes a deep breath.*]

PENNY   You don't think this toxic anger you direct at everyone, especially Lou, has anything to do with the fact that your family is afraid to communicate with you?

LINDA   Whoa, whoa . . . let's not go there. . . .

[MAGGIE *steps towards her.*]

MAGGIE   What did you say?

PENNY   Okay. No one will say it but I will. You spew out such anger all the time. No wonder Erica is afraid to be open with you.

[MAGGIE *inches from* PENNY.]

MAGGIE   You got a nice nose. You ever been hit in the face?

[PENNY, *scared, still stands her ground.*]

PENNY   No. I have not. I'm sure I won't like it. But . . . if that's what you gotta do in order to have a real conversation with me. Do it.

[MAGGIE *stares her down. Deciding what to do.*]

LINDA   Come on, ladies.

[MAGGIE *lights a cigarette.*]

MAGGIE   You think I'm too hard on poor Lou, huh?

PENNY   I do. And I think it's time, for his sake and for Erica's, that you allow him to earn back some of the trust he lost.

MAGGIE   He tell you how he used to drink so much he'd shit in our bed? Often enough I kept a box of Hefty bags by the nightstand so I could throw the sheets in there before they smelled the whole fuckin' house up.

LINDA   Mags.

MAGGIE   Stay outta this, Ma. Or how about that night I come home, and there's Lou, sitting there on the floor, puke all down front of his uniform, so drunk I gotta blink my eyes to see through the fucking whisky stench and he's bear-hugging Erica so tight she's choking. He's so cocked, he can't tell that he has his arm jammed around her throat and she ain't breathing.

[LOU *walks in, senses the tension.*]

LOU   What's going on?

PENNY   It's okay, Lou. Maggie was talking. Go on, Maggie. I'm listening. He had his arm around Erica's throat. . . .

LOU   Why you gotta do this right now?

PENNY   Lou. She's telling me a story and I'm listening. Go on, please. When you're ready.

MAGGIE   Erica . . . she's a little thing, all legs and elbows, and Lou's always been so strong, especially when he has some drink in him and . . . she's turning gray in the face and I say, "Lou, let her go!" And I start pulling his arms, but he's so fucking hammered he doesn't see me, won't let her go. I slap him, kick him, I'm this close to pulling the piece off his hip and shooting his fucking kneecap, but instead I pull a big chunk of hair and skin off of his head and only then—bleeding from his scalp—does he let her go. And what does he do? Does he apologize? Does he ask how Erica is? As she's gasping for her life, he curls in the fetal position and pisses himself. Up to me to get her calm. Up to me to clean the piss and the puke and the blood. Up to me to call his cop buddies so they can cart him off, clean him up, act like nothing ever fucking happened. 'Cause that's what cops do for each other. Us? We're just his family. My mother always says, "Boys will be boys. They always come back." We don't see him for three days. Then he comes back, drunk again, slamming on the door. "Lemme in, Mags!" I switched the locks, of course. Erica's shaking, she's fucking scared of him. I don't blame her, bruises on her neck still purple. So I stick a butcher knife through the screen door and I say, real calm, "You take one more step and I'll kill ya." And I meant it with every inch of me. Did he tell you that, Penny? Huh?

PENNY   Yeah, he did. But that's not who he is now.

MAGGIE   That a fact?

PENNY   People can outrun their demons, Maggie. They can get ahead of the hell they started with and get better.

MAGGIE   Yeah? Well, what about me?

[*The room freezes for a long beat of almost unbearable tension. Finally,* PENNY *hugs* MAGGIE.]

PENNY   I'm so sorry for what you went through.

[MAGGIE *allows herself to be hugged for a beat, then pushes* PENNY *away.*]

MAGGIE   What the fuck are you doing?

PENNY   I was trying to help.

LINDA   Okay, okay. Not to sound insensitive or anything, but that was all very intense and I think we all could use a drink. Except for, you know, him, since he lost privileges or whatever.

LOU   Jesus—

PENNY   I could use a drink too, actually.

LINDA   See? What do you got, Mags?

MAGGIE   Half a bottle of Chardonnay.

LINDA   Maybe if we were in fucking kindergarten. I need something brown.

MAGGIE   Go trudge through the snow to the packie, you need a taste so bad.

LINDA   You know I'm in between checks.

PENNY   I'll spot you.

LOU   You don't need to do that.

PENNY   No, really. It's cool. My treat.

LINDA   She wants to treat, let her treat.

MAGGIE   You're best friends now?

LINDA   Didn't you hear her little, you know, speech there? C'mon. She ain't that bad.

LOU   This isn't a good plan.

LINDA   We'll hit the state store. Could be the fucking apocalypse, they'd still be selling booze.

LOU   That's like twenty minutes in good weather.

PENNY   We bought a giant truck for a reason. Ten months outta the year, that damn thing is middle finger aimed at the environment. But days like this, she proves her worth.

[LINDA *and* PENNY *get jackets on.*]

LOU   Pen, you don't need to do this.

PENNY   Maybe I just need some fucking air, Lou. Let's go, Linda.

[LINDA *pauses, turns. Walks up to* MAGGIE.]

LINDA   You're right, Maggie. You deserved better'n me.

[*She kisses* MAGGIE *on the cheek.*]

Hey, Ohio. You up for pizza too?

PENNY   Heck yeah.

[*She and* PENNY *walk outside, leaving* LOU *and* MAGGIE *alone.* MAGGIE *is stunned from the affection from these two women. Takes her a moment to brush it off.*]

MAGGIE   Anything from the Staties?

LOU   They're on the lookout. I got all my friends on the lookout. But it's a helluva storm out there. Penny's right, though. That thing is a tank. Although it's not a truck. It's an SUV.

MAGGIE   Getting dark outside.

Lou She's only been gone one night.

Maggie A lot can happen in one night. She's not a drinker. Didn't get that gene from your family. But she has stuff that my blood gave her. My sick fucking degenerate bad decision blood.

Lou Can we focus on Erica?

Maggie I'm focusing every cell in my body right now. I'm about to levitate a fucking chair, I'm so focused.

Lou Erica's gonna walk through the door any second, ya just gotta have faith.

Maggie Jesus Christ, Lou. Ya hear ya'self with this Christian bullshit?

Lou Not everybody's gotta be angry like you alla time. Some of us make a choice not ta be.

Maggie Why she *choose* to run off in this weather?

Lou She just wasn't thinking.

Maggie I raised her to think. But off she went. And it's a monstah fucking storm out there . . . you gotta really want to be someplace bad. I mean, I gotta drive to work or my electric is turned off. That's the reality of where I am. But anyone else . . .

Lou I told you not to take on this mortgage.

Maggie What?

Lou Reason you need to drive through a storm, not my fault. I pay what I'm supposed to pay and then some. I told you not to take on this place.

Maggie I didn't say it was your fault. Christ. Ma needed a place, I needed a place, Erica's got her own bathroom. I took a chance. Who shouldn't be able to take a chance on a fucking place to live?

Lou You could rent like the rest of the world.

Maggie You don't rent.

Lou We got two incomes, Mags.

Maggie You don't have my oppressive, ulcer-giving financial obligations, I get it. So why you driving in this fucking storm?

Lou Penny had a doctor thing.

Maggie So she's sick?

Lou She, uh . . . This doctor. He was supposed to give injections today. Her eggs, they can get fertilized and all, but they have trouble finding purchase in her uterus. Looks like it just ain't gonna happen. Me, I'm like fine without another kid. But harder for her, you know.

MAGGIE   I could slice my wrists on the fucking irony.

LOU   Please. Just ease off a bit. Fuckin' A.

MAGGIE   Why don't you tell me when it's okay for me to feel things. That work better for you?

LOU   Jesus Christ. That's not what I mean.

MAGGIE   Poor fucking Lou. Knocked up his loser townie girlfriend, wrecked his fucking future.

LOU   Come on.

MAGGIE   Life got so fuckin' miserable he hadda drink just to get through the day. Ain't his fault he hit rock bottom and she kicked him out. But thank Christ a fuckin' angel flew down from heaven and saved him.

LOU   That's not what I fuckin' say.

MAGGIE   Oh, I'm sure you two got a way sweeter way of saying it. But it's still the same fucking story.

LOU   That night you were telling Penny about . . . there's other details. . . .

MAGGIE   I know the details. You were on patrol and you found a dead kid. It's horrible, but I heard it already. It was in the paper.

LOU   But there's more, Mags.

MAGGIE   Okay. So spill it.

LOU   I will, okay? So there's a noise complaint, we go this apartment. This teenage couple, these drug addicts. Their place is filthy, carpet sticky, real dark. And, uh, I'm looking for the stash or whatever and . . .

MAGGIE   [Cutting him off.] You told me all this, remember? It was one of your steps.

LOU   You just . . . you make it so hard sometimes to . . . you know . . .

MAGGIE   To what?

LOU   To be vulnerable around you.

MAGGIE   Are you fucking kidding me with this shit? Grow some balls, Lou. For Christ's sake.

LOU   "Grow some balls?" See, that's the type of shit I'm talking about right there—

MAGGIE   I guarantee ya, whatever fucking pain ya feeling right now? It pales to what I fuckin' went through!

LOU   This isn't a contest.

MAGGIE   Maybe it is!

[LOU's *phone rings.*]

LOU   [*Looking at Caller ID.*] It's my buddy from the job. You think you can sheathe those claws for a second?

[*Into phone.*]

Hello? Yeah? Come on, Danny. What? Just tell me . . . uh-huh.

MAGGIE   What?

LOU   Uh-huh. Are you sure?

MAGGIE   What the fuck?

LOU   Okay. Okay. Whoa. Okay, slow down. . . .

MAGGIE   What?

LOU   Jesus Christ . . . Listen, there was a big wreck, a nine-car pileup on I-95. Semi went over the divider. . . .

MAGGIE   Was she . . . ?

LOU   Your Honda is in the pileup but . . .

MAGGIE   The Honda, you sure?

LOU   They don't know who was in it. . . .

MAGGIE   Was anyone hurt?

LOU   Dozen emergency vehicles there now. Crawling with EMT and Staties. It's chaos.

MAGGIE   Anyone hurt!

LOU   [*Into phone.*] Tell me what they just said. I don't care, just say it . . . just . . . Oh my God.

MAGGIE   What?

LOU   Oh, sweet Jesus.

MAGGIE   Fucking WHAT?

LOU   [*To* MAGGIE.] Multiple critical injuries, at least one fatality, maybe more.

MAGGIE   Is it her!

LOU   They're working through it. Just happened.

MAGGIE   Is she dead! Oh my god!

LOU   Danny, no, keep me on the line!

MAGGIE   Let's drive down there!

[*She dials.*]

LOU   Danny, hold on. . . . Call them, get my fucking SUV back.

MAGGIE   I'm calling Ma.

LOU   You walk over to the ambulance, Danny!

MAGGIE   It's going to voicemail.

LOU   Gimme your phone. . . .

[*He dials it, hands it back.*]

FUCKING DO IT, DANNY!

[*To* MAGGIE.]

That's Penny . . . she'll answer. Please, Danny. Please.

MAGGIE   It's not doing anything.

LOU   Danny? Hello?

[*Tosses cell phone.*]

Storm fucking with the cell tower. Goddamn AT&T. Fuck. Gimme the fucking landline.

[*He grabs the phone and dials.*]

Danny? Hello? You there? Is it a girl? Is it a sixteen-year-old girl? I can't hear you. Hello? Danny! Danny?

[*The lights flicker as the power surges.*]

Hello?

MAGGIE   Please, please don't lose power right now. Please!

LOU   Hello?

[*With a "pop" the lights go out.*]

MAGGIE   Oh no. Please.

LOU   Oh God . . . *hello*?!

Scene 6.

[*Back in that motel room. The* GIRL *and the* BOY *are entwined beneath the covers. Outside, the dawn sky colors through the windows.*]

BOY   Holy shit, that was . . .

GIRL   You don't even know. There's way more positions than just those two.

BOY Really? Wow. That was my first time, you know.

GIRL Staying up all night?

BOY No, this was my first time doing that.

GIRL No, it wasn't. It was your first, second, and third time.

BOY Right. Sorry. I had a lot stored up. Even with the, you know, practicing since I was thirteen. . . .

GIRL Why do guys do that so much?

BOY You can't really help it. Once you figure it out. Check out how much stronger my left arm is.

GIRL Jeez.

BOY Much better with you, though.

[*He kisses her.*]

GIRL You don't mind kissing me? Even after what I did with my mouth?

BOY I'll always kiss you. You are just perfect in every way.

GIRL Don't say that.

BOY Why not? It's true.

GIRL It's too much pressure. Seriously, don't say that. It's not true and you saying that just makes me feel like shit! So shut the fuck up!

BOY Perfect.

GIRL Shut up.

BOY Perfect.

GIRL Okay. Fine. I'm perfect. Happy?

BOY Yeah. So be honest here. Am I, like . . . ?

GIRL Needy? Yes.

BOY Haha. I mean am I good at stuff? Compared to, like, the other times you . . .

GIRL The best.

BOY Thank God. I know guys, like, want to have sex with every girl, but I honestly and truly can not imagine ever doing that with someone else. It would just, like, pale in comparison.

GIRL You say that now.

BOY I'll say it forever.

GIRL What if it never gets any better than this?

BOY   Whaddya mean? This is just the beginning of how good it'll be.

GIRL   Yeah?

BOY   Yeah.

GIRL   I have an idea. Just to be safe, how about we make a promise to each other right now that no matter what happens, no matter where we end up, we'll do it with each other again when we're old.

BOY   What if we are still together?

GIRL   Just as a backup plan.

BOY   Like what, in thirty years we're like shopping at Market Basket and see each other and like . . .

GIRL   We just have this agreement we made here and only you and me know about it.

BOY   I feel like we're jinxing what just happened, though.

GIRL   Come on, it's fun. We can even come here, to this motel. How awesome will that be?

BOY   What if I have five kids and a wife and stuff?

GIRL   You won't have five kids. That's just selfish.

BOY   Isn't that wrong to do to those theoretical people?

GIRL   Not if the pact was made before we ever met them. We'd have to honor it and it wouldn't be our fault.

BOY   I guess that makes sense.

GIRL   So let's seal it officially.

BOY   How?

GIRL   How else? With blood.

[*She reaches into her purse for a scary-looking buck knife.*]

BOY   We should have a code word too.

GIRL   Yeah. . . . What should it be?

BOY   How about "Rolling Thunder"?

GIRL   What is this a Bruce Willis movie? What about "Dying Wish"?

BOY   What is this a Lifetime movie?

GIRL   What then?

BOY   I got it. Ready? "McSorley's"?

GIRL   "McSorley's." Perfect.

[*They take turns cutting each other's palms and grip their bloody hands together.*]

I hereby bound you to a pact that upon uttering the word—"McSorley's"

BOY   "McSorley's."

GIRL   . . . between us, we shall be obliged to make love to one another. No matter what.

BOY   No matter what.

GIRL   And if we don't honor the pact, we will be shitting on everything that happened between us. . . .

BOY   And that would be like shitting in our own hearts.

GIRL   On my everlasting soul I commit this.

BOY   On my soul too.

[*They clasp hands and kiss.*]

GIRL   I need to tell you something. But I'm scared to tell you. Because this is so nice right now.

BOY   Okay.

GIRL   Okay. So Marty.

BOY   He's done, right? I mean, after we . . .

GIRL   Yes, yes. He's done. I'm yours, I'm all yours. But you need to know that Marty was . . . he was my mother's boyfriend.

BOY   He was?

GIRL   That's fucked up, right?

BOY   I guess.

GIRL   He wasn't the first of my mother's boyfriends.

BOY   Oh. Like you . . . ?

GIRL   The second actually. I don't know why . . . well, I do know why. There's something wrong with me.

BOY   What do you mean?

GIRL   I was thirteen the first time. My mom was dating this guy, Darren. He started looking at me different and I noticed that and I just . . . I didn't want him thinking I was stupid and, like, I was mad at my mom. I like initiated it, but then he didn't tell me not to, so . . . before I knew it we were . . . and then with Marty I was like an expert by then. . . . I still think it messed me up pretty bad.

BOY   Like physically?

GIRL   Like mentally.

BOY   Does your mom know?

GIRL   She'd probably kill herself. She thinks the men just leave her because she's crazy. Which is partially true. You're the only one I've ever told.

BOY   Really?

GIRL   So there it is. I'm really, really damaged and if you want to just, like, leave I'll totally . . .

BOY   There's nothing wrong with you.

GIRL   Then why did I do it?

BOY   Because we do stupid things sometimes when we're young.

GIRL   You never did anything that stupid your whole life. And you're just making fun of me. And if you fucking tell anyone, I swear to God I'll cut you open.

BOY   Listen. I did something really stupid once.

GIRL   What?

BOY   When I was nine I put a Matchbox car up my ass.

GIRL   What?

BOY   Yeah. And I had to go to the hospital to get it removed.

GIRL   You went to the hospital because . . . ?

BOY   You can die from that because the feces pile up and poison you from the inside out. They had to do X-rays and use tools and I got a shot to relax my sphincter and . . . it was really embarrassing. My dad thought maybe I was a homosexual and sent me to a counselor. . . . Anyway, my point is, sometimes, when you're young, you just do really dumb shit. I got out of the shower, saw the Matchbox car, and, and I was like, "Maybe I can fit that up my ass?" and just, you know, it wasn't that hard to get it in there and . . . shit, do you wanna run away from me now?

GIRL   No, not at all. I'm just kind of amazed because that actually makes me feel better.

BOY   You don't ever have to worry about that stuff again.

GIRL   Why?

BOY   Because I'm going to take care of you.

GIRL   Don't say that.

BOY   What? You think because I'm sixteen I can't mean it? Look, we're wicked young, I know. But, like, we can make this work. We really can.

GIRL   How?

BOY   I'll go to college. I can get a good job. But you'll come with me.

GIRL   And go to college?

BOY   If you want to.

GIRL   My grades suck. But I can, like, get a job and cook for us.

BOY   But you should also do more than that, too, you know. Like you should have your own goals.

GIRL   I don't have any.

BOY   Why not?

GIRL   Seriously? Have you seen the women in my life? My mother bounces checks every week, power's off almost as much as it's on, she dates guys that, let's face it, are fucking assholes. . . . She's just, like, never has time to do anything except run in place and I'm like, "Why can't you just *win* one thing, one fucking time, WIN! Instead of just failing at every goddamn thing."

BOY   So you do have a goal.

GIRL   What's my goal?

BOY   Not to be your mother.

GIRL   We're too young.

BOY   So were Romeo and Juliet.

GIRL   You're aware that relationship lasted like three days and six people died?

BOY   Okay, we're Romeo and Juliet with the last couple pages ripped out.

GIRL   Don't lead me on unless you really mean it, okay? I can't take it if you don't mean it.

BOY   I mean it! I am so absolutely sure about this.

GIRL   If I give my heart to you, I do it for life. That's how I work. If it don't work out . . . I don't know if I'll ever get over that. Ya gotta understand that before we go any further, okay?

BOY   I do.

GIRL   Ya sure?

BOY   You are all I've ever wanted and now I have you and I just want to love you forever.

GIRL   Even though I told you that stuff.

BOY   I love who you are, so . . . I guess I love that stuff too. . . .

GIRL   How come you always know the exact right thing to say?

BOY   You don't understand. I've been practicing this scenario in the mirror for several years.

GIRL   That's so fucking cute.

BOY   Let's go home.

GIRL   It's still snowing like crazy out there.

BOY   I'll drive wicked carefully. We'll get back before your ma even gets up to go to work. Nobody will ever have to know about what happened.

GIRL   This feeling. I don't ever want it to end.

BOY   It won't. I promise. Look at me. I will love you forever. Do you believe me?

[*It takes everything in her to show him this moment.*]

GIRL   I believe.

[*They kiss as the snow falls outside the window.*]

Scene 7

[*Power is still out. It's dark outside now. The scene is lit by a dark gray light through the window and a smattering of candles and flashlights.* MAGGIE *is pacing like a caged animal. There is a cell phone, a blackberry and a home phone on the table in front of her. After a beat,* LOU *bounds inside shivering and covered in snow and out of breath.*]

LOU   Still no signal. I ran up and down the fucking street. Power's out in the whole neighborhood.

MAGGIE   E-mail them on that thing again.

LOU   I did. Five times. Just sits there in the outbox.

[*A cell phone rings and* LOU *snatches it up.*]

Hello? Hello? I can't hear . . . hello?

[*He slams it down.*]

Goddammit!

MAGGIE   She's my only tether to this world. . . . If she's gone, I'm walking into my mother's bathroom and swallowing a whole fucking bottle of Trexall.

LOU   Please, don't even say that.

Maggie   Erica's all I got. Without her, I got no reason to exist.

Lou   She's okay. Just . . . put out positive thoughts.

Maggie   I don't got no positive thoughts left. Only the truth. The ugly, disgusting, heartbreakin' fucking truth that everything I touch turns to shit.

Lou   That's not the truth.

Maggie   You been paying attention these last seventeen years?

[*NOTE: these next seven lines are overlapping, messy.*]

Lou   Yeah, I have, and you're // not seeing shit clearly right now—

Maggie   Lay it on the fuckin' table—admit you think I'm a goddamn loser who fucked up your whole life.

Lou   Stop.

Maggie   Admit it.

Lou   Enough with this. // Please.

Maggie   Admit it. // Admit it. // Admit it. // Admit it.

Lou   Shut up. // Shut up. // Shut the fuck up! // Can you please just be quiet for two fucking seconds and let me talk?

Maggie   Fine.

Lou   Okay?

Maggie   Fine.

[**Lou** *paces for a beat. He's never spoken about this before.*]

Lou   So, that night I hurt Erica . . . you know . . . earlier, when I found that kid. Something happened when I . . . I thought it was a doll dropped down there, behind the dryer, ya know? She musta been cold and crawled back there and . . . no more than two years old, this little lost girl just lying there . . . not moving and . . . I scooped her up. She's, like, ice cold, stiff, and . . . all I can think about is our Erica. How fucking delicate they are, how easy it is to just ruin them, and . . . I had seen dark things before, Mags. On the job, you see things . . . but this . . . it was like God reached inside my heart and my soul and pulled on a loose thread and everything inside me just tore all open . . . and I just, like . . . I lost it, Mags. I took off her dirty pajamas and I opened my shirt and put her inside . . . skin on skin . . . and I walk outta there. Two uniforms found me sitting on a swing set few houses down. I don't know how much time went by. They had to pry my arms open. I broke. Because I saw the world for what it really is. Hopeless. And I couldn't handle that. I broke, Mags. And it had absolutely nothing to do with you.

MAGGIE   I never wanted you to be a cop, Lou. I always said you were too sensitive for that.

LOU   It was a good job. We needed a good job.

MAGGIE   You always want to save people. Sprint right in. But you can't shoulder the reality of it.

LOU   I'm better now. I really am. I haven't had a taste in five years. You think I'm too weak to carry the weight of this Erica situation? I'm not. Go ahead. Do it.

MAGGIE   Go ahead and what?

LOU   Unload on me.

MAGGIE   With what?

LOU   There's gotta be something.

MAGGIE   I don't . . . there is. Okay . . . I was cleaning my car last week and I stick my hand between the cushions and guess what I find?

LOU   What?

MAGGIE   Lenny.

LOU   That little red superhero toy from the Happy Meal.

MAGGIE   You remember, right?

LOU   Of course I remember. Cheapest thing ever but it was her, like, her best friend. She made a little house for it out of my hat box.

MAGGIE   We'd buy her nice shit, when we could afford it, but always she went back to Lenny. Cheap-ass Chinese-sweatshop-made Lenny. For years, in her pocket . . .

LOU   I musta painted his mustache back on fifty times.

MAGGIE   I was so dumb I didn't even know how poetic it was her being in love with something so simple. She lost him right around the time we split up.

LOU   I know.

MAGGIE   Nine years old and it was real pain, Lou, as real as anything we're feeling right now and I was so in my own world . . . I couldn't even . . .

LOU   I called MacDonald's headquarters. They said they couldn't send a new one. They had moved on.

MAGGIE   I didn't know you did that. That was real nice of you.

LOU   And all along, Lenny was in your car, huh?

MAGGIE   Stuck between the seats.

LOU   What did she say when you showed her?

[MAGGIE *walks over to a drawer and opens it. She pulls out a tiny wrapped present.*]

MAGGIE   I was gonna put him under the tree.

[*She places the present on the table in front of* LOU.]

Open it. . . . She might be gone, Lou. Our little girl might be gone from this earth. I close my eyes and I don't feel her no more. And you are her father and you gotta face what that means and bear that weight with me.

[*He opens the box. Something inside the box lights against his face.*]

LOU   It's beautiful.

[MAGGIE *kisses him.*]

Don't . . .

MAGGIE   Lou . . .

LOU   Please . . .

[MAGGIE *holds her hand up and grips* LOU'*s hand, creating the same image as* BOY *and* GIRL.]

MAGGIE   "McSorley's."

LOU   Shit. "McSorley's."

[*After a moment,* LOU *kisses her. She straddles him and they make love clumsily through their clothes.*]

[*In the darkness on the side of the stage, a light illuminates the* GIRL *and the* BOY *from the motel. Their younger selves, watching from the night they made that promise so many years ago.*]

[MAGGIE *and* LOU *move together . . . making sad, mournful noises. . . . After a few moments, their movements speed up, slow, then the lights dim on the* BOY *and* GIRL *and they disappear into darkness.*]

MAGGIE   Seems like just last week we were in that wicked little apartment over that garage on Mammoth Road. She was so tiny she fit in the hood of your sweatshirt.

LOU   I had just started the Academy. Had our whole lives ahead of us. And I messed it all up.

MAGGIE   I loved you more than you will ever be loved by another human being. But I had to make a choice. And I chose Erica.

LOU   I know.

MAGGIE   It hurt a lot when you got remarried.

LOU   I'll never love anybody the way I loved you, Mags. I used it all up on you. But with Penny, I'm at peace.

MAGGIE   You deserve to be happy, Lou.

LOU   So do you.

MAGGIE   Yeah.

LOU   You're perfect, Mags.

MAGGIE   Don't say that.

LOU   Perfect.

[*A diesel engine approaches and flashing red lights appear outside, through the snow, coming from the street. The light bounces through the window, all over the living room. After a moment, the front door quietly opens and a teenage girl in a jacket stands in the doorway, silhouetted by the streetlight outside. The wind whips behind her, blowing in snow as she takes a step inside and stands still in the darkness. The red light flashing behind her. She looks like young* MAGGIE, *only a little different. Same actress but there is something more contemporary about her hair . . . what she's wearing . . . her posture. She rushes into* MAGGIE's *arms.*]

ERICA   I'm so sorry, Mom. I messed up.

[*Power is restored with a pop.* PENNY *and* LINDA *rush inside past* LOU. *The red lights fade as that diesel engine drives off.*]

LINDA   Why's a goddamn ambulance out there?

PENNY   Erica—?

[PENNY *rushes towards* ERICA, *who is still embracing* MAGGIE. *She stops, knows it's not her place.*]

MAGGIE   It's okay, Penny.

[MAGGIE *moves aside so* PENNY *can give* ERICA *a quick hug.*]

LINDA   Why the fuck didn't you call me?

MAGGIE   She just walked in.

PENNY   Where have you been?

ERICA   Boston.

LINDA   Boston, in this weather? Are you fuckin' stupid?

ERICA   [*Getting hugged by* LINDA.] Ow. I have a fractured elbow.

MAGGIE   Jesus Christ, kid.

ERICA   My friend Crystal, you know her, she was in a real bad place because of this jerky frat guy and she wanted to go to this party at Northeastern, so I had Jeremy drive us // all together, so we could keep an eye on her.

EVERYONE   [*Yelling out after hearing his name.*] Who's Jeremy? / Who the fuck is Jeremy? / Jeremy who? / Fuck is Jeremy?

ERICA   Stop yelling at me.

LOU   Who is he, Erica?

ERICA   You mean besides a terrible driver? He's just a guy in my grade I've been spending time with.

LOU   Are you two sexually active?

ERICA   Jesus, bad enough I almost died, you have to embarrass me in front of everybody?

PENNY   [*Losing it.*] Why the FUCK didn't you call us, Erica?

ERICA   [*Pauses for a second, shocked.*] My phone died. It's not my fault. I told you guys I need a new phone. Nobody ever listens to me.

MAGGIE   Sit your ass down, Erica. Right now.

[ERICA *sits.*]

ERICA   Am I really in so much trouble?

MAGGIE   I'm two seconds from grabbin' you by the fucking hair and draggin' you outside to (beat some fuckin' sense into ya—)

[*Catches herself, takes a breath.*]

We're all gonna have a talk. A real long talk. But not right now. Right now you're gonna sit here and me and your dad and your gramma and your step-mom, and we're all just gonna get our breath back. And be thankful.

ERICA   But seriously, you gotta let me just be myself sometimes. I'm going to make mistakes. It's part of growing up. But you didn't raise a friggin' idiot, Mom. Im so much better than, like, every other girl I know. What?

[MAGGIE *and* LOU *stare at her.*]

LOU   I want to kill her so bad right now, Mags.

MAGGIE   I know, Lou. Me too. I want to bash her little fucking face in.

[*And life resumes in* MAGGIE'*s apartment as we fade to black.*]

———————————

NEW COUNTRY

by

Mark Roberts

Production History

New Country was originally produced by Fair Trade Productions and Kelcie Beene Cooper at the Cherry Lane Theater in New York, in association with Rattlestick Playwrights Theater. It was directed by Mark Roberts and David Harwell, with set design by David Harwell and lighting design by Tito Ladd.

Cast

PAUL   Malcolm Madera
CHUCK   Jared Culverhouse
OLLIE   Stephen Sheffer
JUSTIN   David Lind
UNCLE JIM   Mark Roberts
SHARON   Sarah Lemp

Biography

Mark Roberts is a playwright, actor, and television producer currently residing in Brooklyn, New York. His published works include *Parasite Drag*, *Rantoul and Die*, and *Where the Great Ones Run*, all of which have been produced in various theaters around the country. In television, Mark was an executive producer and head writer for *Two and a Half Men* for seven seasons, executive consultant on *The Big Bang Theory* for three seasons, and creator of *Mike and Molly*, where he served as executive producer for the first seventy episodes.

———

[Lights up on an upscale hotel suite. Through the window we see the Nashville skyline. There's a sitting area with a sofa, coffee table and two chairs, a flat-screen TV, and a fully stocked bar and mini-fridge. A hallway leads offstage to the bedroom and bath. Pacing the room is PAUL, *fifties, confident and in control. He's dressed in an expensive Western-style suit and bolo tie and talking on his cell phone in a thick Southern accent. Standing behind him listening is* CHUCK, *forties, nervous, and high-strung. He is also dressed in a Western-style suit and also speaks with a thick Southern accent.]*

PAUL   *[Into phone.]* Listen to me, darlin', 'cause I'm shootin' arrow straight with you right now. You cannot get riled at a twenty-five-year-old man for acting stupid, irresponsible, and crazy-reckless. That's just inherent behavior at that stage of life and how that particular package comes wrapped. Man's gonna do whatever he damn well pleases, and truthfully, it's unfair on your part to burden him with things like designated curfews and accountability. Like handin' a scarecrow a book of matches then gettin' miffed when he comes home in an ashtray.

[*Pause.*]

Well, disagree all you want, but that ain't gonna turn water into wine or give frogs the right to vote. Need to let that boy be who he is and stop tryin' to strap a saddle on him.

[*Pause.*]

No, I am not "attempting to dismiss or invalidate your feelings." I'm just sayin' they're unfounded, wrong-headed and flat-out goofy. The storm clouds overhead are all imagined, in your noggin', pre-weddin' jitters, that I guarantee will part and pass the minute the car's draggin' cans and you're shakin' rice out of your hair. Alright? Alright, then. See you at the church.

[*Hanging up.*]

Eight months tops, then that milk is gonna curdle and sour.

CHUCK   Didn't feel the need to address my issues, huh?

PAUL   [*Exasperated.*] No, Chuck, I did not.

CHUCK   [*Sarcastic.*] Slipped your mind, I reckon?

PAUL   Nope. Just felt there were bigger fish to fry.

CHUCK   Did you now?

PAUL   I did. So, I prioritized. That okay by you?

CHUCK   [*Shrugging.*] Hey.

[*Pause.*]

CHUCK   Not a complicated point I'm trying to make here.

PAUL   Mountain out of a mole hill, friend. Mountain out of a goddamn mole hill.

CHUCK   I disagree, think it's a valid concern that warrants discussion.

PAUL   And we have discussed it a-plenty.

CHUCK   Okay, fine, forget it.

[*Beat.*]

"None is so blind as he that will not see."

PAUL   See what? What is it I'm not seeing, Chuck?

CHUCK   Nothing, forget it, moving on.

PAUL   Enlighten me.

CHUCK   [*Angry.*] Said, moving on.

[*Pause.*]

PAUL   [*Sighing.*] You are unhappy with the pairing.

CHUCK   Yes, I am. Very, very displeased.

PAUL   Is what it is, buddy boy.

CHUCK   Just tell me how's come I get stuck with the fat chick? Huh? Explain that to me.

PAUL   That's truly your issue here? What this whole crazy conniption is about?

CHUCK   Not a conniption, and it's a goddamn reasonable question.

PAUL   No, it's, uh, it's really not.

CHUCK   That's your opinion.

PAUL   Here it is: He picks three guys to be groomsmen, she chooses an equal number of bridesmaids. Pairing is decided after the fact.

CHUCK   Well, clearly a flawed process.

PAUL   The process is flawed?

CHUCK   Deeply, deeply flawed.

PAUL   Do understand it's completely random.

CHUCK   Please. An event like this? Where every minute detail is discussed to fuckin' death?

PAUL   Listen . . .

CHUCK   Please.

PAUL   So you're saying they purposefully, perhaps even spitefully, paired you with that heavy-set gal?

CHUCK   Heavy set? She's two teats shy of bein' bovine. And I got no idea why they did what they did. Women in a room, somewhere. Who knows why they do half the shit they do?

PAUL   Look, nobody's asking you to create a life with this lady. Just stroll down the aisle, she veers left, you turn right, "I do, I do, sayonara."

CHUCK   Point I'm trying to make, get a word in edgewise, is the pairing should at least be plausible.

PAUL   "Plausible," how? What's that even mean, "plausible"?

CHUCK   Romantic occasion such as this . . . ?

PAUL   Yes?

CHUCK   . . . Want to at least create the illusion that we're actual couples.

PAUL   The fuck for? Everybody knows we're not real couples, don't give a shit.

CHUCK   Once again, your opinion. Me, I believe a certain amount of plausibility helps facilitate, you know . . . a mood.

PAUL   What kind of mood you talkin' about?

CHUCK   A joyous, romantic, wedding-type fucking mood. And nobody is ever going to believe that I'm linked to that chub-a-lub-a- ding-dong.

PAUL   Come on now. She's got a cute face.

CHUCK   Yeah, restin' on four chins. Like a pumpkin plopped on a stack of tires.

PAUL   Very personable, I thought.

CHUCK   Hey, you're tipping the scale at two-fifty and change, you can't be snotty. And if you're so enamored, you yolk her up and yank her down the aisle.

PAUL   We can't trade women. Okay? This is how Lindsey wanted us paired and that's just the way it is.

CHUCK   Lindsey. Who let her decide everything, anyway?

PAUL   She's the bride, asshole. Jesus. Can't you just be a get-along guy for once in your life?

CHUCK   I get along, go fuck yourself. And it's easy for you to be pliable, you drew the hot cousin with the tramp stamp and big jugs.

PAUL   Nothing to do with it.

CHUCK   Bullshit. Meanwhile, I'm sashayin' with Buffalo Gal, everybody shooting me pity eyes because I drew "the fat straw". People see she's not in my league, makes them uncomfortable and I believe, truly believe, it detracts from the actual ceremony.

PAUL   You're a complete and total dick, man.

CHUCK   Well, that's a whole other conversation.

[*Pause.*]

PAUL   Fine. Feel that strongly about it, talk to Justin. Not like he doesn't know his sister has a weight problem.

CHUCK   Wait, what? What are you talking about?

PAUL   That stack of tires is Justin's sister.

Chuck   No, huh-uh, I met the sister. The prison cook with the maroon hair and Junior Mint mole on her eyelid.

Paul   That's a wart and that's the oldest. Your gal's the younger one, from a different daddy. Did you speak to her at all at the rehearsal dinner?

Chuck   Yes, of course, I engaged.

[*Beat.*]

Little bit. She was pretty focused on her food. Brought out that tri-tip, thought she was gonna come. His sister, really?

Paul   How do you not know this shit? Been working with the man for five years.

Chuck   Hey, I handle contracts, A and R, and the label. You're the one in charge of hand-holdin', publicity, and private life.

Paul   [*Sighing.*] Add on weddin' planner, couples counselor, and every other degrading task that son of a bitch throws my way.

Chuck   Speaking of which, how much longer do we gotta sit here and wait for "Uncle Pig Farmer"?

Paul   [*Looking at his watch.*] Should be en route. Car picked him up at the airport ten minutes ago, with a cooler of Dr Pepper and three rolled joints.

[*There's a knock at the door.* Chuck *crosses to it.*]

Chuck   President's suite and an Escalade for some Kentucky hog jockey, too cheap to rent a fuckin' car.

Paul   Can't rent a car, no license. Five DUI's in two years. Last one they give him, he was on a ridin' lawn mower.

Chuck   Great. The whole *Hee-Haw* gang.

[Chuck *opens the door, revealing* Ollie, *an aggressive, slightly effeminate, twenty-year-old bellboy. He's carrying a gift basket filled with food and liquor. He also speaks with a strong, Southern accent.*]

Ollie   Greetings, gentlemen. Pardon the intrusion. Just wanted to let you know your guests are starting to trickle in downstairs.

Chuck   Be there shortly.

[*Re: basket.*]

What's all this?

Ollie   A few snacks and goodies for Mister Spears and entourage to help celebrate his impending nuptials.

CHUCK   Great. Set it wherever.

[OLLIE *crosses to the bar area.*]

OLLIE   Imported cheeses, chocolates, and charcuterie. Plus assorted breads, crackers, five different kinds of Italian olives, dried fruit, and three gourmet mustards. Brown, spicy brown, and wasabi. Also a bottle of Knob Creek sippin' whiskey, which every true Justin Spears fan knows is his preferred libation.

[*Looking around.*]

By the way, is the guest of honor here yet? Perhaps in the shower, or . . . ?

[PAUL *crosses to him, taking out a wad of bills.*]

PAUL   Thanks a bunch and thank the management for us.

[*He offers* OLLIE *a twenty.*]

OLLIE   Oh, no tipping allowed, hotel policy.

PAUL   [*Pocketing the cash.*] Even better.

OLLIE   Plus, I happen to be one of those aforementioned fans. Actually, I was the one who gave the manager the inside scoop on the Knob Creek.

PAUL   Appreciate it.

OLLIE   He was gonna toss in a bottle of Jack Daniels, figuring that's what all country stars drink. But I swiftly corrected his heinous, idiotic misstep.

PAUL   Great.

[*Beat.*]

Thanks again.

OLLIE   And for clarification, when I say I'm a "fan" I do not mean one of those pathetic lost souls lollygagging, starry-eyed around the tour bus hoping Justin will peer out a window and offer up a half smile, maybe a casual nod. Or pining away at a concert, throwing themselves at the lip of the stage, praying that he'll make eye contact or anoint them with a few drops of his sweet, blessed perspiration. No, my definition of "fan" would be more along the lines of someone who has a spiritual, almost divine connection to his music and artistry. A "soul mate" would probably be a more accurate description of mine and Justin's . . . relationship.

[CHUCK *and* PAUL *stare at him.*]

PAUL   Autographed T-shirt?

OLLIE   Already own two signed T-shirts, nine autographed eight-by-tens and seven used guitar picks that he's discarded on various stages in and around Davidson County.

CHUCK   Build a creepy shrine at this point.

OLLIE   [*Laughing.*] Hardly.

[*Seriously.*]

My simple mementos have been lovingly, respectfully mounted on a crushed velvet backing and framed in museum-quality glass. Hung in my home office, above my desk. Something to gaze at as I seek inspiration for my own work, my own music.

PAUL   Uh-huh.

[*Beat.*]

You said one of those mustards is wasabi?

OLLIE   What I don't have and would appreciate more than monetary compensation is contact information for Mister Spears, to present him with a demo tape of my songs to enjoy, perhaps inspire.

PAUL   Yeah, unfortunately, we can't accept unsolicited material from unknown songwriters.

OLLIE   Not unknown.

[*Laughing.*]

At all.

[*Seriously.*]

I'm a regular fixture at all the open-mike nights and writer's roundtables in Nashville proper, have been written up in several music-related blogs, and I play second lead guitar with the house band at the Sukho Thai restaurant in Opryland.

PAUL   Sounds like you're well on your way. But honestly, I can't accept your demo.

[*Shrugging.*]

Legal thing.

OLLIE   [*Deliberate.*] I'll just end up selling those songs to another established artist and you're gonna spend the rest of your life kicking yourself.

PAUL   [*Quickly.*] And that will be something I have to live with.

[*Beat.*]

Like so many things.

OLLIE   Right. Hm. Right.

[*Pause.*]

You know, I believe I will take that twenty dollars.

[PAUL *hands him a twenty.*]

PAUL   Course you will.

OLLIE   [*Snippy.*] Enjoy the cheese.

[*He exits.*]

CHUCK   God, I hate this town.

PAUL   Town's fine. It's the people in it what fucks it up.

[PAUL's *cell phone rings. He looks at the caller ID.*]

Jesus, this is startin' to get real fuckin' old.

CHUCK   Lyndsey again?

PAUL   She's called seven times since we left the rehearsal dinner.

CHUCK   Just hit "ignore."

PAUL   I'm hittin' "Ignore."

[*Taps the phone.*]

Tell you what, biggest mistake was her quittin' that job. Now she's just idling, too much damn time on her hands.

CHUCK   Eatin' bon-bons and bitchin' and moanin'.

PAUL   Justin's dumb idea for her to give notice. I told him to leave it be, let her have some purpose in life, but he thought it looked bad on him, her workin'.

CHUCK   Well, I say the minute he gets that ring slid past knuckle number two, he needs to knock her up and shut her up, put an end to all this nonsense.

PAUL   Oh, I wouldn't be tossin' a youngster into that mix. No, sir. Not the salve I'd be rubbin' on that particular wound.

CHUCK   I disagree. You throw a kid into the equation, something to distract her, she won't have the wherewithal to care for it and concern herself with her husband's constant lies and infidelities.

[*Smiling.*]

She'll prioritize.

PAUL   So, you're advisin' usin' a baby as kind of a rodeo clown? A human diversion to keep the bull from stompin' and gaugin' the cowboy?

CHUCK   Crudely put, but essentially, yes. And, hey, if that kid is born with some kind of special needs . . .

[*Winking.*]

even better.

PAUL No, Chuck, no.

CHUCK Nothing heinous, like muscular dystrophy or his little heart's on the outside. Talking a slight speech impediment or ADD. You know, something that's not life threatening, but taxes her time and attention. Tourette's, maybe. Be a hoot, right? Little kid screamin' "cocksucker" all the time.

[CHUCK's *cell phone rings. He looks at the caller ID.*]

Oh shit, she's callin' me now. What do I do, what should I do?

PAUL Ask her why she paired you up with that fat girl.

CHUCK Seriously?

PAUL No, not seriously.

CHUCK Should I hit "Ignore"?

PAUL No, you should give your phone to me.

[*Trading phones.*]

And call Justin on mine.

CHUCK What am I supposed to say?

[CHUCK *dials the phone.*]

PAUL Tell him we're in his uncle's room and the party can't start without him.

[*Into phone.*]

Hey, Pumpkin pie. No, it's Paul. Oh, really? Huh. Must have picked up the wrong phone. So, what's up? No, not yet. Guessing he's on his way, though.

CHUCK Machine.

PAUL [*Into phone.*] Well, you know everything that I know. He left the rehearsal dinner, home to change clothes, then due here.

CHUCK [*Into phone.*] Hey, Justin, what's up, buddy?

PAUL [*Into phone.*] I'm not lying to you, sweetheart.

CHUCK [*Into phone.*] Mind checkin' in soon as you get this?

PAUL [*Into phone.*] Look, gonna offer up a little "tough love" here.

CHUCK [*Into phone.*] No biggee, just touchin' base.

PAUL [*Into phone.*] Gotta stop this jealousy and mistrust.

CHUCK   [*Into phone.*] Can't start the shindig without you.

PAUL   [*Into phone.*] 'Cause if you're this unhappy now, should just cancel the whole deal.

CHUCK   [*Into phone.*] Gonna be fun, son, hum-dinger.

PAUL   [*Into phone.*] Preacher, party, and press.

CHUCK   [Into phone, chuckling.] All gonna end up in jail, probably. Anyway, call me back.

[*Beat.*]

This is Chuck, by the way.

[CHUCK *hangs up and pockets the phone.*]

PAUL   [*Into phone.*] Listen, I understand your concerns. I get it. No, I wouldn't want the type of marriage my folks had, neither. Fought like two birds on a bread crust.

[*Pause.*]

Really? No, I didn't . . . didn't know that. Was aware your mama had passed, but never knew . . . circumstances.

[*Covering the phone, quietly to* CHUCK.]

Jesus Christ.

[*There's a knock.* CHUCK *crosses to the door, still watching* PAUL.]

PAUL   [*Into phone, sincerely.*] Listen to me, it's all gonna work out. It will, I promise you. Gotta quit worryin' yourself. Spend your whole life looking for bad, eventually it's gonna show up.

[CHUCK *opens the door, revealing a* MAN *wearing a long, black trench coat and a rubber "Obama" mask. He's holding an automatic assault rifle, which he points at them.*]

MAN   [*Screaming in a muffled voice.*] Hit the deck, motherfuckers!

CHUCK   Jesus Christ!

MAN   Grab some fuckin' floor!

[CHUCK *and* PAUL *hit the floor. The* MAN *brandishes the gun back and forth between the two of them.*]

CHUCK   Take whatever you want, no trouble.

MAN   [*Pointing the gun.*] Trouble?

CHUCK   No, no! No trouble! Said no trouble!

PAUL   No trouble at all!

[*The man makes a guttural, growling sound as he points the gun back and forth between the two men. Pause. He laughs and pulls off the mask. It's* JUSTIN. *He's twenty-five, handsome, and speaks with a thick Southern accent.*]

JUSTIN   Understand you crackers didn't vote for me.

PAUL   Son of a bitch!

CHUCK   Cocksucker!

[JUSTIN *glares at him.*]

[*Smiling.*]

I mean, you rascal.

JUSTIN   [*Laughing.*] Should have seen your damn faces.

[JUSTIN *tosses the mask on the couch.*]

PAUL   I'll bet.

CHUCK   Joke's on us. Jesus. Good one.

JUSTIN   That goes in my top five, for sure. Right?

CHUCK   Almost beats that "toaster in the pool" stunt, you pulled.

[CHUCK *and* PAUL *stand,* PAUL *tosses his cell-phone to* JUSTIN.]

PAUL   Fiancée, funny man.

JUSTIN   [*Smiling.*] Dropped to the floor like two little girls.

[PAUL *smiles, nods and crosses to the bar.* CHUCK *exits down the hall.*]

PAUL   Yeah.

[*To* CHUCK.]

You okay?

CHUCK   No, I might've pooped a little.

JUSTIN   [*Laughing.*] Fuckin' classic.

PAUL   One for the books.

[*Pointing at the phone.*]

Bride-to-be.

JUSTIN   Oh, right, right.

[PAUL *takes the gun from* JUSTIN, *crosses to the sofa, and sits.*]

[*Into phone.*]

Hey, baby. What's up? No, there's no commotion, just messing with the guys, is all. Little bit of fun.

PAUL   Big fun.

JUSTIN   [*Into phone.*] No, I didn't get no messages. I had my phone turned off. Am so telling you the truth. Lyndsey, don't start in with your bullshit, I'm in no mood for it.

PAUL   [*Quietly.*] Be nice now.

JUSTIN   [*Into phone.*] Hang on.

[*To* PAUL.]

What was that?

PAUL   Sayin' be sweet, she was worried sick about you.

JUSTIN   Uh-huh. Overstepping a little bit here, ain't you?

PAUL   Justin, come on, she's a nervous bride, night before the wedding. . . .

JUSTIN   [*Interrupting.*] And that concerns you, how? Huh? How is that any of your business?

[*Pause.*]

PAUL   Reckon it's not.

JUSTIN   Reckon right. Don't pay you to be my mama, nursemaid, or little angel on my shoulder. I'm a grown-ass man. The grown-ass man who signs the checks, in fact. Your checks. We clear?

PAUL   Justin, what's the matter with you?

JUSTIN   [*Angry.*] Asked you, are we clear?

[*Pause.* PAUL *shrugs.*]

That a "yes"?

PAUL   No. That's a "yes, sir."

JUSTIN   Good. Good. [*Into phone, crossing downstage.*] Still there? No, nothin', just remindin' Paul who the boss is.

[*Laughing.*]

He forgets sometimes.

[PAUL *mouths the words "fuck you," then brings the rifle up slowly, quietly aiming it at the back of* JUSTIN's *head. He peers through the scope, following* JUSTIN *with the barrel as he paces downstage.*]

JUSTIN   [*Into phone, charming.*] Look, baby, you get this way every time I got a tour on the horizon. Start frettin' over nothing and reading and believing all that tabloid nonsense. Told you a hundred times, I love you. All I want, all I need in life, is you.

[*Looking at his watch.*]

Love of my life, sweetheart. Yes, I promise tonight will be super low-key. No strippers or hookers, none of that mess. Yes, I'll leave my phone on all night. I promise.

[*Pause.*]

Alright. Love you. Bye-bye.

[JUSTIN *hangs up the phone and faces out, not looking at* PAUL, *but aware of what he's doing.*]

Nice feel to it, don't it?

PAUL   Indeed it do.

JUSTIN   Not much kickback, neither. Four-year-old could fire that thing, not even swallow his gum.

[PAUL *lowers the gun.* JUSTIN *turns to look at him.*]

PAUL   Accumulatin' quite the arsenal these days.

JUSTIN   That one was a gift, actually. Prototype, ain't even in stores yet.

PAUL   Nice.

[*Beat.*]

Secret admirer?

JUSTIN   No secrets.

[*Pointedly.*]

Larry Meyer give that to me.

[*Pause.*]

PAUL   Sweet on Larry Meyer now, are you?

JUSTIN   Too soon to tell.

[*Beat.*]

He is sure sweet on me, though.

PAUL   "Froggie went a courtin' and he did ride."

JUSTIN   [*Singing.*] "Uh-huh."

[*They smile at each other.*]

PAUL   Should have just shot you when I had the chance.

JUSTIN   Well, you're not the kind that can actually pull the trigger, are you?

PAUL   Might surprise you.

JUSTIN   Haven't so far.

[JUSTIN *crosses to* PAUL *and grabs the barrel of the gun to take it.* PAUL *holds onto it, not letting go.*]

PAUL   There was a time when a man's word actually meant something in this life. He told you he was going to do something, honor something, he did just that. Word was his bond, his currency.

JUSTIN   That right?

PAUL   Damn right. Because his reputation, his character was on the line. And that mattered more than anything. Certainly more than a few gold statues or a couple of silly-ass magazine covers.

[JUSTIN *takes the gun.*]

JUSTIN   I like getting free shit, Paul. Shoes, watches, guns, cars. Whatever people want to give me, I am more than happy to take. See, my old man was one of those "word is his bond" kind of guys. Thought if he broke his back, worked hard, did his best, the world was going to take care of him, reward him, somehow.

[*Beat.*]

Know what his reward ended up being? An ass full of tumors and a homeless man's funeral. But, he stayed a man of his word. Would have written that on his tombstone, if we could have afforded to buy him a fuckin' tombstone.

PAUL   Listen, you got a grievance, son, let's talk about it, figure it out and get past it.

JUSTIN   I'm tired of talkin'. Thinkin' may be time for a change.

[*Pause.*]

PAUL   Wasn't for me, you'd still be scufflin' up and down Music Row wearin' taped-up boots and playin' for winks and quarters.

JUSTIN   [*Sarcastic.*] Probably still be swimmin' in my mama's belly, if you hadn't shown up with a lantern and a road map.

[CHUCK *crosses in from the hallway.*]

CHUCK   Better sell BVDs in the gift shop, otherwise I'm "going commando".

[*Pause.*]

Everything copacetic?

JUSTIN   Everything is peachy.

[*Beat.*]

So, how many assholes you got comin' to this soiree, anyway?

CHUCK   Just a few execs from the label, they'll be your biggest assholes. VIP area will be mostly us, your uncle, and a few handpicked pieces of eye candy.

PAUL   [*To* JUSTIN.] Room for Larry Meyer, you want to invite him.

CHUCK   Larry Meyer?

JUSTIN   [*Smiling, to* PAUL.] Thanks for your permission, but I already did.

PAUL   Great. Two of you can find a dark corner somewhere and get snuggly. Maybe as a wedding present he'll even give you a "reach-around."

CHUCK   [*Laughing, unaware.*] "Reach-around."

JUSTIN   [*To* PAUL.] Gonna make this real easy, ain't you?

PAUL   On the contrary.

[*The door bursts open and* UNCLE JIM *enters. He's sixty, with a long, thick white beard and bad teeth. He's dressed in a work shirt, camo pants, red suspenders, and a baseball cap. He's speaks in a heavy, almost unintelligible Southern accent and has a lost childlike quality about him.*]

UNCLE JIM   Hey, who let all you fuckers in my room?

JUSTIN   Uncle Jim!

UNCLE JIM   The serious partyin' may now commence.

JUSTIN   The trouble we been waitin' for.

UNCLE JIM   [*Holding up his hands, clearing his throat for attention.*] Old bull and a young bull standing on top of a hill. Below is acres of pasture, filled with hundreds of beautiful, grazing dairy cows. Young bull says to the old bull, "Hey, let's run down there and fuck seven or eight of them cows." Old bull says, "No, let's walk down and fuck them all."

JUSTIN   The man, the myth.

UNCLE JIM   "Fuck them all."

[JUSTIN *puts the gun on the sofa and crosses to* UNCLE JIM, *giving him a hug.*]

JUSTIN   Glad you could make it, partner.

UNCLE JIM   Wouldn't have missed it for the world, all the tea in China.

[OLLIE *enters, carrying a garbage bag filled with clothes and an inflatable sex doll.*]

OLLIE   Sir, where would you like your . . . luggage.

UNCLE JIM   [*Irritated.*] In the bedroom, weird little fucker.

Ollie   Yes, of course.

[*To* Justin.]

Hello.

[Uncle Jim *grabs the blow-up doll, as* Ollie *exits down the hall.*]

Uncle Jim   Give me her.

[*Re: doll.*]

Name is Wanda June Whitmore, boys, and she is up for anything and everything. Three hot, hungry holes, no waiting. So enjoy yourselves. But, hey, no "water sports" or "Dirty Sanchezes". She's still a good Christian gal and her folks are still alive.

[Uncle Jim *puts the doll on the couch as* Ollie *crosses out of the hall, towards the door.*]

Justin   [*Laughing.*] Favorite livin' relative, right fuckin' there!

Uncle Jim   [*To* Ollie.] Told you downstairs I was kin to him, didn't I, little shit-ass?

Ollie   You did, sir, and I sincerely apologize.

Uncle Jim   Judgin' a book by its cover was your *modus operandi*. I dress how I dress and my teeth are my teeth.

Ollie   [*To* Justin.] Just tryin' to maintain your security, sir.

[Justin *crosses to him.*]

Justin   No worries.

Ollie   Lot of crazies tryin' to get next to you.

Uncle Jim   Callin' me crazy now? I'll torch this whole fuckin' building.

Justin   [*To* Jim, *laughing.*] I got this.

Uncle Jim   [*To* Ollie.] Nothin' left of you but a femur bone and a butt plug. I'll do it too, I'm a wild card.

Justin   [*To* Chuck.] Get him some weed. Jim, you want some weed?

Uncle Jim   Oh, I'd love some weed.

[Uncle Jim *crosses to* Chuck.]

Chuck   [*Holding up a pocket vaporizer.*] Locked and loaded.

Uncle Jim   Smoked what was in the car.

Chuck   Three joints?

Uncle Jim   I got glaucoma, fucker. What are you, a narc?

[UNCLE JIM *grabs the vaporizer and takes a big hit.*]

JUSTIN   [*To* OLLIE.] Appreciate you lookin' out for me.

OLLIE   It's my job, happy to do it. By the way, I love your music.

JUSTIN   Thank you. What's your name?

UNCLE JIM   [*Exhaling.*] Name is Fuck-with-Me-Ever-Again-and-I'll-Teach-You-the-True-Meaning-of-Pain. That's his name.

JUSTIN   [*Laughing.*] Actually, no, that'd be your name, Jim.

[*Pause.*]

UNCLE JIM   Oh, right, right, that would be my name.

[*To* CHUCK *re: vaporizer.*]

Reload, fucker! Reload!

[CHUCK *refills the vaporizer from a small bag of weed.*]

OLLIE   [*To* JUSTIN.] "Ollie" Oliver Scott Junior. Singer-songwriter, lead guitar and vocals.

JUSTIN   Music man, huh?

OLLIE   Oh, yes. It's my passion, my life, really.

[PAUL *crosses towards* OLLIE, *taking a wad of bills out of his pocket.*]

PAUL   Thank you for everything, son.

OLLIE   I told you, no tipping.

[*To* JUSTIN.]

Keeps trying to throw money at me.

JUSTIN   You're lucky, I have the exact opposite problem with him.

PAUL   Don't hold back, Justin, tell me how you feel.

JUSTIN   [*To* OLLIE.] Thanks a bunch and best of luck with your music.

OLLIE   Speakin' of which.

[*Handing him a CD.*]

Couple of the tracks are still a little rough.

PAUL   Wait, whoa, whoa, whoa.

OLLIE   Haven't done the final mix yet. . . .

PAUL   Son, I told you we cannot accept unsolicited material.

OLLIE   [*To* JUSTIN.] Just need a break is all.

PAUL   Gotta go through proper channels. Can't just hand this man—

JUSTIN   [*Interrupting.*] I got this.

PAUL   Justin.

JUSTIN   [*Sharply.*] I'll handle it.

[*Pause.*]

PAUL   Fine. You handle it.

[JUSTIN *takes the CD from* OLLIE.]

JUSTIN   Be proud to give it a listen.

OLLIE   Really?

JUSTIN   After my honeymoon, of course.

OLLIE   Of course.

JUSTIN   No promises now.

PAUL   None whatsoever. And everybody here heard that.

JUSTIN   Yeah, Paul, we heard it, so shut the fuck up.

PAUL   [*Threatening.*] Come again?

UNCLE JIM   I didn't hear shit, so don't be showin' up at my door with no babies or subpoenas.

[*To* CHUCK.]

Is the liquor free?

OLLIE   [*To* JUSTIN.] You've always been an inspiration. Real role model to me. Times when I've faced adversity or been goin' through a rough patch, I'd ask myself, "How would Justin handle this?" "What would Justin do?"

UNCLE JIM   [*To* CHUCK.] Just threw up a little in my mouth.

JUSTIN   [*To* OLLIE.] Lookin' forward to hearin' your songs.

PAUL   [*Loudly.*] Strictly as a courtesy, personal favor, that in no way obligates Mister Spears or his publishing company, which I still own ten percent of, to purchase or record anything on that disc. We clear on that?

JUSTIN   Crystal clear, Matlock. And thank you again, for your concise legal expertise.

[PAUL *glares at* JUSTIN.]

OLLIE   Thank you, Mister Spears.

JUSTIN   Call me Justin.

OLLIE   Justin.

[*They smile at each other a beat, then* OLLIE *exits.*]

PAUL   Gonna keep tossin' these little "pissy missiles" my way, or are we gonna have us an actual sit-down?

JUSTIN   On the docket, to be certain. But not tonight, baby. Last night of freedom, gonna have some fun. Right, Jim? You up for some fun?

UNCLE JIM   Hell, yes. Reason I flew in all the way from Jabez.

[*Beat.*]

Hey, is it gonna be just booze and weed tonight, 'cause I'd love a little Oxy-Contin?

JUSTIN   No, no "Oxy" tonight, partner.

UNCLE JIM   Oh, just a smidge, take the edge off.

JUSTIN   Can't be blurry tonight, son, 'cause downstairs we got a room full of hot, sexy Southern bitches, all waiting for you and a sneaky-peak at that "one-eyed anaconda."

UNCLE JIM   [*Chuckling.*] "Anaconda."

[*To* PAUL *and* CHUCK.]

He's exaggeratin', it ain't that long. Thick as shit, though, seriously, like a tuna can.

JUSTIN   Blondes, brunettes, redheads. And first pick is yours.

UNCLE JIM   Well, I ain't finicky when it comes to the poon-tang. Whatever's on my plate, I'll eat. Black, Asian, Mexican, Methodist . . .

JUSTIN   [*Laughing.*] Hey, tell 'em about that one gal, that Injun gal, you used to go with.

UNCLE JIM   Don't say "Injun." Politically correct term is "Native American." Pawnee to be precise. Called herself "Pretty Feathers." And pretty she was. Until she'd knock back a couple cans of Coors beer. Then she'd turn into crazy-red-eyed-devil-bitch.

JUSTIN   [*Laughing, to* PAUL *and* CHUCK.] Seriously. Ran him over with her fuckin' car.

UNCLE JIM   Shit wasn't funny. Hit me hard, flew up and over the top of that vehicle and landed facedown in the hog wallow, out cold. Luckily, a neighbor saw the whole deal and drug me out. Otherwise, I'm certain them hogs would've eaten me alive. They'll eat anything warm. Course, so will I.

[*Laughing.*]

Get it? "Anything warm"? Everybody get that?

[PAUL *nods.*]

CHUCK   I get it. Very funny.

JUSTIN   [*To* UNCLE JIM.] Skippin' the best part, man. The police report, tell that part, fillin' out the police report.

UNCLE JIM   Oh, right, right. This is good, real good. When they asked me to give a description of the driver, you know, make and model of the car what hit me, I said, "It was a Pawnee, driving a Cherokee." True story. Absolutely true. Cop thought I was fuckin' with him, but I wasn't, no sir, just tellin' the natural truth.

PAUL   Probably ought to start headin' downstairs, Justin. Got people waitin'.

JUSTIN   [*Angry.*] Let 'em fuckin' wait. It's my party, right?

PAUL   [*Smiling.*] And I'll cry if I want to.

JUSTIN   [*To* UNCLE JIM.] Hey, tell 'em about that other one, the midget one!

UNCLE JIM   No, no, I'm pretty tired, boy, and nobody wants to hear about that.

JUSTIN   Sure they do.

[*To* PAUL *and* CHUCK.]

You guys wanna hear about her, don't you?

[PAUL *sighs and shrugs.*]

CHUCK   [*Unsure.*] Absolutely, love these stories.

PAUL   Your Uncle's tired, Justin. You okay, Jim?

JUSTIN   He's fine, leave him alone!

[*To* UNCLE JIM, *forcefully.*]

Now, you met that midget when the Ice Capades came through town, right?

UNCLE JIM   Wasn't the Ice Capades, it was Disney on Ice." She was performing in the role of Jiminy Cricket. And please don't call her a midget. Politically correct term is "little people."

[*To* CHUCK.]

And little she was. No bigger than a booger. Only time in my life I ever got a blow-job when both people was standing up. True story.

JUSTIN   [*Laughing and clapping.*] Here we go.

UNCLE JIM   Shit you not. We played this game where that little mite would start from all the way across the room and barrel straight at me, mouth agape, and she'd gobble it all, balls deep with nary a tooth scrape, hand to God.

JUSTIN   Do it, show 'em, show 'em how she'd run at you.

UNCLE JIM   No, no, no.

JUSTIN   Come on.

UNCLE JIM   Not now, I'm weary.

JUSTIN   [*Ugly.*] Really? First-class airfare and a hotel suite doesn't buy a guy a couple of fuckin' chuckles?

[*Pause.* UNCLE JIM *looks at him.*]

UNCLE JIM   Alright, boy, whatever you want.

[*To* CHUCK *and* PAUL.]

The whole procedure would put you in mind of that playground game "Red Rover, Red Rover." But, you know, the X-rated version.

JUSTIN   [*Clapping.*] Here we go!

UNCLE JIM   And it was pretty comical, 'cause, you know, she had them legs, them itty-bitty legs, no bigger than ham hocks. And she'd start out from across the room, take her a minute to hit her stride, but once she did, she could fly like the wind. And then, "pop," over the lips and past the gums, gulp. Nine times out of ten, too. Only once did I ever poke her in the eye, or rather she poked herself in the eye, you know, with my dick.

[JUSTIN *laughs,* UNCLE JIM *sits, exhausted.*]

JUSTIN   [*To* PAUL *and* CHUCK.] Unbelievable, right? Fuckin' insane.

PAUL   Fuckin' insane.

UNCLE JIM   [*Disoriented, looking around.*] What the hell was her name, anyway? Can't remember her name, for the life of me. Wasn't really Jiminy Cricket, was it?

[*Pause.* UNCLE JIM *mumbles to himself, lost.*]

PAUL   Alright, we should head on down. Jim, you okay?

JUSTIN   He's fine. [*To* UNCLE JIM.] Tell about that fat chick you dated, you know, the one from the post office.

UNCLE JIM   [*Upset.*] No. No more. I'm tired, boy. And don't call her a "fat chick." Politically correct term is "morbidly obese." Doesn't sound much better, but there it is. Do remember her name. Sweet Jolene from Abilene. Took her ten minutes to get out of her car, twice that long to get out of her britches.

[UNCLE JIM *laughs, then starts to shake, convulse, finally going into a full diabetic seizure.*]

JUSTIN   Oh Christ, I'm outta here.

[JUSTIN *crosses to the door.*]

Paul   What's happenin'? Is he okay?

Justin   He's havin' one of his fuckin' fits. I can't watch this shit.

[Justin *opens the door.*]

Paul   Seriously, are you guys fooling around?

Justin   Give him some orange juice or a Kit Kat bar, he'll be fine.

[*Shouting.*]

Heading downstairs, Jim.

[Justin *exits.* Uncle Jim *convulses and slides off the couch onto the floor.* Paul *runs to him.*]

Paul   Holy shit, Justin! This is a seizure? Diabetic seizure?

[*To* Chuck.]

Get some juice out of the mini-bar.

Chuck   Better call somebody, we should call somebody.

[Chuck *runs to the mini-fridge.*]

Paul   Get the goddamn orange juice. Hang on, Jim, just hang on.

Chuck   No OJ. Just apple or Sunny D.

Paul   Whatever, bring.

[*To* Uncle Jim.]

Be fine, you're gonna be fine. Goddammit, Justin.

[Chuck *runs over with the juice.* Paul *takes it and puts it to* Uncle Jim's *mouth; he spits and writhes.*]

Paul   Come on now, let's get some juice in you. Jim! Come on, take a sip. You need the sugar. That's it. There you go. Little more. Good man. Good man.

[Uncle Jim *slowly comes out of the grand mal and his muscles stop twitching. Long pause.*]

Chuck   Should I call 9-1-1?

Paul   Just wait. [*To* Uncle Jim.] Drink a little more for me. There you go. There you go, partner. Sip it. Just sip it slow.

[Uncle Jim *looks around the room.*]

Uncle Jim   What happened? Where am I?

Paul   Hiram Hotel, Nashville, Tennessee.

Uncle Jim   Oh, Nashville.

[*Beat.*]

Am I with Barbara Mandrell?

PAUL   [*Smiling.*] No, sir.

UNCLE JIM   Oh.

[*Beat.*]

Any of the Mandrell sisters?

PAUL   [*Smiling.*] Afraid not. Just in town for your nephew's wedding.

UNCLE JIM   Oh, okay, right. That's right. You any kin to me?

PAUL   No, sir.

UNCLE JIM   Oh.

[*Beat.*]

Who the fuck are you then?

PAUL   Just a friend.

UNCLE JIM   [*Realizing.*] Oh shit, Justin's party, ruined the boy's party?

PAUL   No, no, you didn't ruin anything.

UNCLE JIM   [*Crying.*] Damn fits. What have I done, what have I done?

PAUL   Everything's fine. Drink your juice, some more of your juice.

[UNCLE JIM *drinks. Pause.*]

UNCLE JIM   Justin don't like it when I have one of my spells. I think it embarrasses him.

PAUL   Yeah, well, fuck him.

[UNCLE JIM *slaps* PAUL *hard across the face.*]

UNCLE JIM   That's my family.

[*Pause.*]

PAUL   Sorry. You're right. I'm sorry.

UNCLE JIM   Since you kept me from slippin' into coma, I'll cut you some slack. But don't ever talk against that boy when I'm within earshot.

PAUL   Understood.

UNCLE JIM   Alright, then, movin' on. Help me get up.

[PAUL *and* CHUCK *lift him to his feet.*]

UNCLE JIM   [*Eyeing his crotch.*] Didn't piss myself. Good. I'll take that as my silver lining.

CHUCK   You want to see a doctor or something, Jim?

UNCLE JIM   No, I'll be fine. You fellows oughta get goin' to your party.

CHUCK   Not comin' with us?

UNCLE JIM   Huh-uh. I'm gonna stay here, order a strawberry milkshake, take a bath, and then go to bed.

CHUCK   Gonna miss all the fun.

UNCLE JIM   Oh, I'll probably watch a little porn, too.

PAUL   You sure about the doctor?

UNCLE JIM   Yes, I am sure. Go on, now.

[*Beat.*]

Please.

PAUL   You know what, maybe I'll just hang up here too.

UNCLE JIM   Unnecessary, friend.

PAUL   Not really in a party mood myself.

UNCLE JIM   [*Quietly.*] Get the fuck out.

[PAUL *nods, then he and* CHUCK *exit.* JIM *lets out a deep, mournful sigh and looks around the room, lost, whimpering like a child. He notices the blow-up doll laying on the sofa. Pause.*]

UNCLE JIM   Do not waste thy piteous gaze on me, Wanda June. For the man you see before you is not the man I am. And most assuredly, not the man I was.

[*Crossing to the bar and picking up a bottle.*]

Man I was stood tall and upright, pillar strong and confident. His boyish face framed by long golden tresses that smelled of youthful exuberance and Pert Plus Shampoo and Conditioner. Man I was had a beautiful, bright-white smile, conveyin' confidence, ambition, and a future filled with possibilities. Possibly. Possible. Pumpkin pie.

[*Drinks.*]

Man I had eyes the bluest of blue that sparkled in the sun and viewed the world as a joyous, wondrous playground, filled with all the promises of God.

[*Pause.*]

But shit happens, my dear. Twenties give way to thirties, thirties blend into your forties, forties melt into fifties, and the rest is just a series of five-year blinks all the way to the fuckin' grave.

[*Drinks.*]

The once lustrous hair has now vanished. Replaced by a dry, barren, near-dead scalp. The pearly smile is now a mouth full of chipped, cracked, yellow-brown bitin' bones. Stained from years of instant coffee, filter-less cigarettes, and swallowin' the shit of a thousand lesser men. And the eyes, once sparklin' with dreams, have now faded. Milked over by a lifetime of heartache, struggle, and plain old rotten luck.

[*Pause.*]

I apologize, Wanda June. Afraid I'm not very good company this evening.

[*He crosses to the couch and sits.*]

Old bull and a young bull, standin' top of a hill, pasture below is filled with beautiful, grazin' dairy cows.

[*He picks up the gun.*]

Young bull says, "Let's run down there and fuck seven or eight of them cows." Old bull says "No, let's walk down . . . and fuck 'em all."

[*Pause.*]

Fuck them all.

[*He sticks the barrel of the rifle into his mouth, placing a thumb on the trigger. Long pause.*]

[*Opening his eyes.*]

Nope. Huh-uh. Can't do it. Cannot do it. For the life of me, Wanda June, can't even kill myself.

[*Tossing the gun on the sofa.*]

Know why? Tell you why. No blessed follow-through. Nary a thimble full. Not proud of that fact, but there she lies.

[*A knock at the door, he turns and looks at it. Pause.*]

[*Turning back to the doll.*]

Get my toes right up to the goal line, inches away, then just stop and stare at the uprights. Slack-jawed, dead-eyed, two fingers stirring in my butt-hole. Pitiful. Pitiful and pathetic.

[*Another knock, he looks at the door. Pause.*]

[*Turning back to the doll.*]

Been riding the brakes my entire life, Wanda June. Make myself sick, seriously. Never finish a goddamn thing I start. Which explains them unopened tapes on speaking Spanish and that dust-covered ukulele I got resting under my sink.

[*Another knock. He looks at the door, stands, and crosses towards it. He opens it slowly, revealing* SHARON, *an attractive woman in her thirties. She's strong-willed and aggressive. Dressed in a leather jacket, jeans and carrying a motorcycle helmet. She speaks in a strong Southern accent.*]

SHARON   James Byron Spears the Third?

UNCLE JIM   Last time I checked.

[*She shoves the helmet into his hands and crosses in.*]

SHARON   Born January nineteenth, nineteen and fifty-one?

UNCLE JIM   Premature, kneeling breech, brung me out C-section.

SHARON   Dropped out of Jabez High School a third of the way through your junior year, sporting about a D-minus average.

UNCLE JIM   Ain't "book smart," sue me. You a collection agency of some sort?

[*She peers out the window.*]

SHARON   Four years military, Army specifically and equally unimpressive. Went in buck private, came out buck private.

UNCLE JIM   [*Shrugging.*] Politics, sunshine. Listen, is this about the late payment on my lawn mower? 'Cause I called that girl and told her this month was gonna be tight.

SHARON   Upon discharge, you moved back home, scrambled around, dead-end job to dead-end job. Truck driver, fry cook, carnival worker.

UNCLE JIM   Nickel toss and dunk tank were my territories. And carnival work ain't dead-end, now, it's just seasonal.

SHARON   Arrested several times, petty offences mostly, always alcohol related. Drunk driving, drunk and disorderly, public drunkenness.

UNCLE JIM   I'm a fuckin' drunk, what do you expect? But listen up, you "repo" that Lawn Boy and I got no way to get around.

SHARON   Single, never married, no children to speak of.

UNCLE JIM   [*Smiling.*] None that I know about. Seriously though, you followed me out of state over two late payments?

SHARON   Engaged to be married, however briefly, to one Darlene Patricia Reifstack, now deceased. Killed in an automobile accident just outside of Somerset.

UNCLE JIM   [*Quietly.*] Poplarville.

Sharon Other driver hit your car head-on. You walked away with a few minor cuts and bruises. Unfortunately, Darlene died in the ambulance on the way to the hospital.

Uncle Jim Lost consciousness on the drive. Wasn't pronounced legal dead until the next morning.

Sharon Sorry.

Uncle Jim I was holding one hand, her mama was holding the other.

[*Beat, then exploding.*]

Just who the fuck are you, lady?

Sharon [*Pointing.*] Good question. Eternal question, really. "Who the fuck am I?"

Uncle Jim [*Tossing the helmet to her.*] Ain't playing charades with you, missy.

Sharon Understood, understood.

[*Pause.*]

Name is Sharon Mary Warfel, middle child of Dennis and Inez Warfel. Thirty-five years of age, as of exactly two days ago.

Uncle Jim [*Sarcastically.*] Happy belated.

Sharon Thank you much. I own most of a two-bedroom, ranch-style home here in Nashville and have been employed by same city for over five years as a decorated officer of the law.

Uncle Jim Cop, shit.

[*Pointing.*]

That's how you're privy to all my pertinents, isn't it?

Sharon Like you, also did a stint in the military, also Army. Three years active duty, but unlike you, I came out with stripes on my shoulders.

Uncle Jim Whoop-dee-do, Sergeant Fury.

Sharon Was also engaged to be married, however briefly, to one Justin Eugene Spears, son of Henry Carl Spears, your brother, making my former fiancée, lying piece of shit that he is . . .

Uncle Jim My nephew.

[*Beat.*]

Woman scorned, got it. Listen, if you're here to kill the boy, he ain't on premises. He's with his wife-to-be and her folks . . . at an "undisclosed location."

Sharon   He's downstairs with his sycophants, drinking a Corona Light, eating a chimichanga and laughing at his own fucking jokes.

Uncle Jim   Jesus, you're good.

Sharon   Recited your entire life history upon entry, you don't think I know who's in this fucking building.

Uncle Jim   Point taken.

Sharon   And if I wanted to kill that son of a bitch, he'd already be dead. As would the ex-con-junkie-snitch that I framed into doin' the deed.

Uncle Jim   Not that you've put any kind of thought into it or anything.

Sharon   What can I tell you, Jim. May I call you Jim?

Uncle Jim   Your world, Sheriff.

Sharon   We "scorned women" handle rejection in a lot of different ways. Some gals take to the couch, balled-up, crying, watching *Fried Green Tomatoes* and gnawing on a log of cookie dough. Others of us buy eleven hundred dollars worth of surveillance equipment, study our exes every waking move, then find a stone-cold-killer-smack-addict who'll cut their "former's" throat from ear to ear, make it look like a failed robbery attempt, and won't be missed when they vanish from the face of the fucking earth.

Uncle Jim   Thin blue line, Jesus Christ.

[*Beat.*]

Now, by telling me all this, you're gonna have to eliminate me now, ain't you?

Sharon   Haven't pondered "collateral damage," but I'll let you know.

Uncle Jim   Prefer to be surprised. Just make it quick, like *Old Yeller*. Scratch my ears, point me towards the mountains, and squeeze one into my skull.

Sharon   Well, I'm probably gonna let you slide.

Uncle Jim   [*Pissed.*] Course you will, 'cause that's the way my luck's been fucking running lately.

[*Beat.*]

And why ain't you down in the bar harassing your "ex" instead of up here busting my sixty-three-year-old balls?

Sharon   He's about due, just bidin' my time. Besides I wanted to meet the infamous Uncle Jim. Living legend to hear Justin tell it and the only relative I ever heard him speak fondly of.

Uncle Jim   Rest of the family's a bunch of assholes, so I'm just candy corn in a bucket of shit. Count your blessings you didn't marry into that.

SHARON   Never given the option, Jim. Was assured many times of its imminence, but that tree never bore fruit. Shit.

[*Re: vaporizer.*]

This your paraphernalia?

[SHARON *crosses, sits and examines the vaporizer.*]

UNCLE JIM   No. I don't know who that belongs to, I don't ever touch that stuff. And if I did, I'd use a one-hitter, pipe, or roll myself "a spliff."

[*Beat.*]

I mean, you know, if I ever did.

SHARON   Relax, don't give a shit, just wanna know who's mouth's been on it.

[*She takes a pill bottle full of weed out of her pocket and loads the vaporizer.*]

UNCLE JIM   Oh. Well, hard to tell. World we live in, can't really figure whose mouth's been on anything anymore.

SHARON   Take my chances.

UNCLE JIM   Just like the rest of us.

[*Beat.*]

So, they stop screening you cops or you got some kid you're blackmailing for clean piss?

SHARON   You watch too much *Law and Order*, Jim.

UNCLE JIM   Can't help it, fucking thing's always on.

SHARON   If you must know, I'm takin' a little sabbatical from active duty. So, no more "mandatory's" for me.

[*She takes a hit.*]

UNCLE JIM   Uh-huh.

[*Pause.*]

So, what happened make you walk away? See some bad shit? That it? Stumble into a brains-on-the-wall type crime scene that's haunting your sleep and underlining the despicable, heinous nature that is man?

SHARON   [*Shaking her head.*] No.

UNCLE JIM   No.

[*Beat.*]

Find yourself privy to an ugly cover-up involvin' dirty cops and government officials? And when you ratted out the whole bunch to I.A. your fellow officers turned on you and set you up to take the fall?

SHARON   [*Exhaling.*] Nope.

UNCLE JIM   Nope.

[*Beat.*]

Find a trunk full of unmarked hundred-dollar bills that nobody knows about and will never be missed and now you're gonna buy a little sports bar in Pompano Beach and spend the rest of your days sipping daiquiris and playing Texas hold 'em?

SHARON   No.

UNCLE JIM   No. You knocked up?

[*Pause.*]

SHARON   Oh, no. Definitely not. Just time to move on, buddy boy. Greener pastures. A new life of unknown adventures and infinite possibilities.

[*Beat.*]

Possibly.

[*Beat.*]

Possible.

UNCLE JIM   [*Quietly.*] Pumpkin pie.

[*Looking around.*]

Fuckin' bugged.

SHARON   Wherever the shifting winds shall take me, there I will go. No plan, no escape route, well, possibly an escape route.

[*Re: The gun, mask, and doll.*]

What is all this shit?

UNCLE JIM   Huh? Oh. That's a rubber mask of the President, a semi-automatic rifle, and a blow-up sex doll.

SHARON   Uh-huh.

[*Beat.*]

Yours?

UNCLE JIM   The gun and the mask are not my property. I am, however, the owner of that inflatable lady.

SHARON   [*Smirking.*] Proud owner?

UNCLE JIM   Oh, I wouldn't say that.

SHARON   Jesus.

[*Examining the doll.*]

Please tell me you don't actually have sex with this thing.

UNCLE JIM   I don't actually have sex with that thing. Bought it more as a party favor, you know, joke type deal, no intimate intentions whatsoever.

SHARON   Sweet lord, what kind of man would seriously stick his penis into one of these contraptions?

UNCLE JIM   Guessin' your top answer would be "lonely man." Followed by "horribly disfigured man" or "smells like dog shit man."

SHARON   Men. Jesus. Perfect woman, though, right? No brains or heart to speak of. Just two holes, no parents, periods, or problems.

[UNCLE JIM *takes the doll from her.*]

UNCLE JIM   Three holes, actually, and she is not without her problems. Speakin' specifically about the quality of her hair and her air-valve, which in my opinion, are both very, very shoddy.

[UNCLE JIM *tosses the doll down the hallway, looking at* SHARON *sheepishly. Pause.*]

SHARON   [*Picking up the gun.*] Guessing this hardware to be Justin's property.

UNCLE JIM   Safe bet. Boy sure loves the guns, don't he?

SHARON   Almost as much as he loves himself.

[*Pause.*]

You know it was me that taught that asshole how to shoot.

UNCLE JIM   That right?

SHARON   Damn right. Master Marksmen Award, three years running, best shot on the force.

UNCLE JIM   Good for you.

SHARON   [*Sarcastically.*] Oh yeah, real good for me. Surrounded by nothing but sexist, old-South, fat-ass, cracker po-lice, calling me "Annie Oakley" and "Calamity Jane." Most of them couldn't a run half a block without "stroking out" or hit a fucking urinal if they were pissin' with five dicks.

UNCLE JIM   [*Chuckling.*] Five dicks.

[*She stares him down; he stops chuckling.*]

SHARON   Ridiculous world of men. Who's fucked-up idea was that?

[*Beat.*]

Anyway, Justin was always messing around with my twenty-two, playing Sundance Kid. Finally, I took him to the range and taught him how to fire it, before he killed one or both of us.

[*Beat.*]

Got pretty good, too. Nowhere near my level, but passable.

UNCLE JIM   Well, his daddy and me weren't no kind of sportsmen, so glad somebody taught him how to shoot.

[*She stands and crosses towards him, pointing the gun at his face.*]

SHARON   [*Angry.*] I taught that son of a bitch everything. How to shoot, shit, fight, fuck, and bake banana bread. When I met that worm-hole, he couldn't put his boots on without tipping over. I fed him, tended him, babied him, and gave him seven years of my life. Seven good years, seven goddamn important years, turns out. Only to get lied to, cheated on, and tossed aside like a used rubber on prom night.

UNCLE JIM   My mama used to add pecans to her banana bread. Tasted just like Christmas.

[*He smiles and grabs the barrel of the gun, putting it into his mouth. A beat. She pulls it away. Pause.*]

SHARON   Live in your own little world, don't you, pal?

UNCLE JIM   Well. Beats the one they give us.

SHARON   True enough. True enough. Everything sure looked better in the catalog.

[*Beat.*]

Fuck it. Moving on. So, what are we drinking, Jim?

UNCLE JIM   Shit, anything and everything. As you surmised from my dossier, I am not finicky in the alcohol department. So, lady's choice.

SHARON   [*Picking up a bottle.*] Te-qui-la.

UNCLE JIM   Good choice, lady. Little Mexican mayhem, *mi amigo*. Gonna need salt or lime to get that down?

SHARON   Don't even need a fucking glass.

[UNCLE JIM *crosses to the couch.* SHARON *opens the bottle and drinks.*]

UNCLE JIM   Low maintenance, I like that. Meaning, I appreciate that. Ran with this one gal, insisted on a specified receptacle or utensil for everything she ever ate, everything she ever drank.

SHARON   Death by formality, huh?

UNCLE JIM   Bull's-eye. Water had to be drunk from a water glass, wine from a wineglass. Salad forks, butter knives, soup spoons, and go fuck yourself. Me, I'm like you, no frills. I'll drink beer out of a work boot and eat cereal out of a baseball cap. I mean, it's not preferable, just saying I don't give a shit.

[*She hands him the bottle.*]

SHARON   To not giving a shit.

UNCLE JIM   Drink to that. Hell, spent my whole life drinking to that.

[*He takes a long, loud, gulping drink.*]

SHARON   Jesus, *hombre.* That's a good way to kill yourself.

UNCLE JIM   Certainly more expedient methods, but I'm fairly cowardly.

[*She looks at him; he chuckles and takes another long, gulping drink.*]

SHARON   Didn't your mama teach you to share?

UNCLE JIM   Oh, right, sorry. Your turn at the pump.

[*He wipes off the bottle and hands it to her. Long pause.*]

Listen, not to contradict you or nothing, but you didn't teach that boy everything he knows.

SHARON   [*Smiling, knowing.*] No, I did not teach him how to play the guitar.

UNCLE JIM   You did not. I did that, that was me. First three chords he ever learned, come from me, that was all my doing.

SHARON   On an old Silvertone, right?

UNCLE JIM   Sears and Roebuck, acoustic Sunburst with a white pick guard. G, C, and E. First three chords, G, C, and E. Over and over again. Tell you what, though, two weeks time, that boy knew half a dozen different chords. Playing whole songs, strumming that thing better than I ever did. Just picked it up and ran.

SHARON   He's a natural.

UNCLE JIM   That's for certain. Gifted and talented young man, good at whatever he puts his mind to, really.

SHARON   Well . . .

UNCLE JIM   And not just the guitar neither. Good at sports, all kinds of activities.

SHARON   Yep.

UNCLE JIM   Just one of them people, you know, one of them special, touched-by-God kind of people.

SHARON   Uh-huh.

UNCLE JIM   Excelled at everything, basketball, football, baseball . . .

SHARON   He fucked my best friend in our bed while I was at work.

[*Pause.*]

UNCLE JIM   [*Quietly.*] Hockey, bowling, horseshoes . . .

SHARON   Used to blame myself for all that. Figured I was doing something wrong, you know, lackin' in some way. Couldn't just be that he was a selfish taker, despicable shit, with no regard for other people or their feelings. Couldn't be that he's too special.

[*Pause.*]

But who gives a shit, right? I don't give a shit.

[*She drinks.*]

UNCLE JIM   [*Quietly.*] I don't give a shit neither.

SHARON   So, you still play, guitar, I mean?

UNCLE JIM   Oh, no, no. I give that old one of mine to Justin, keepsake. Never thought to replace it, truthfully, wasn't that good to begin with.

SHARON   Saying you just quit?

UNCLE JIM   No, yeah, yes, I did, I quit, just quit.

[*Pause.*]

Did purchase a ukulele a while back but . . . don't even know what I did with that thing.

[*Beat.*]

And truthfully, I don't give a shit.

[*Pause.*]

SHARON   I don't give a shit, neither. Can't all be world-famous superstars, right? Riding around in limos, spying billboards with our faces on them.

UNCLE JIM   S'right. Gotta have regular people, too. People to pick the fruit, put out the fires, and clean the vomit off the Tilt-a-Whirl.

SHARON   Can't believe you were actually a fucking "carny."

UNCLE JIM   Respectable work. Plus, you get to travel, you're paid in cash. Only negative is the heat, the smell, and the people.

[*Beat.*]

So, how about you?

SHARON   How about me what?

UNCLE JIM   Are you, you know, musically inclined at all?

SHARON   Don't play any instruments, if that's what you mean. Clarinet, a little in high school, but no guitar or nothing.

[*Beat.*]

Used to sing quite a bit, here and there.

UNCLE JIM   Did you now? Like in church or the Sweet Adelines. . . ?

SHARON   [*Angry.*] No, not in church or the Sweet fucking Adelines! In a band, man, in a country band. A good country band.

UNCLE JIM   Oh, okay. Sorry.

SHARON   That's how I met Justin in the first place. He'd come see us play, follow us around from bar to bar. First in-town gigs he ever got were my doing.

UNCLE JIM   That right? You still involved with all that or . . . ?

SHARON   No. Jim. I am not.

[*Drinks.*]

I quit. Gave it all up. Walked away. Only room for one star in our particular galaxy and it certainly wasn't gonna be me.

[*Beat.*]

Not that I'm bitter about it or anything.

UNCLE JIM   Well, probably better off, you know, tough racket. Dog eat dog.

SHARON   Dog eat dog, indeed. Besides, didn't have time to pursue my music and work forty hours a week, to pay our rent. Add on bein' Justin's cheerleader and doormat and there was no time for me at all. No time. Focus had to be completely on him, his career. His happiness.

[*Beat.*]

His fucking happiness.

UNCLE JIM   Never too late, you know, get back into it, singing and all that, if you really wanted to.

SHARON   I believe the ship has sailed on my music career. Easier to chase that dream when you're younger. You know, twice as dumb and half as afraid.

UNCLE JIM   What are you talking about? You're still a young woman, full of piss and vinegar, got plenty of life ahead of you.

SHARON   Well, let's just call that "the third opinion."

[*Pause.*]

'Sides what if I tried and failed, found out I wasn't good enough? Be right where I am now, but with nobody else to blame it on.

[*Sighing.*]

What's done is done. Is done.

[*Pause. She takes a drink.*]

UNCLE JIM   When I was a youngster, I wanted to be Evel Knievel.

SHARON   [*Smiling.*] That right?

UNCLE JIM   Sailing a motorcycle through the air, over cars, busses and flying all the way across the Snake River Canyon.

SHARON   Boyhood dream, huh?

UNCLE JIM   Quickly soured after jumping my Stingray off the roof of our house and shattering my jaw on the handlebars.

SHARON   That'll do it.

UNCLE JIM   Three months wired shut, sucking beef bouillon through a Silly Straw. Ample time to reevaluate my dreams of becoming a world-famous daredevil. And any time I get too full of myself, open my mouth too wide, I hear that little click in my mandible, reminding me of my limitations. My poor, pitiful limitations.

[*Pause.*]

SHARON   [*Mocking.*] Waah!

UNCLE JIM   Hey, fuck you.

SHARON   You let one broken jaw stop you from pursuing your dreams?

UNCLE JIM   Ever had your jaw broke? Once is more than plenty, and you go out of your way to make sure it never fuckin' happens again.

SHARON   Need to climb back on that hog, Jim. Real hog this time, though. Seriously, I got my Triumph parked right outside.

[*She picks up the helmet.*]

UNCLE JIM   A motorcycle? Shit, that ain't never, never gonna happen.

SHARON   [*Tossing him the helmet.*] You'll be fine, wear my helmet, protect that weird little head of yours.

UNCLE JIM   [*Tossing it back.*] Fuck you, my head ain't weird. Your head's weird.

SHARON   Just a few wheelies around the parking lot. Let's do it.

UNCLE JIM   No, no, I'm pretty fucked up, even for me.

SHARON   Don't have to jump any cars or anything, few laps around the perimeter.

UNCLE JIM   If you wanna kill me, just pick up that rifle and shoot me in the face.

SHARON   Come on. You'll be fine, it'll be fun.

UNCLE JIM   No, no, you do it and I'll watch.

SHARON   Okay, forget it. I understand you're scared. Too old for that kind of thing, anyway.

[*Pause. She smiles.*]

UNCLE JIM   You goading me?

SHARON   Little bit.

UNCLE JIM   Petunia, I could finish the rest of that bottle and half of another, eat a plate of biscuits and gravy, beat you in a straight-up foot race, then love you till your eyes bug out.

SHARON   Promises, promises, old-timer.

UNCLE JIM   Fine, I'll bite your bait.

[*Standing.*]

But if I live, you're singing me a song.

SHARON   [*Smiling.*] Deal.

UNCLE JIM   Alright. Grab that helmet so I don't split open my weird little head.

SHARON   You'll be fine.

[*She puts the helmet on him.*]

UNCLE JIM   My luck, I'd crash, not die, and end up a drooling vegetable. Kid at my grocery store ran his Harley into a parked car. Now he's got oatmeal brains and more stitches than a baseball.

SHARON   [*Tightening the strap.*] Just keep this on.

UNCLE JIM   Last week I saw him talking to a can of hominy.

[*Dramatically.*]

And I don't want that.

SHARON   Ain't gonna let nothing happen to you. Trust me, James Byron.

UNCLE JIM   Ain't heard a woman call me that in a hundred years.

[*Pause, choking up.*]

I was holding one hand, her mama was holding the other.

[*She puts her hand on him.*]

SHARON   What's your favorite song, partner?

UNCLE JIM   No favorites, just anything by Hank Senior. See, I like old country. Everything new is shit.

SHARON   Well, you're in luck, because I like old country, too.

[*The door opens and* JUSTIN *and* OLLIE *enter, playing grab-ass.*]

JUSTIN   . . . better finish what you started, girl.

OLLIE   You're terrible.

[*They see* SHARON *and* UNCLE JIM.]

SHARON   [*Laughing, to* JUSTIN.] Well, proclivity's consistent but your preference seems to have shifted.

JUSTIN   Surprise attack, huh? Some things never change.

SHARON   They certainly do not.

OLLIE   [*To* JUSTIN.] Everything okay?

JUSTIN   Be best for you to run along now.

SHARON   [*Shaking her head.*] Boy, if I had a nickel . . .

OLLIE   [*To* JUSTIN.] Seriously, security's just a phone call away.

JUSTIN   Scram, faggot!

OLLIE   Excuse me?

[*Pause.*]

Fine. Whatever you say, Mister Spears.

[*Beat.*]

You folks have yourselves a pleasant evening.

[OLLIE *crosses out.*]

SHARON   That's gonna cost you a nice dinner and a new pair of Tony Lama's.

JUSTIN   Figured you'd have a little more class than to pull a stunt like this. But, I've learned to lower my expectations when it comes to women and their ridiculous behavior.

SHARON   Good thing you've switched to little boys then. They'll do exactly what you tell them, plus you all can trade underpants.

UNCLE JIM   [*Chuckling.*] Underpants.

[*Standing.*]

I better give you folks some privacy. . . .

JUSTIN   Sit down, Jim.

UNCLE JIM   [*Sitting.*] Okee-dokee.

JUSTIN   Need somebody in the room, witness, in case communication goes south and this bitch decides to scream "rape."

SHARON   Ain't here to fight with you, Justin. But call me "bitch" one more time and you'll be rapin' yourself with your own dick. Meaning I'll snap it off with my bare hands and ram it up your ass with a hammer.

UNCLE JIM   I'd listen to her, boy.

JUSTIN   Shut up.

[*To* SHARON.]

State your business, then skedaddle.

SHARON   Straight to the point. I like that. Show's confidence. And way sexier than when you'd lay your head on my lap, crying about some gig you'd lost or a mean old label that passed on your demo.

JUSTIN   Ain't nobody passing on anything anymore, sweetheart. Case you haven't noticed, I'm an industry now. Global, worldwide.

SHARON   You are Mickey fucking Mouse, to be certain. Guessing you pay somebody now to brush the sweat stains off your good Stetson and wipe your pee-pee off the toilet seat.

JUSTIN   Learned to straddle the bowl and my Stetson's pristine, because I ain't sweating anything, baby.

SHARON   Sure you're not. People like you can't be bothered with things like a conscience, morality, or even the tiniest shred of human decency.

JUSTIN   What do you want to hear? I'm sorry I'm successful? I regret that all my years of struggle and hard work paid off for me?

SHARON   I don't want to hear that, 'cause it'd be bullshit. What I'd like from you is a simple acknowledgement of my contribution to your life, your success.

JUSTIN   You know, I recall writing a couple of checks that you refused to take, so beyond that I don't know what I can do.

SHARON   Say "thank you." That's what you can do. Climb off your pedestal for one second, look me in the eyes, and say "thank you." "Thank you for takin' care of me when I needed somebody to take care of me." "Thank you for believing in me when nobody else did." "Thank you for not turning your back on me, when everybody else had." Just acknowledge the fact that other people, me especially, played a part in getting you where you are right now.

[*He stares at her blankly. Pause.*]

JUSTIN   How about a framed gold record? That'd be pretty cool, right?

[*She slaps him hard.*]

SHARON   Fuck you. Who do you think you're talking to, big shot? I took you off the street and kept you afloat for years—

JUSTIN   [*Interrupting.*] Anything else?

[*She takes a key out of her pocket.*]

SHARON   Key to our storage unit. I'm leaving town and there's some stuff in there you might actually want.

JUSTIN   I don't want any of that shit.

SHARON   You don't take it, I'm gonna toss it.

JUSTIN   Toss it then.

SHARON   [*Sighing.*] You might want to take a look at it first. It's stuff from early on, early on with us. Pictures, boots, old stage clothes.

JUSTIN   You hang on to it. Be worth a pretty penny one day.

SHARON   [*Angry.*] No. Thank you. I am not hanging on to anything. Pissed away years doing that. And all it took were two different doctors saying the same two words to make me realize how much time I have truly wasted.

[*Pause.*]

JUSTIN   What were the two—?

SHARON   [*Angry.*] First one was ovarian.

[*Pause.*]

Alright, okay, there it is, what are you gonna do? "Too many kids in the world anyway." Right? Wasn't that your mantra?

JUSTIN   [*Quietly.*] Tough break.

SHARON   Yes. It is, isn't it? It is a tough break. But luckily, it ain't my first, in fact, it's turned into kind of a theme.

[*Pause.*]

Anyway, heading to Knoxville to stay with my mom. Doing my treatments there.

[*She stares at* JUSTIN. *He looks away.*]

Say something. Please say something. Don't just stand there with that dumb-ass smirk on your dumb-ass face.

[*Shouting.*]

Say something!

UNCLE JIM   Truly sorry for you, ma'am. Young woman like yourself, dealt a hand like that, don't make no sense. Folks always try to find some kind of meaning during these difficult times, but that's just folly. Feeble attempts to insinuate purpose to the random, hateful misfortunes of life.

SHARON   [*To* JUSTIN.] The random, hateful misfortunes of life.

[*Pause.*]

Now I know who the real poet in your family is.

[JUSTIN *glares at* UNCLE JIM. SHARON *puts the key in* JUSTIN's *shirt pocket.*]

Enjoy your honeymoon.

[*Pause.*]

Nice to meet you, James Byron.

[*She exits.*]

UNCLE JIM   Nice to meet you. Sharon Mary.

[*Long pause.*]

Never got to hear her sing.

JUSTIN   Strictly amateur.

UNCLE JIM   We're all amateurs, boy. Sooner you grasp on to that fact, better off you'll be.

JUSTIN   Spilled the beans about writing all my songs, didn't you?

UNCLE JIM   That's your takeaway from all that?

[*Crying.*]

No. I didn't say anything. Your secret's safe. Besides, I've never written a song in my life. I'm just a poor, ignorant hog farmer that learned you to play the guitar.

[UNCLE JIM *stands, picks up the gun, and crosses towards the hallway.*]

JUSTIN   Where you going?

UNCLE JIM   Going to bed.

JUSTIN   Why you takin' the gun?

UNCLE JIM   Gonna kill myself again.

JUSTIN   Stay up awhile, have a drink with me.

UNCLE JIM   I've had enough for one night, more than enough.

JUSTIN   Come on, you're here on my dime, least you can do—

UNCLE JIM   [*Exploding, pointing the gun at* JUSTIN.] Fuck you, boy! I am not your court jester, trained monkey, or one of them hired lackeys you got tying your ballet slippers! We clear?

JUSTIN   Yes, sir.

UNCLE JIM   Yes, sir, is right!

[*Crying.*]

I'm your kin, your elder, and I'll paint these walls with your fucking brains you ever talk to me that way again!

[*Long pause.*]

JUSTIN   Sorry, Uncle Jim.

[*Quietly.*]

I'm a fucking asshole.

UNCLE JIM   Indeed, you are. Top five I've ever met, truthfully. Praying it'll pass.

[*Starts to leave, stops.*]

Need to ask you a question. Did you love that woman?

JUSTIN   I don't know.

[*Smirking.*]

I've loved a lot of women, Jim.

UNCLE JIM   [*Pointing the gun.*] I'll ask again.

JUSTIN   Said I don't know. Think maybe. At the time I thought I did.

UNCLE JIM   What about the gal you're marrying tomorrow? You love her?

JUSTIN   I don't know. How do you ever really know if you love someone?

UNCLE JIM   Usually you don't until it's too late. Until they're snatched away from you. Then you know.

[*Lost.*]

Then you know for certain.

[*Pause.*]

G'night, nephew.

JUSTIN   Night.

[*A knock at the door.*]

UNCLE JIM   Your little boyfriend probably circled back. Have fun sodomizing each other. I'll be in my room with six pillows covering my head.

[**UNCLE JIM** *exits down the hall. Pause.* **JUSTIN** *takes the key out of his pocket and looks at it.*]

JUSTIN   [*Quietly.*] Stuff from early on. Early on with us.

[*Another knock.* **JUSTIN** *pockets the key, then crosses to the door and opens it.* **PAUL** *and* **CHUCK** *enter.*]\

PAUL   Had the key card changed without a proper breakup. That's just spiteful now. Isn't that spiteful, Chuck?

CHUCK   Inconsiderate and spiteful.

JUSTIN   Alright, don't start in, I'm in no mood. Let's all just have a drink and talk this thing out.

PAUL   You wanna talk it out now?

CHUCK   [*To* **PAUL**.] So, now he wants to talk.

JUSTIN   Been friends a long time, no reason in the world to piss that all away.

PAUL   You hear that, Chuck? He's telling us he wants to stay friends. That's sweet. Isn't that sweet?

CHUCK   Precious and sweet.

JUSTIN   Don't wanna make a big deal out of it. Had a good run, everybody made a lot of money. You're still standing up at my wedding, this here, this is just business.

PAUL   So, you're advising us to focus on the good times and ignore the kitchen knives we got quivering in the middle of our backs?

CHUCK   Stabbed in the fucking back.

JUSTIN   Yes, that's what I'm advising.

[*Beat.*]

Or you boys can keep actin' like a couple of assholes, we can all lawyer up and burn the house down. Either way, I'll still be sitting at the top of the charts and you fellows will be booking dead Opry stars into county fairs.

[*Pause.*]

You cunts decide.

PAUL   Oh, now, no call for that, Justin. That's ugly. Hateful and ugly, isn't it, Chuck?

CHUCK   Very hateful and extremely ugly.

JUSTIN   Fine, see you bitches at the deposition.

PAUL   [*Holding up his iPhone.*] Course, not as ugly as this thirty seconds of video I got with America's favorite singing cowboy sucking on some bellboy's "peeder."

CHUCK   [*Holding up his iPhone.*] You know, I got the same video. And that is ugly.

[JUSTIN *looks at them, taken aback.*]

PAUL   And that judgment call is not based on the act itself or in any way meant as a homophobic slur. To each his own. Right, Chuck?

CHUCK   Absolutely. Live and let live.

PAUL   We're basin' our assessment more on the angle of the phone and the harsh fluorescent lighting in that service elevator.

CHUCK   Very unflattering.

PAUL   Suppose we could correct some things with a little digital magic. Smooth out the color, eliminate the glare. We'll do what we can if we decide to go viral with this thing. But careful to preserve the unmistakable image of one Justin Spears on his knees, in a public place, fellating another man with astonishing fluidity.

CHUCK   And that little bellboy is hung like a racehorse. Which I think explains his aggressive and confident demeanor.

PAUL   He'll make a nice addition to our little roster of stars. Justin, did you get a chance to hear his music? Did he happen to hum or sing while you were licking on him like a Popsicle?

JUSTIN   Said he had a song on his iPhone he wanted me to hear.

[*Pause, then smiling.*]

Fine. What's it going take to make it go away?

PAUL   Oh, it ain't going away. Nor are we. See, you, me, and Chuck are married now. For life.

[*Holding up his phone.*]

This here's our pre-nup. Which I've already e-mailed to my home computer as well as Chuck's.

JUSTIN   Think I'm gonna stay in business with you after this stunt?

PAUL   Well, you could tell me to go fuck myself, run downstairs, dump this whole mess into Larry Meyer's lap. But he might not find your new relationship as alluring when he gets a look at your dirty little dowry.

CHUCK   On your knees in an elevator . . .

PAUL   Pressing the down button on some innocent young boy who claims you took advantage of him, manipulated him with drugs, alcohol, and the sweet promise of stardom.

JUSTIN   Gonna blackmail me now? After everything I've done for you?

PAUL   When you were playing in shit dives for ten bucks and two free drinks, it was me and Chuck standing in the back of the room, supporting you. When you had no money to buy a new shirt, make your rent or eat a hot fucking meal, it was me and Chuck who provided. And now you think you can just toss us aside. Discard us, like some woman. No. Huh-uh. That ain't never gonna happen. Because right now, in this particular scenario, you're the woman. You're the bitch.

CHUCK   [*Blow-job gesture.*] In more ways than one, Sugar Lips.

[*Pause.*]

JUSTIN   Fuck you, two-bit scumbag assholes.

PAUL   No, sweetie pie. Fuck you.

CHUCK   Yeah, yeah, fuck you.

[*Exploding.*]

And your big fat sister, too.

[JUSTIN *lunges at* CHUCK. *They slap at each other, then fall to the floor, wrestling.*]

[PAUL *takes a cigar out of his pocket and bites off the tip as they roll around.*]

JUSTIN   Son of a bitch!

CHUCK   Cocksucker! Cocksucker!

JUSTIN   Fuckin' kill you!

PAUL   [*Calmly.*] Break it up. Chuck. Come on now. That'll do.

[CHUCK *starts choking* JUSTIN.]

CHUCK   My last girlfriend was a fucking model, homo!

[*A loud gunshot is heard offstage.* PAUL *and* CHUCK *run down the hall.* JUSTIN *crosses to a chair and sits.* PAUL *and* CHUCK *cross in, carrying* UNCLE JIM *by his arms. He is in mid-seizure, clutching the rifle and still wearing the motorcycle helmet, which now has a bullet hole and powder burn on it.*]

PAUL   [*To* CHUCK.] Grab some juice! Jim, stay with us, buddy, come on.

[CHUCK *runs to the bar.* UNCLE JIM *falls to the floor.* PAUL *tries to grab him and the gun.*]

CHUCK   Get that gun away from him.

PAUL   Got a death grip on it.

[*There's a knock at the door,* CHUCK *crosses to* PAUL *with the juice.* PAUL *takes it as* CHUCK *pulls the gun away from* UNCLE JIM.]

PAUL   Jim, sip some of this juice now! Justin, answer the door.

[*Beat.*]

Answer the fucking door!

[JUSTIN *crosses to the door as* PAUL *and* CHUCK *struggle to get* UNCLE JIM *to drink the juice.*]

PAUL   Come on, Jim. A little more, sip on a little more.

[JUSTIN *opens the door, revealing* OLLIE. *He crosses in.*]

OLLIE   Did someone fire a fucking gun up here?

JUSTIN   Accident. My uncle had a seizure, diabetic . . .

OLLIE   Do I need to call a doctor?

JUSTIN   No, no doctor.

OLLIE   What about the police?

JUSTIN   Don't need to call anybody. It's taken care of.

OLLIE   So, no need to involve the authorities in this or any other improprieties?

JUSTIN   Under control.

OLLIE   Good. Good to hear. No reason in the world for things to get ugly. That just wastes everybody's time. Right?

JUSTIN   [*Seething.*] Set me up.

OLLIE   Set yourself up. But I'm confident you and I will get past this itty-bitty rough patch in our relationship. You'll find, Justin, that I have a very forgiving and empathetic nature.

JUSTIN   And you feel okay gaining entry this way?

OLLIE   Whatever I need to do to get my foot in the door. Seizing the opportunities as they

[*Smiling.*]

arise.

JUSTIN You're gonna do real well in this world.

OLLIE Means a lot coming from you. One of my peers.

[*Pause.*]

Well, if you gentlemen have this handled, I'll be downstairs giving the manager my notice.

[*To* JUSTIN.]

You need a Tic-Tac. Faggot.

[OLLIE *crosses out, leaving the door open.* UNCLE JIM'*s seizure subsides. He looks at* PAUL. *Pause.*]

PAUL You okay, partner?

UNCLE JIM Did I ruin the party?

PAUL No, it's fine. Everything's fine.

UNCLE JIM Where am I?

PAUL Hiram Hotel in Nashville, Tennessee.

UNCLE JIM Nashville.

[*Beat.*]

Am I with Barbara Mandrell?

PAUL [*Smiling.*] No, sir.

UNCLE JIM No, sir.

[*Beat.*]

Any of the Mandrell sisters?

PAUL Sorry.

UNCLE JIM Dare to dream. Otherwise, got a head full of nightmares.

[*Pause.*]

Only looked away from that road for a split second, one careless glance. Spied a gi-normous raccoon inching up a radio tower. Turned back, saw nothing but headlights.

[SHARON *crosses in quietly and stands in the doorway. She and* JUSTIN *stare at each other.*]

Everything broke apart. Whole world shattered. Windshield, dashboard and that little face and body. I kept reaching out, flailing to hold it back, keep it at bay. But I was too weak and the impact was too powerful. Finally, I give up, surrendered to it, turned away, closed my eyes, and prayed to God to take us both, not just kill her and leave me to carry that around.

[*Pause.*]

He must not have heard me. Bigger fish to fry, I reckon.

SHARON   Always bigger fish somewhere.

UNCLE JIM   [*Wiping his eyes.*] Sharon Mary.

JUSTIN   Had a feeling you'd circle back.

SHARON   Know me pretty well.

JUSTIN   Lot left to say, I reckon.

SHARON   Not on my end. Come back for my helmet is all.

[*She crosses to* UNCLE JIM.]

UNCLE JIM   Thing will stop a bullet, sorry to say.

[*She looks at the hole in the helmet and smiles sadly. Pause.*]

SHARON   Why don't you come tag along with me, Evel Knievel? Keep me company. I could use a little company.

UNCLE JIM   Might could be coerced. Trusting your invitation is sincere.

[*Pause. She looks around the room, uncomfortable, then smiles.*]

SHARON   [*Singing.*] "Well, I'm a rolling stone all alone and lost, and for a life of sin, I have paid the cost . . ."

UNCLE JIM   [*Quietly.*] When I pass by . . .

SHARON   [*Singing.*] "When I pass by, all the people say, just another guy on the lost highway."

UNCLE JIM   Just a deck of cards.

SHARON   [*Singing.*] "Just a deck of cards and a jug of wine, and a woman's lies made a life like mine. Oh, the day we met, I went astray, I started rolling down that lost highway."

[*Pause. He stands.*]

UNCLE JIM   I'm your huckleberry.

SHARON   Let's roll.

UNCLE JIM   Need to take it slow, though, until I get the feel of it.

SHARON   If you're insinuating yourself in the driver's seat, that ain't never, ever going to happen. You'll be "sitting bitch."

UNCLE JIM   Fine with that, too.

JUSTIN   [*To* UNCLE JIM.] Not coming to my wedding?

UNCLE JIM   I'll come to the next one. And the only amateur in this room, boy, is you.

[UNCLE JIM *crosses to the door.*]

PAUL   Been a long time, Sharon.

SHARON   Not long enough, prick.

[*To* JUSTIN.]

Give Miss Tennessee my best. I hope you two are very happy together.

JUSTIN   Don't mean that.

SHARON   Fucked-up thing is, I do. After all your bullshit, I still wish you well and never want any harm to come to you.

JUSTIN   Appreciate it.

SHARON   No, you don't.

[*Beat.*]

But one day you will.

[SHARON *crosses out,* UNCLE JIM *starts to follow, then turns back.*]

UNCLE JIM   Old bull and a young bull standing top of a hill . . . well, you know the rest.

[*To* PAUL *and* CHUCK.]

Gentlemen.

[UNCLE JIM *exits. Pause.*]

CHUCK   She's looking good.

PAUL   Always did.

CHUCK   Sounded good, too.

PAUL   Always did.

[*To* JUSTIN.]

Well. Better get some sleep. Big day tomorrow.

JUSTIN   [*Distracted.*] Big day?

PAUL   Wedding day.

CHUCK   Getting married in the morning, son.

JUSTIN   Right. Wedding day.

PAUL   Joyous occasion.

CHUCK   Blessed and joyous.

JUSTIN   Yeah, listen, about tonight, I'm not really interested in Larry Meyer.

PAUL   No?

JUSTIN   Hell no. Just felt good to be, you know, pursued.

PAUL   Having somebody else wanting you. Certainly get that.

CHUCK   Understand that inclination.

JUSTIN   But it don't mean nothing.

PAUL   Hey, we've been together a long time, three of us.

CHUCK   And sometimes you just want something fresh and new.

PAUL   Untainted, you know, unencumbered, by all that history.

CHUCK   Bittersweet history.

JUSTIN   [*Emotional.*] Truth is, my daddy never showed me no kind of love growing up, and so—

PAUL   [*Interrupting.*] Don't matter.

[*Beat.*]

And I don't care.

[PAUL *crosses menacingly towards* JUSTIN. CHUCK *follows suit.*]

It don't matter and I don't care. It don't matter and I don't care. It don't matter and I don't care.

[*Beat.*]

Don't matter.

[PAUL *grabs* JUSTIN *in a bear hug.* CHUCK *does the same.*]

CHUCK   Don't care.

[PAUL's *phone rings; he looks at the caller ID.*]

PAUL   Bitch.

[*Smiling.*]

I mean, "bride to be."

JUSTIN   Can you handle that for me?

PAUL   Proud to. Be my honor and pleasure, Mister Spears.

CHUCK   Honor and pleasure.

[JUSTIN *stares at the two of them, then exits down the hall.*]

PAUL   [*Looking at the phone.*] Pick a lie. Any lie.

CHUCK   No need to fabricate. Tell her he went to bed.

PAUL   Ain't never going to swallow that.

CHUCK   Why not? It's the truth.

PAUL   Pilgrim, we passed the truth about two hundred miles ago.

[*Into phone.*]

Hello, darling, how are you? What? No, he ain't here right now. Honestly, I don't know where he is. Did you try him on his cell phone? Huh. Well, that's a mystery, to be certain, but I wouldn't worry your pretty little head about it. I'm sure everything is fine, with him, with you, with me, everything is going to be just fine. Just fine for everybody.

[*The lights slowly fade.*]

NICE GIRL

by

Melissa Ross

Photograph by Larkin Clark

Production History

Nice Girl was originally produced by Labyrinth Theater Company (Mimi O'Donnell, artistic director; Danny Feldman, executive director) in May 2015. The cast was as follows:

Cast

Donny   Nick Cordero
Josephine   Diane Davis
Francine   Kathryn Kates
Sherry   Liv Rooth

The director was Mimi O'Donnell.

Biography

Melissa Ross's plays include *Thinner Than Water, You Are Here, Do Something Pretty, A Life Extra Ordinary, Nice Girl,* and *Of Good Stock. Thinner Than Water* and *Nice Girl* were both originally produced by Labyrinth Theater Company. *Thinner Than Water* is included in the anthology *New Playwrights: Best Plays of 2011,* published by Smith and Kraus. *Of Good Stock* received its world premiere at South Coast Repertory as a part of the Pacific Playwrights Festival, followed by a subsequent production at Manhattan Theater Club. Melissa has had readings and workshops with the Amoralists, the Cherry Lane Theater, Colt Coeur, Dorset Theater Festival, the Gift Theatre, Iama Theatre Company, the Juilliard School, Labyrinth Theater Company, LCT3, Manhattan Theater Club, Montana Rep, New York Stage and Film, the New Group, South Coast Repertory, Rattlestick Playwrights Theater, and the TheatreWorks Palo Alto New Works Festival. She has received commissions from South Coast Repertory and Manhattan Theater Club. Melissa is a graduate of the Lila Acheson Wallace Playwriting Program at the Juilliard School, a two-time winner of the Le Comte de Nouy Prize, and is a proud member of Labyrinth Theater Company.

Characters

Jo   37, a secretary
Francine   68, her mother
Sherry   34, Jo's co-worker
Donny   38, a butcher

Time and Place

A middle-class suburb of Boston.

Fall 1984

The Text

A slash in the middle of a line indicates overlapping dialogue. Internal punctuation inside of a sentence should serve as a guide for emphasis and intention and not be considered true stops. A beat is a quick shift in thought— a momentary breath—and should not be given *too* much significance. Pauses have a bit more weight. Silences should be allowed to linger.

ACT ONE

[*A simply furnished and neatly kept home in a small suburb of Massachusetts outside of Boston. It's not a wealthy suburb. This is not the Massachusetts of the Kennedys. And it is not terribly poor or blue collar. It is decidedly exactly-in-the-middle class. And it's happy to be that way. This is a town that doesn't color outside of the lines.*

There is a living room and an adjacent kitchen. A staircase leads to an upper floor. A small screened-in porch with an outdoor set. A glider. Some slightly rusted chairs. All with the same flowered cushions. Faded from years in the sun.

The furnishings are clean but old. A mix of relics from generations past. And a few new things here and there. Not cluttered. And kept nicely. The house was built sometime in the fifties. And has been updated only as needed since then. So. A new fridge next to the original stove.

The entire play should take place here. All settings should be created from and suggested by the house itself. A kitchen counter becomes a supermarket's butcher shop. A table and chairs turn into an office break room. But the general feeling should be that wherever we go. We're still here.

Jo gets ready for work. Drinking coffee. Reading the paper. Busying herself in the kitchen.

FRANCINE *drinks coffee at the kitchen table and watches television. She wears a nightgown. Perhaps a housecoat. And slippers. This is her everyday attire. Even in this ensemble, she looks neat and put together. She wears lipstick.*

They are in the midst of what appears to be their every morning ritual.]

One

Jo   I'm leaving money over here by the microwave/OK?

FRANCINE   Yeah yeah.

Jo   You gotta call the taxi an hour before/you wanna go.

FRANCINE   Yeah yeah.

Jo   And it takes a half-hour to get to Dr. Elliot's.

FRANCINE   I know I know. Stop nagging me/to death.

Jo   Not *nagging*, Ma. *Reminding.*

FRANCINE   I don't need all this. Constant. Looking after/you know.

Jo   Yeah yeah.

FRANCINE   I don't!

Jo   Fine I'll. Move out then.

FRANCINE   Go ahead. Whado I care for.

Jo   What wouldja do if I moved out, Ma.

FRANCINE   Whatever I want. I'd do just fine.

Jo   [*A little laugh.*] Sure you would.

FRANCINE   I would do whatever I want whenever I want so. So screw you.

Jo   Yeah OK so maybe I'll go to work today and I won't ever come back. Whadya think of that.

FRANCINE   Be fine with me!

[*Beat.*]

You wouldn't really do that Jo. Not really you wouldn't.

Jo   You push my buttons enough, Ma. I may just walk out that door and never come back. And then what/would you do.

FRANCINE   You don't have the guts.

Jo   Try me. Push one more button and see. Go on. I dare you. Push it.

[*Pause.*]

Now who doesn't have the guts. Huh?

[*Beat.*]

You wanna egg or a bagel.

FRANCINE   Bagel. But just a half.

Jo   OK.

[Jo *begins to slice a bagel.*]

FRANCINE   Don't cut it like that you'll slice your/hand up.

Jo   I know howta cut a bagel!

[*She cuts her hand.*]

Damnit.

FRANCINE   I/told you.

Jo   Shut it.

FRANCINE   Is it bad?

Jo   No/I'm fine.

FRANCINE   Don't get blood on my bagel.

Jo   [*Shoots her a look.*] I *won't.*

[*She puts the bagel in the toaster and begins to tend to her hand.*]

FRANCINE   [*Beat.*] You'd really just leave without saying good-bye? You wouldn't do that, Josephine.

Jo   Maybe.

FRANCINE   Where would you go?

Jo   . . . Paris . . .

FRANCINE   Paris? By yourself?

Jo   Maybe I/will maybe.

FRANCINE   Whadya gonna do in *Paris*?

Jo   Eat delicious food. See. Art.

FRANCINE   [*Beat.*] Your father took me to Paris for our third/anniversary.

Jo   Yeah I know.

FRANCINE   Bought me the most gorgeous clothes. You should go through the boxes in the basement. Take whatever you want.

Jo   What I want your old clothes for.

FRANCINE   Styles come back. I had this dress with a nipped-in waist. Looked just like something I saw on TV/the other day.

Jo   Or maybe. Spain.

FRANCINE   My waist was so small the dressmaker hadda take it in. Nineteen inches around. She couldn't believe anybody hadda waist/that small.

Jo   Or maybe Milwaukee.

FRANCINE   What're you talking about?

JO   Places I could go.

FRANCINE   Who goes to *Milwaukee*?

JO   Me maybe. Or Australia . . . Australia takes twenty-four hours to get to. It'd be like. Getting a day of my life back.

FRANCINE   Not really.

[*Pause.*]

Maybe I'll come too!

JO   [*A little laugh.*] No thank you!

FRANCINE   Come on! It'll be fun! You and me take a nice trip.

JO   Can't wear a nightgown and slippers on an airplane, Ma.

FRANCINE   Smart mouth.

JO   You *can't*.

FRANCINE   I know that!

[*Beat.*]

Way people dress nowadays who the heck cares anyway. People wear dungarees everywhere.

JO   It's the style, Ma.

FRANCINE   People useta make/an effort.

JO   Uh-huh.

FRANCINE   Dress nice on the airplane. Men in ties. Women got their best furs on./Not like now.

JO   I laid your clothes out nice on the bed.

FRANCINE   What'd you do that for?

JO   As a friendly reminder.

FRANCINE   What's so friendly about it.

[*Beat.*]

You treat me like I'm a moron.

JO   I do not.

FRANCINE   You and your father both useta think you were so smart. With your college degrees and your fancy-schmancy things/you know.

JO   Don't have a college degree, Ma.

FRANCINE   Just *about*.

JO   Not even a year's worth.

FRANCINE   Well. You're still smart.

[*Beat. No response.*]

You hear me Josephine? You're still a/very smart girl.

JO   I hear you Ma! I hear you!

[*Silence. Coffee drinking. Bagel eating. Newspaper reading. TV watching.*]

FRANCINE   What time you coming home tonight?

JO   What time do I always come home.

FRANCINE   Six-thirty.

JO   So . . . There you go. Why'd you ask?

FRANCINE   Just. Making conversation.

[*Pause.*]

You got a phone call yesterday.

JO   You take a note?

FRANCINE   Forgot . . .

JO   How many times do we haveta go over this? You wanna answer the phone you gotta/write down a message.

FRANCINE   It's my house! I can answer the phone if I want to without/ getting permission!

JO   Fine! But you gotta take messages!

FRANCINE   I got a good memory though.

JO   OK so who called?

FRANCINE   A woman.

JO   That's. Extraordinarily helpful, Ma.

FRANCINE   It was about the reunion.

JO   Oh. Jeez. Forgot about that.

FRANCINE   You gonna go?

JO   Haven't decided yet.

FRANCINE   Go! You should go! You never go anywhere!

JO   I go plenty of places.

FRANCINE   Where do you go? Besides imaginary trips to. *Milwaukee.*

[*Beat.*]

Maybe you'll get a romance going.

Jo   With *who*?

Francine   Somebody at the reunion!

Jo   [*A little laugh.*] Yeah. Maybe.

Francine   People reconnect at reunions all the time. I read an article in *People* magazine/about that.

Jo   They're all married Ma.

Francine   How do you know?

Jo   Cuz most people my age live around here are married!

Francine   Maybe somebody's a widower?

Jo   [*Laughs.*] Maybe.

Francine   Or divorced? Lotta people get divorced/these days.

Jo   Yeah sure.

Francine   Get a new dress. Get a nice hairstyle.

Jo   Maybe.

Francine   You gotta good figure when you don't dress like a schlump. You should put yourself together more.

Jo   Like you?

Francine   *I* always have lipstick on. Even when I'm just in the house. Because/you never know.

Jo   You never know.

Francine   And I'm an old lady honey. I don't need to put myself together. But you're young.

Jo   No I'm not.

Francine   You're younger than me.

Jo   Younger than *you* isn't. *Young.*

[*Beat.*]

Maybe we'll go to a movie tonight Ma. Whadya think huh? See what's playing at South Shore Plaza. Go to Brighams after. Get a cone?

Francine   See how I feel later./But maybe.

Jo   Yeah sure.

[*Beat.*]

Get dressed today Ma. Nice sweater. Pair of slacks.

FRANCINE   Nothing fits.

Jo   It does so fit. What I set out/for you fits.

FRANCINE   I gotta lose ten pounds. After the change you put it on in the belly. I never/had a belly.

Jo   You gotta get dressed if you're going to/Dr. Elliot's.

FRANCINE   Don't push!

Jo   Fine. OK.

[*Beat.*]

OK.

[*Beat. An idea.*]

Hey Ma how 'bout this. I come home and you're all dressed nice. I'll.

[*Beat.*]

I'll go to the reunion. How's that.

FRANCINE   What do I care if you go to the reunion or not.

Jo   [*A sigh.*] I donno. I just thought.

[*Beat.*]

Never mind.

[*Beat.*]

I gotta go to work I'm gonna be late. I'll/see you later.

FRANCINE   Jo? Josephine?

Jo   Yeah what Ma.

FRANCINE   Maybe. Maybe I will OK? Get dressed nice.

Jo   OK.

FRANCINE   You're gonna come back. Right? You're gonna come back after work. You're not gonna leave like you said/you might.

Jo   I donno Ma. Maybe. Maybe I will.

[*She exits.*]

Two

[*A slightly sad and bare office break room.* SHERRY *and* Jo *sit at a table.* SHERRY *is very little in stature—but big everywhere else. Big hair. Feathered on the sides. Frosted. Big nails. Big earrings. Big voice. Big shoulder pads.* SHERRY *smokes Virginia Slims.* Jo *sips a Tab. They are in mid-conversation.*]

SHERRY   So he goes. Get this right? He goes. I gotta tell you something. Can I be honest with you?

JO   No. Lie to me.

SHERRY   That's what *I* said.

JO   Oh yeah?

SHERRY   Yeah! Exactly like that too!

JO   Ha.

SHERRY   So he goes. I kinda. Get this. I kinda. Have a *wife*.

JO   What's kinda mean?

SHERRY   That's what *I* said!

JO   Really?

SHERRY   Yeah you and me. We're like.

[*She points back and forth between them.*]

JO   Well. What else *could* you say.

SHERRY   I mean I could've said.

[*She lowers her voice.*]

Fuck you you fucking dickwad asshole.

[*Raises it back.*]

But I didn't.

JO   Yeah. Why stoop down/to his level.

SHERRY   Cuz his kid was there.

JO   Oh!

[*Lowers her voice.*]

He brought his kid?

SHERRY   Yeah. Messed up right?

JO   Who *does* that?

SHERRY   Apparently *this guy*. Apparently *this guy* does that. I think he brought her to you know. *Guarantee* that I wouldn't cause him any kinda. *Bodily harm.*

JO   Wow so he said that? Right in front of her?

SHERRY   Said what right in fronta who?

JO   Said that to you about having a wife. In front of his kid. Said that about the/kid's *mother*.

Sherry   No no no she was in the car.

Jo   The *wife* was in/the car?!?

Sherry   No no no the *kid*. The *kid* was in the car.

Jo   Where were you having the conversation?

Sherry   Driveway of my apartment. Kid stayed in the car like. Five feet away.

Jo   You know he had a kid?

Sherry   I didn't know he had a wife!

Jo   Yeah but people can have kids and no wife.

Sherry   No I didn't know he had neither. He's got two kids. He just brought one with him. Girl. Like thirteen fourteen. Pretty. Saw her through the window. You know what that means, right?

Jo   Huh?

Sherry   Means the wife's pretty too.

Jo   Oh. Yeah. Probly.

[*Beat.*]

How long were you with him?

Sherry   Six months.

[*Beat.*]

Six months and I didn't know any of this. I mean. He met *my* kid. *My* kid loves him. So he didn't just fuck *me* up. He fucked up my *kid*. Fucking sonofabitch.

[*Beat.*]

I thought I did it right this time too you know. Didn't sleep with him too soon cuz you know how they get right?

Jo   Huh?

Sherry   Men.

Jo   Oh yeah right sure. *Men.*

Sherry   Yeah so. I made him wait. A whole freaking month before I even let him inside my apartment.

[*She lowers her voice.*]

And then another two dates till I let him do it with me. And he *still* lies to me and screws me.

[*Beat.*]

And he's a *urologist.*

Jo   What's that.

Sherry   It's like a gyno. For men.

Jo   Oh.

Sherry   Yeah. Kinda married my ass.

Jo   Uh-huh.

[*Pause.*]

What does that. Mean?

Sherry   What does what mean.

Jo   Kinda. Married.

Sherry   I mean. It means. He's. I mean it means he's. Separated? And they don't live together or nothing. But he's not divorced. Yet. But they will be./ Someday.

Jo   How do you know?

Sherry   How do I know what?

Jo   I mean how do you know if it's true cuz he lied before so/he could lie again.

Sherry   Cuz he *loves* me that's why! He might be a lying piece a shit but he's a lying piece a shit who/*loves* me!

Jo   I didn't mean that.

Sherry   I mean the whole thing stinks like garbage but. I'm not so *deluded* I'd. Freaking. I mean.

[*Beat.*]

You think he's lying? About loving me.

Jo   No no I/didn't mean.

Sherry   Cuz now you've got me wondering all kindsa stuff I wasn't thinking/about before.

Jo   Sorry.

Sherry   I mean it's bad enough I gotta think about getting this *wife* outta the picture and how my whole life's been shattered pulverized into bits. But at least if he *loves* me it's not all a freaking *waste*, you know? At least then I've got some kinda *hope* or something. At least I got *something*. Cuz otherwise I got *nothing*./And that's horrifying.

Jo   I think. He loves you. I don't know what I was saying.

Sherry   You really do?

Jo I really. Do.

SHERRY [*An exhale.*] Good. I feel better.

[*Pause.* SHERRY *lights another cigarette.* JO *sips her Tab.*]

You like that crap? Tastes like piss.

Jo It's OK. I'm. Trying to lose a couple pounds.

SHERRY I gain and lose the same five over and over again.

Jo [*A little laugh.*] Yeah me too.

SHERRY You should do Jane Fonda. You do Jane Fonda?

Jo Uh/no.

SHERRY I got the tapes—I'll bring 'em in/for you.

Jo Yeah OK.

SHERRY Cuz you really don't need to lose too much. You just wanna tone up. Make everything *tight.*/You know?

Jo Sure.

SHERRY Everything I eat goes straight to my ass. But I can eat whatever I want so long as I do/those tapes.

Jo Great! Thanks!

[*Silence.*]

SHERRY You think I'm a bad person.

Jo Why would I think that.

SHERRY I donno. Cuz of what I just told you.

Jo No.

SHERRY You ever with a married guy?

Jo No.

SHERRY This is my *third.*

Jo Oh./Huh.

SHERRY First one was intentional. Second was accidental. And this one was. I mean he's not *really* married.

Jo I mean he/kinda is?

SHERRY Can I tell you something?

Jo OK.

SHERRY Me and him? We were talking about having a baby together.

Jo *Oh.*

SHERRY   Yeah. I woulda been one of those women you see on TV you know. Who have kids with married guys and they don't even know and so the whole time they're a second freaking family.

JO   It's. A lot.

SHERRY   Yeah.

[*Beat.*]

Yeah.

[*Pause.*]

You're easy to talk to. You're a good listener.

JO   Thanks.

SHERRY   I don't know you but I feel like I could really open up to you. I feel like I can tell you shit and you won't judge me.

JO   I guess?

[*Beat.*]

We. Know? Each other.

SHERRY   Whadya mean.

JO   I mean. We've been working together for. Almost five years.

SHERRY   Yeah but we've never *talked*. Not like this. And I mean. I'm telling you real deep confidential personal crap in the break room of our *office*.

JO   That's true.

SHERRY   Like. Jo. Is that short for something like. Joanne?

JO   Josephine.

SHERRY   See! I didn't know that!

[*Beat.*] Sherry's short for Sherilyn.

JO   Oh that's a. Pretty name.

SHERRY   It's all right. Better than Sheryl. Sheryl would've sucked. Ass.

JO   [*Beat.*] I gotta. Cousin named Sheryl.

SHERRY   Uh-huh . . . That's. Nice.

[*Beat.*]

See we're getting to know each other.

[*Pause—smokes—sips.*]

You think it's messed up that I still wanna have a baby with him. Even though I know what I know?

Jo　Oh uh/I donno.

Sherry　Cuz I'm so freaking fertile I could get that fucker to make that shit happen whenever I want.

Jo　I think that's maybe. Not such a good idea.

Sherry　Yeah. Yeah you're probly right. You're smart Jo. You got a good head on your shoulders.

Jo　Sometimes.

Sherry　And you're *nice*. You're a really nice girl. You're somebody I should be friends with.

Jo　Oh/OK.

Sherry　When I first met you no offense I thought you were a snotty asshole. But now that I know you. I gotta say. I think you're terrific.

Jo　Thanks.

Sherry　We should go do something together. Sometime. You and me.

Jo　Like do what.

Sherry　Like go out sometime after work. Go meet guys.

Jo　Oh/sure maybe.

Sherry　Cuz if I go home after work it's so fucking depressing I wanna kill myself. You know what I mean?

Jo　[*A little laugh.*] . . . Yeah . . .

Sherry　Like let's go tonight. We/can go tonight.

Jo　Oh . . . I donno if I can.

Sherry　Whaddya mean??? It's Friday night!!!

Jo　Yeah/I know.

Sherry　Whadya gotta do that you can't go out? Watch freaking *Falcon Crest*?

Jo　[*A little laugh.*] No/I gotta.

Sherry　There was a plane crash. Everybody died.

Jo　I gotta go to the store. Gotta cook dinner for/my mother.

Sherry　*After* that. We could go out *after* you do everything else you/gotta do.

Jo　Maybe?

Sherry　Fuck maybe. Say *yes* Jo. How many times a day do you say yes? To something *you* wanna do and not something somebody *else* wants you to do.

Jo [*A little laugh.*] I donno. Not a whole lot.

SHERRY You and me all day we gotta do crap for.

[*She lowers her voice.*]

These old idiots, right? I don't even know what they do all freaking day that they gotta keep us running around getting coffee the way they do while they sit on their asses.

Jo They're accountants. It's an accounting firm.

SHERRY I know *that*. I'm talking about what they *do*. Half the time I walk into Itzkowicz's office he's staring at the freaking *wall*.

Jo [*A little laugh.*] Yeah.

SHERRY [*A little laugh.*] Idiots. They're all idiots. So you and me. We gotta stick together. I mean. I found out my freaking boyfriend was *married* yesterday. So. I need to go unwind. And *you* need to come with me. I'm not taking no/for an answer.

Jo Yeah I donno.

SHERRY Come on! *We* are gonna go out. And we are gonna get shit-faced. And I'm gonna go home with somebody I don't know. And it's gonna be a wicked fucking pissa time.

Jo . . . Okay . . .

SHERRY Yeah!

Jo [*Beat.*] Yeah!

SHERRY You and me we're gonna go out on the town gonna go to the city even maybe gonna meet some guys gonna have fun gonna say yes Jo. OK? We're gonna say yes.

Jo To what.

SHERRY To *everything*.

[*She puts out her cigarette and exits.* Jo *sits and sips her Tab.*]

Three

[*A supermarket meat counter.* DONNY *and* Jo *stand on opposite sides.*]

DONNY I got some chops? Real nice. Good marbling. You want? I got 'em in back.

Jo Veal or lamb?

DONNY I got both but. Right now I'm talking about the veal.

Jo   I/donno . . .

DONNY   They're this thick. Haven't put 'em out yet. I'd be getting 'em for you special.

Jo   I donno how I feel about. *Veal.*

DONNY   You don't haveta *feel* anything about it. You just gotta eat it.

Jo   Yeah but I mean. How they *make* veal.

DONNY   Whadya mean how they make it. I'm a butcher. *I* make it.

Jo   Yeah but. I donno. Veal is. I mean it's. Babies taken away from their mothers.

DONNY   It's meat. It doesn't have a mother.

Jo   Everything that's dead now had a mother sometime. It's. I donno I can't. It's too sad.

[*She starts to cry.*]

DONNY   You crying?

Jo   Huh?

DONNY   You crying about the *veal?*

Jo   No.

[*She is.*]

No.

[*Beat.*]

Uh.

[*Pause.*]

What else you got that's good?

DONNY   Hamburg? Ground it fresh this morning. With my own hands.

[*He holds up his hands with one finger down.*]

Fuck. When did that happen?

Jo   *Tease.*

DONNY   You gotta be fucking shitting me! What??? Where'd it go? I mean it. I had all ten/this morning.

Jo   Yeah yeah.

DONNY   [*He puts it back up.*] Oh there it is. Thank freaking god.

[*Beat.*]

Imagine if I did that? Ground my fingers up in the hamburg in the morning and then sell it to you in the afternoon.

Jo   That'd be pretty messed up.

DONNY   Yeah. Ha. Yeah it would be.

[*Beat.*]

I'd uh. Never do that. Not like./Not really.

Jo   Oh yeah no. I know you. Wouldn't.

[*Awkward pause.*]

DONNY   So, uh . . .

[*Beat.*] Hey! How's your ma doing? Haven't seen her/in a while.

Jo   Oh! Yeah well. She stays in a lot/these days.

DONNY   Huh.

Jo   She's got a. Weak. Constitution.

DONNY   That doesn't sound so good.

Jo   [*A little laugh.*] Eh. It is what it is/you know.

DONNY   Sure sure.

[*Awkward pause.*]

Jo   Are you . . .

[*Beat.*]

You gonna go to the twentieth/you think?

DONNY   Oh! That's coming up/isn't it?

Jo   Yeah.

DONNY   I donno. You going?

Jo   I was thinking maybe.

[*Beat.*]

I ran into Marybeth Dougherty.

DONNY   Oh yeah? How's she doing?

Jo   She's *organizing* it.

DONNY   She would be.

Jo   Yeah right?

DONNY   Jeesh. Just thinking about Marybeth Dougherty's getting me stressed.

Jo   Me too.

Donny   I'm thinking of skipping it.

Jo   Oh yeah?

Donny   I mean. I didn't like most of those people then. Don't think I'm gonna like 'em any better now/you know?

Jo   Yeah yeah sure.

Donny   And since me and Kathy split. If she goes. I don't know if I wanna go. So.

[*Beat.*]

So uh. You want the uh. You want the hamburg?

Jo   Yeah OK.

Donny   You want that with or without my index finger.

Jo   Ha ha. Without please.

[*Beat.*]

Actually—lemme take a look at those chops.

Donny   Oh yeah?

Jo   Yeah. If they're as good as you say they are. They must be something.

Donny   They're gorgeous. Really. You're gonna fall in love.

[*He goes in the back. She waits. And waits. She smooths her skirt. She tucks her hair behind her ear. She awkwardly looks around. He returns with a piece of meat on a piece of butcher paper.*]

Huh? Right? Whadya think of that huh?

Jo   That's a. That's a real good looking piece of meat.

Donny   Well thank you.

Jo   Ha ha.

Donny   You blushing Jo.

Jo   Yeah. Yeah probly. I uh. Blush easy.

Donny   It's pretty.

Jo   No. It's not.

Donny   It is. World like this nowadays? It's nice that there are still girls who are. Shy enough to blush.

Jo   [*Beat. A smile.*] Thanks?

Donny   [*A smile.*] Sure.

[*Beat.*]

So listen. You know what I'd do? If it were me?

Jo Huh.

Donny I'd get the chops and I'd stuff 'em with breadcrumbs. A little prosciutto. A little provolone. Give it a nice sear. Chop up a little fresh parsley. A little hot pepper. Do a. Like a wine sauce maybe?

Jo Wow. You make that up in your head just now?

Donny Yeah I. I like to cook.

Jo Sounds good. But.

[*Beat.*]

My ma's. She gets heartburn a lot/and so.

Donny Oh.

Jo She can't eat spicy food so/much.

Donny Yeah well. Maybe/not then.

Jo Yeah so I think I should probly just. Stick with the hamburg/for today.

Donny Sure. Sure.

[*Beat.*] Do you uh. Do *you* like spicy food?

Jo [*A little laugh.*] Uh . . . Yeah? I guess/I do?

Donny So maybe I'll make you a veal chop one of these days. Like how I was describing.

Jo Oh.

Donny Could I do that?

Jo If you want I guess.

Donny If I did would you cry or would you eat it?

Jo [*A little laugh.*] I donno. Maybe a little of both.

Donny OK.

[*Beat.*]

That'd be OK.

[*Slightly awkward pause.*]

So. Uh. How much hamburg you want?

Jo Little over three-quarter pound I think.

Donny All right then.

[*He measures out the meat.*]

You know what I think?

Jo Huh?

Donny I'm thinking maybe I throw a little pork in there? Mix it all up. You'll have a meatloaf that'll knock your socks off. I'd say veal too. But. I know you got a lotta feelings about that so.

[*He wraps up the meat and then hands it to her.*]

Shhh . . . On me.

Jo Oh. I couldn't. Take it/for free.

Donny Keep it down would ya?

[*He laughs.*]

It's a. Thank you for uh. Keeping me company.

Jo OK. Thank you.

Donny Sure.

Jo Nice seeing you Donny.

Donny Yeah you too Jo.

[*She walks away. He follows her with his eyes—appreciates the back view.*]

Four

[Jo*'s making dinner.* Francine*'s watching television.* Francine*'s wearing the same outfit she wore earlier.* Jo*'s dressed up a little.*]

Francine So we're not going to the movie then.

Jo What do you think.

Francine You said a movie maybe. And a cone after./From Brigham's.

Jo Did you get dressed?

Francine I did. I got dressed and then I got back in this to be comfortable.

Jo Shoulda taken a Polaroid then. So you'd have *proof.*

Francine I was looking forward to a movie.

Jo Oh well. Sucks to be you then.

Francine What kinda lousy language is that?

Jo Sorry Ma. It is terribly unfortunate then. To be *you.*

[*Cooking. TV watching. The celebratory sounds of a game show.*]

Francine What're you making.

Jo   Meatloaf.

Francine   Yuck.

Jo   You don't like meatloaf.

Francine   Not really.

Jo   Since when.

Francine   Since always. Too much stuff going on.

Jo   In *meatloaf*?

Francine   The way you make it there is.

[*Beat.*]

What else you got?

Jo   I got *meatloaf.*

[*Silence.*]

Francine   [*Beat.*] Whodja say you were going out with?

Jo   Girl from work.

Francine   I know her?

Jo   Nope.

Francine   She from here?

Jo   Brockton, I think. Stoughton maybe?

Francine   Where you going?

Jo   Club or something.

Francine   What kinda club.

Jo   Oh jeez Ma./I donno.

Francine   You wearing that?

Jo   Yeah/I think.

Francine   It makes you look like you're trying too hard.

Jo   I'm not trying for anything, Ma. I'm just. Going out/for a drink.

Francine   You look like you wanna go home with somebody.

Jo   Maybe I do./Maybe I will.

Francine   Don't you dare.

Jo   Come on Ma! When's the last time I did/something like that.

Francine   Don't you even make fun about that. You could get hacked/into bits!

JO   Oh jeez.

FRANCINE   Like that poor girl in that movie! What's the name'a that movie. With that pretty actress always dresses/like a man.

JO   *Looking for Mr. Goodbar.*

FRANCINE   What?!

JO   *Looking for Mr. Goodbar,* Ma!

FRANCINE   Nice girls don't go to bars looking for sex/like that.

JO   OK!

[*Silence.*]

FRANCINE   Whadjou say this girl's name is again?

JO   Sherry.

FRANCINE   What kinda name is that?

JO   It's her *name*.

FRANCINE   Who the heck names their kid *Sherry*?

JO   Who the heck names their kid *Josephine*?

FRANCINE   You were named after my dear brother./You know that.

JO   Yeah I know I know.

FRANCINE   You should be grateful. To be named. After somebody good as/ he was.

JO   Yeah OK.

FRANCINE   You *should*.

JO   OK!

[*Silence.*]

FRANCINE   She gonna come in?

JO   Who?

FRANCINE   *Sherry.*

JO   What would she do that for?

FRANCINE   Just to be social. We can make a little cocktail maybe. Put out the good candy.

JO   No thanks.

FRANCINE   Call her up on the phone. See if she wants to/come in.

JO   She's probly left/already Ma!

FRANCINE   Come on go ahead and call!

JO   Oh for Chrissake.

[*She takes a small slip of paper out of her purse.*]

FRANCINE   You calling?

JO   I'm looking for the number. Calm down.

[*She dials the number. Beat. She hangs up.*]

Yeah I got the machine. She's probly already/on her way.

FRANCINE   So when she honks the horn tell her to come in.

[*No response.*]

Josephine.

[*No response.*]

You hear/me?

JO   Yeah I. Hear. You.

[*Beat.*]

I'll think about it.

[*Pause.*]

What Dr. Elliot haveta say.

FRANCINE   Huh?

JO   Dr. Elliot. Ma. What he/haveta say.

FRANCINE   Oh . . . Yeah. I didn't go.

JO   Whadya mean you/didn't go?

FRANCINE   You were supposed to leave me a Post-it on the television to remind me!/And you didn't!

JO   We talked about it before I left this morning and I gave you money for a taxi. Whadja think that was for?

[*No response.*]

Ma.

[*No response.*]

Well I'll call them tomorrow/and reschedule.

FRANCINE   I don't wanna go!

JO   You don't have a choice!

FRANCINE   I'm not strong enough to go there/by myself!

Jo   You don't wanna go see Dr. Elliot because you know damn sure he's gonna give you a clean bill of health gonna tell you that there's nothing/ wrong with you.

FRANCINE   That's not true!

Jo   He's gonna tell you you aren't sick anymore. Gonna tell you that if you wanna sit around in a bathrobe all day and do nothing that's your choice. Because all of us—you, me, and everybody in Dr. Elliot's office—we all know that you are nothing but absolutely one hundred percent *fine*.

[*Beat.*]

Except you can't hear for shit.

FRANCINE   I heard that.

Jo   *Good.*

[*Beat.*]

Donny Moretti was asking about you today.

FRANCINE   Who's that.

Jo   Donny Moretti Ma. I went to high school/with him.

FRANCINE   The butcher?

Jo   Yeah. That's what/he does. Yeah.

FRANCINE   Why's the butcher asking about me.

Jo   He just asked how you were./That's all.

FRANCINE   What does he need to know from my business for.

Jo   It was just small talk. It was.

[*Beat.*]

He.

[*A little laugh.*]

I think he was flirting with me kinda.

FRANCINE   Oh yeah?

Jo   Yeah I.

[*Beat.*]

I think he maybe asked me out/on a date.

FRANCINE   Isn't he married?

Jo   Separated.

FRANCINE   Separated's still married.

[*Beat.*]

I don't think he's a nice person.

JO   *Why.*

FRANCINE   He lit Mrs. Rosenthal's cat on fire.

JO   Oh for/Chrissake, Ma.

FRANCINE   What kinda person does that to a cat???

JO   He was ten!

FRANCINE   It's not a nice thing to do!

JO   He was considered to be a big catch when we were younger. He was the best-looking guy in school. And smart. He went to a pretty good college.

FRANCINE   Good as you? He go to a school as good as the/one you went to.

JO   I don't remember.

FRANCINE   So what's he doing working as a butcher then if he's so smart huh.
[*She laughs.*]

JO   What.

FRANCINE   That's why I got meatloaf!

JO   That's not why at all/shut your mouth.

FRANCINE   He give you something free?/Because if he did.

JO   I didn't get anything for *free.*

FRANCINE   Because if he did. He's expecting something free back.
[*No response.*]

Josephine.

JO   *What.*

FRANCINE   Are you hearing what/I'm saying to you honey.

JO   Yes Ma yes. I heard you. Something free/something free back.

FRANCINE   The way men are.

JO   Forget I said anything about it, Ma. Okay?
[*Silence.*]

FRANCINE   What time are you coming back?

JO   Late.

FRANCINE   What are the neighbors gonna think. You coming home late/like that.

Jo   I got you some potato salad, Ma. You can have it with/the meatloaf.

Francine   I don't like this. Keeping company with married men. Going out to nightclubs with loose women till god knows/when.

Jo   Sorry you don't/approve, Ma.

Francine   *You* are a lovely nice girl with good/values.

Jo   Meatloaf goes in for an hour and/a half.

Francine   The kinda men you meet in those bars don't want anything serious./They're just.

Jo   I'm setting the timer.

Francine   They just want somebody to run around with. They aren't looking for a nice girl like you/sweetheart.

Jo   I am not a *girl* anymore, Ma! I am a grown *woman*!

[*Silence.* Jo *starts to cry.*]

Francine   Josephine? You all/right honey?

Jo   I'm fine.

Francine   What I say?

Jo   I'm putting the meatloaf/in the oven.

[*She puts the meatloaf in the oven and sets a timer.*]

Francine   You should be proud of who you are/honey.

Jo   Goes in till it's just/pink in the middle.

Francine   You hear me? You should be proud of who you are.

Jo   Yeah well. I'm *not*.

[*The sound of a car on gravel—a horn from outside.*]

I gotta go.

Francine   Invite her in for a minute. Please? Honey? Invite her in.

Jo   [*A beat. A decision.*] No.

[*She grabs her purse and exits.*]

Five

[*A bar. Loud-ish music.* Jo *and* Sherry *stand like they are for sale. Vaguely listening to the music. Talking to each other while constantly assessing the room. They talk slightly over the music but not screaming.*]

Sherry   So what he say! I mean what'd he say specifically!

Jo   Said he'd cook for me or something sometime.

SHERRY   That's so cute. That's so freaking adorable.

Jo   Yeah?

SHERRY   Wicked fucking cute! You don't think?

Jo   I donno . . . Yeah. Sure. Yeah.

SHERRY   A butcher huh?

Jo   Yeah over at Morse's Food Mart. Near work.

SHERRY   That's a good job. People always gotta eat, you know.

Jo   Yeah. Yeah that's true.

[*Music playing. Head bobbing.*]

SHERRY   Itzkowicz grabbed my ass today. Can you believe that shit? Didn't just brush by it or nothing either. He got a really good hold on it. A nice solid. Cupping.

Jo   When did he do that?

SHERRY   Called me in to take a letter and when I turned around to leave he. You know. He. Made like AT&T and he reached out and touched someone.

Jo   He's almost eighty.

SHERRY   I don't care how old he is—he does it again it I'm gonna cut it off.

Jo   His hand?

SHERRY   [*Laughs.*] Yeah. Can you imagine? Come in all sweet and nice with my freaking pad and pen. "Yes Mr. Itzkowicz? What can I do for you, Mr. Itzkowicz?" And then he reaches out to grab my ass and I whip out a machete and slice his freaking hand off. And then he goes "I just wanted a pencil" or something. Wouldn't that be hilarious.

Jo   [*A little laugh.*] Ha. Yeah. "I just wanted a pencil."

SHERRY   "Pencil this asshole! Kabam. You don't got an arm no more!" Jerkface.

[*They laugh. Drinking. Head bobbing.*]

Jo   What'd you say this was again?

SHERRY   Fuzzy navel. Good, right?

Jo   Very. Sweet.

SHERRY   I went to Club Med after my divorce with my sister and we drank these till we puked and then we passed out. We had a wicked pissa time. I'm telling you. My sister's an asshole but. She's good to get fucked up with.

[*Drinking. Head bobbing.*]

I think I wanna go home with *that* guy.

Jo   What guy?

Sherry   The guy talking to us earlier. He's wicked hot right?

Jo   Oh. Yeah?

Sherry   You see anybody you like?

Jo   I donno. It's kinda dark? Hard to see people. And the people I do see all kinda look a little. Sad.

Sherry   Yeah well. It's a singles bar. You gotta just get a little shitfaced so you can ignore the stank of. Desperation. Permeating in the air.

[*A sad little laugh.*]

Jo   You really do that? Go home with people you don't know?

Sherry   I mean I have. Yeah. Done that.

[*Beat.*]

Why you haven't?

Jo   Naw never.

Sherry   It's not that bigga deal. Sometimes it's fun. And sometimes it sucks balls. And sometimes you wish you didn't. But whatever it is. You just. Do it.

[*Beat.*]

How long've you lived at home?

Jo   Easier question is how long've I *not* lived at home.

Sherry   And what's that?

Jo   Eight months. Eight months almost twenty years ago.

Sherry   Oh . . .

[*Silence.*]

Jo   I know that's very strange.

Sherry   Yeah. I mean yeah it is. A little strange.

Jo   I didn't set out for that it. Just happened.

Sherry   Where were you those eight months?

Jo   College. I went to college for a./Little while.

Sherry   Oh yeah. Where'd you go?

Jo   Oh I uh. I went to Radcliffe?/College.

Sherry   Shut the fuck up!

[SHERRY *laughs.* JOSEPHINE *laughs.*]

You're shitting me!

Jo   [*A little laugh.*] Nope it's the truth.

SHERRY   You went to fucking Harvard???

Jo   [*Correcting her.*] Radcliffe.

SHERRY   Same difference.

Jo   Yeah the boys at Harvard didn't think so.

SHERRY   I hadda cousin went to Massasoit Community but. Fucking Harvard?!?

Jo   [*Correcting her.*] Radcliffe.

[*Beat.*]

It's no big deal. I was barely there a year.

SHERRY   Why?

Jo   Oh my uh. My father? He got sick and. And my Ma she needed help taking care of him? So. I came home. And then after he died. She still needed help. Paying the bills. Taking care of the house. And I fell behind in my classes and I uh. Lost my scholarship/and uh.

SHERRY   Aw Jo.

Jo   Oh no it's OK. It's not so bad. It's just what happened you know?

[*Beat.*]

Eventually it was too late to go back. And so I. Yeah I.

[*She shrugs.*]

Never left home.

[*Beat.*]

Sorry. That all sounds so weird when I say it/out loud but I.

SHERRY   No it's OK. I got stuff too. We all got stuff.

Jo   [*A little laugh.*] Yeah.

SHERRY   [*A little laugh.*] Yeah.

[*Beat.*]

So.

[*Beat.*]

So uh.

[*Beat.*]

I think? I'm gonna go talk to that guy/over there.

Jo   Oh! Yeah sure.

Sherry   Maybe get him to buy us another round. See if he's got a cute friend or something I can send over. You be into that?

Jo   If he seems nice/yeah sure.

Sherry   I'll feel him out. I'm on a mission to get you laid. We gotta clean out those pipes of yours before they dry up for good.

Jo   [*A slight laugh.*] Ha. OK.

[Sherry *bends over at the waist and flips her hair back and exits.* Jo *sits awkwardly. She smooths her hair. She fixes her blouse. She bobs a bit to the music—and then feels self-conscious and stops. She thinks someone waves at her and waves back. She squints. She's not sure the wave was for her.* Donny *enters abruptly—laughing. He was the one who was waving.*]

Donny   Of all/the crazy?!?

Jo   Hey there!

Donny   I thought that was you!

Jo   Yeah, it's. Me!

Donny   I couldn't tell for sure cuz it's so/dark in here.

Jo   It's so dark in. Here./Yes. It is.

Donny   Small world.

Jo   . . . Yeah . . .

[Awkward pause.]

Jo/Donny   You wanna sit?/You wanna drink?

[*They laugh.*]

Donny   You uh. Need a refill?

Jo   OK.

Donny   What're you drinking.

Jo   Fuzzy navel.

Donny   Oh. You're one'a *those* girls, huh.

Jo   [*Not sure what that means.*] Uh-huh.

Donny   OK. Be right back.

[*He leaves. She quietly turns away and reapplies her lipstick. She leans over at the waist and flips her hair like* Sherry. *She waits. She waits. She waits. He returns.*]

A fuzzy navel for the lady.

[*He lifts his shirt.*] And . . . I got you a drink too.

Jo   Ha. Yeah. Jokester.

DONNY   I try. I'm not so funny unfortunately. More corny than anything, right?

Jo   Oh I wouldn't say that.

DONNY   Yeah cuz you're sweet so. I'll say it for you.

[*Beat.*]

So.

[*Holds up his glass to toast.*]

Cheers!

[*Drinks.*]

I can't get over how I'm seeing you again after I just/saw you earlier!

Jo   I know!

DONNY   My buddies made me come out here but. It's weird. Doing this again after splitting/with Kathy.

Jo   Oh sure. I'll bet.

DONNY   The rules are different? Since. The last time I was doing this and. I donno. It's a little embarrassing./Being here.

Jo   Yeah.

DONNY   I woulda rather gone to a. Celtics game or something.

[*Beat.*]

You like basketball?

Jo   A little.

DONNY   You know who Larry Bird is though, right?

Jo   Everybody knows who Larry Bird is.

DONNY   . . . Yeah . . .

Jo   . . . Yeah . . .

[*Pause.*]

So! You and Kathy. You gonna get divorced you think?

DONNY   Oh I uh. Think so?

[*Beat.*]

I donno I've. Been with her my whole life./You know?

Jo   Yeah.

DONNY   We've got kids. I.

[*Beat.*]

I miss my kids. I miss seeing 'em every day.

Jo   Sure.

DONNY   But they're teenagers. Gonna go off and then. It's just gonna be me and her and. I mean. I'm in therapy. We're in therapy. But. I think we're fighting to keep something going that's. Already gone.

[*Beat.*]

Sorry. I'm not being all that fun to be/around am I.

Jo   No! No you're fine!

DONNY   Lately I'm a. Bit of a downer.

[*Pause.*]

You come here alone?

Jo   No I came with a friend but. She's talking to somebody so./I don't know if she's.

DONNY   You wanna. Ride home/maybe?

Jo   Oh I.

DONNY   I've been drinking club soda/all night so.

Jo   Oh.

DONNY   Yeah I'm. I'm not drinking these days I. I get a little sad lately. When I drink so . . . I'm not/right now.

Jo   Sure.

DONNY   Jeesh, that was too much? Information?/But. I can.

Jo   That's OK.

DONNY   Drive you home and not get in an accident or anything. That's what I was/trying to say.

Jo   I'd like. That.

DONNY   OK.

[*Beat.*]

OK.

[*He gets up.*]

I just gotta take a leak/before we go.

Jo   OK.

Donny   What the fuck. Sorry. I gotta. If you'll excuse me. I gotta go to the men's room. I'll. Be right back. Don't go anywhere.

Jo   Where would I. Go?

[*An awkward laugh. He exits. She sits and waits.* Sherry *pops back in.*]

Sherry   How ya doing???

Jo   Oh . . ./Uh. Okay?

Sherry   I saw you talking to somebody. But it's so dark I couldn't see what he looks like.

Jo   Oh yeah, funny! It's the guy I was telling you about.

Sherry   The butcher!

Jo   Shhhh . . ./Yeah.

Sherry   Nobody can/hear me!

Jo   He's gonna drive me home so I. You don't haveta/worry about me.

Sherry   Lookit you.

[Jo *laughs.*]

I'm impressed. Very impressed.

[*She makes her back-and-forth hand gesture between the two of them again.*]

You and me Jo. I'm telling you. You and freaking me.

[*Beat.*]

Don't do anything I wouldn't do.

Jo   OK.

Sherry   And for the record. I'd go home with him so. There you go.

[*She exits.* Jo *laughs. Does the hand gesture back to* Sherry, *who is now offstage. A mutual laugh that fades into a smile. That fades into the awkwardness of now being alone. A moment. She waits. Not sure what to do next.*]

Six

[*The porch outside of* Jo *and* Francine's *house.*]

[Jo *and* Donny *sit in the dim light on opposite sides of the glider. Every once in a while. They glide.*]

Donny   So . . .

Jo   Huh?

DONNY   Oh.

[*Beat.*]

Sorry.

Jo   For what?

DONNY   I uh. I broke the quiet.

Jo   [*Genuinely.*] S'OK.

DONNY   The quiet was nice.

Jo   Uh-huh.

[*Beat.*]

S'nice to talk too sometimes.

DONNY   . . . Yeah . . .

Jo   Yeah.

[*Beat.*]

What were you gonna say?

DONNY   Oh. Huh. Nothing.

Jo   OK.

[*Silence.*]

DONNY   I was gonna say something about it being nice out, you know. And then I thought. What kinda A-hole makes a comment like that? Talking about the weather! So corny, right?

[Jo *laughs.*]

So I uh. Yeah. That's what I was. Gonna say.

Jo   It *is* nice out though isn't it? For fall? A little cold but. Not too much.

DONNY   You want my jacket?

Jo   Oh! I wasn't. Hinting.

DONNY   No I/know I just.

Jo   If I take it then you'll be cold.

DONNY   I'm OK. Here.

[*He puts his jacket over her shoulders—it swallows her up.*]

Jo   Thanks.

DONNY   Uh-huh.

[*Beat.*]

Just so ya know. Guys like it when ladies get cold and we give 'em our jackets. Makes us feel useful so. Don't feel bad when it's offered. Just take it.

Jo OK.

DONNY I wasn't trying to criticize you or anything. I just. So you know. For the future.

[*Silence.*]

Jo You decide about the reunion yet?

DONNY No. You?

Jo No.

[*Beat.*]

I think maybe I wanna go I think.

DONNY Yeah?

Jo I think?

DONNY [*Beat.*] Maybe we could. Go together.

Jo [*A little too eagerly.*] Oh!/Yeah. Maybe.

DONNY If you want.

Jo [*More nonchalantly.*] Yeah sure.

DONNY [*Beat.*] Maybe it'd be. Fun maybe.

Jo . . . Yeah . . .

DONNY Yeah.

[*Beat.*]

Probly not though.

Jo [*Laughs.*] No probly not.

DONNY Probly gonna be a lotta people trying to prove something you know? Trying to pretend they're somebody they aren't. I mean you ever.

[*He stops himself.*]

Jo I ever what.

DONNY Naw never mind.

Jo No I wanna hear what you/gotta say.

DONNY It's stupid but. You ever think maybe you were sposed to be somebody else and. You got sidetracked. And. You didn't know it till it was too late?

Jo [*A little laugh.*] All the time.

DONNY   I mean. I didn't think I'd be working at my uncle's grocery store.

JO   I didn't think I'd be living at home.

DONNY   You went to college. Didn't you go to college?

JO   For a little while.

DONNY   Why'd you come home?

[*She shrugs.*]

Shit happens, right?

JO   Yeah.

[*Beat.*]

You did too.

DONNY   Yeah. Kathy got pregnant. So. I came home. Did the right thing.

JO   Shit happens.

DONNY   Yeah.

[*He laughs.*]

Like the poster, right? With the freaking cat. Hanging in the tree? You ever see that?

JO   Nope.

DONNY   It's hilarious. A cat. Hanging in the tree. "Shit happens."

[*An awkward laugh.*]

Fuck. I'm such a loser.

JO   No you're not.

DONNY   No. I am. It's okay.

[*Beat.*]

My kid. My oldest. He's gonna be eighteen and he. He looks at me like "Please god don't let me turn out like that." I know it cuz I looked at my old man the same way. And I don't blame him. I don't wanna be me much neither.

JO   [*Beat.*] I think you're OK.

DONNY   Yeah?

JO   I think you're just fine.

DONNY   You too.

[*Pause.*]

So I was. Uh. Do you maybe wanna.

[*She suddenly and abruptly grabs him and kisses him.*]

FRANCINE   [*From off.*]

Josephine???

[*Lights on in the house.*]

Jo   [*Under her breath.*] For Chrissake.

[*To* FRANCINE]

What?!?

FRANCINE   That you?

Jo   Who else would it be???

FRANCINE   A burglar maybe?

[*She opens the screen door.*]

Jo   Not a burglar./Go back to bed.

FRANCINE   What're you doing out on the porch?

[*Sees* DONNY.]

Oh. Hello.

DONNY   Hullo.

FRANCINE   Didn't know you had company.

Jo   Well./Now you do so.

DONNY   I uh. I brought Josephine home. From the bar. I wasn't drinking./So you know.

FRANCINE   Oh. Well that was nice of you.

[*Pause.*]

I'm gonna get back to bed. Sorry/to bother you.

Jo   OK.

FRANCINE   You coming/Josephine?

Jo   Not just yet.

FRANCINE   What's that?

Jo   I said. I'm not. Coming in. Just yet.

[FRANCINE *doesn't move.*]

I said I'm gonna stay out here with my guest but. *You. You* can. Go inside.

[FRANCINE *still doesn't move.*]

Not a suggestion, Ma.

Francine   Close out the lights and make sure you/lock the door.

Jo   Got it.

[**Francine** *exits. Pause.*]

Sorry.

Donny   For what?

Jo   That was. Disrespectful.

Donny   Trust me. I gotta mother too.

[*Pause.*]

Anyway . . .

[*He gets up.*]

I should uh. Get going/anyways.

Jo   Yeah OK.

Donny   But I. Hadda good time with you tonight Jo.

Jo   [*A little laugh.*] Yeah?

Donny   Yeah. So we'll go to the reunion next week maybe? Huh? Whadya think?

Jo   I think I like that idea.

Donny   You think or you know?

[*A little laugh from both of them.*]

G'night Josephine.

Jo   G'night.

[*An awkward pause. He steals a kiss. Another awkward pause. He walks away. The headlights illuminate her for a moment. The car drives away. Jo sits for a moment. Breathing in the air. Taking in the glorious joy of the evening.* **Francine** *appears at the doorway.*]

Francine   [*Beat.*] It's too late for you to be outside with a man. The neighbors/will.

Jo   Will what, Ma? Say bad things about me? They do anyway.

Francine   They do/not.

Jo   They're nice to my face but I know they say all kindsa crap about me behind my back.

Francine   Like what.

Jo   Old Maid. Spinster.

Francine   They say no such thing. That is all/in your head.

Jo   It's like just the sight of me makes them. Sad.

Francine   All people think is that you are lovely girl./And good-hearted.

Jo   And *sad*. S'OK, Ma. All I'm saying is.

[*She shrugs.*]

I don't really care much what the neighbors think of me and what I do anymore. That's all.

Francine   [*Pause.*] I'm gonna/go to bed.

Jo   Why didn't you ever make me go back to school.

[*No response.*] Huh, Ma. After Daddy died./When I still coulda.

Francine   *Make* you. Whaddya mean/*make* you.

Jo   Just answer the question.

Francine   It was too *late* honey. You lost your/scholarship.

Jo   So community college./Something anything.

Francine   This is crazy talk.

Jo   I *still* coulda. I coulda. *Done* it if you.

[*Beat.*]

If you had.

[*She stops herself.*]

Francine   If I what.

Jo   Nothing nevermind.

[*Silence.*]

Francine   I'm gonna go to sleep.

Jo   OK.

Francine   You coming?

Jo   In a minute.

Francine   It's getting late/you shouldn't.

Jo   I *said* in a minute.

Francine   [*Beat.*] Shut the lights before/you go to sleep.

Jo   I will.

Francine   And remember to/lock the door.

Jo   Yeah OK.

328 BEST PLAYS OF 2015

[FRANCINE *goes back inside. The door closes.* JO *sits in stillness waiting for the lights to turn out inside, leaving her in a pool of light from the street lamps and porch light. And then, when she's sure she's completely alone—a small silent scream of frustration that turns into quiet self-contained tears—that slowly build and build until she is sobbing as silently as she can. After a moment—she realizes she's still wearing* DONNY's *coat. This awareness seems to soothe her a bit. She wraps it up around her. She takes a deep breath. And buries herself deep inside the coat.*]

End of Act One

ACT TWO
One

[*The break room.* JO *drinks a Tab as before.* SHERRY *smokes.*]

SHERRY So then he goes. Get this. He goes. "I *miss* you."

JO What's *that* about.

SHERRY Right?!? But I'm such a sap I start to fucking cry! This was all on the phone. We were talking on the phone all freaking night like this. Talking. And then *not* talking. Like. Sometimes? We'd just be on the phone like that together. Nobody saying anything cuz there's nothing to freaking say. Both of us just. *Listening.* To *nothing.*

[*Beat.*]

It's a fucking mess. We're both wicked messed in the head about it. On our own *and* together. It's a fucking pissa. Lemme tell ya.

[*Beat.*]

So. Yeah. *That* happened.

[*Beat.*]

Whadya think I should do?

JO Oh I. Uh. I'm not the one to ask/I don't think.

SHERRY Why not?

JO This seems a bit out of my. Realm? Of. Understanding.

SHERRY You're a person aren't you.

JO Yeah/sure.

SHERRY You're a woman, right?

JO I/mean yeah.

SHERRY   So I'm asking you. Woman to woman. What would you do.

JO   [*Beat.*] I've never. Been in love before.

SHERRY   Never?

JO   I mean I've dated. I've gone on dates you know. But I've. Never had something so. *Intense*. Like what you got with this guy. That's all.

SHERRY   Oh. OK.

[*Beat.*]

That's. That's *sad*, Jo.

JO   Eh it is what it is.

SHERRY   No it's sad. It's really sad. Everybody should fall in love. It's like voting. It's a right we all should have.

JO   I guess?

SHERRY   I mean. When it's over it sucks. But even the messed up parts are. Wonderful.

[*Pause.*]

Aw Jo.

JO   Huh.

SHERRY   That made me so sad all of a sudden.

JO   Oh don't be! I'm OK. You don't haveta be sad 'cuz/of me.

SHERRY   OK.

[*Beat.*]

OK.

[*Beat.*]

So! You take that guy home with you the other night?/The butcher?

JO   To my mother's? No.

SHERRY   Your house too.

JO   . . . Yeah . . .

SHERRY   You go home with *him*?

JO   No. He just drove me home and. We sat out on the porch.

SHERRY   [*Slightly confused.*] Oh. That's. That's nice.

JO   [*Beat.*] I kissed him.

SHERRY   Oh yeah?

Jo   Yeah I. Grabbed him and I kissed him.

Sherry   Lookit you! Good for you!

Jo   . . . Yeah . . .

Sherry   That's sweet. So many people fuck first ask questions later.

Jo   I guess?

[*Beat.*]

We're uh. We're gonna go to the reunion together./I think.

Sherry   Like a date or like. Carpooling?

Jo   Oh. I donno? A date I think?

Sherry   When's it at.

Jo   Thursday.

Sherry   Not the weekend???

Jo   No.

Sherry   Maybe it was cheaper to get the place or something.

Jo   Maybe. Yeah maybe.

Sherry   Probly that's what it is. Where they having it?

Jo   Charlie's Saloon. At the Chestnut Hill Mall.

Sherry   *Fancy schmancy.*

Jo   [*Laughs.*] I guess. It's just a burger place.

Sherry   Yeah but. Ladies in Chestnut Hill always look at me like I got crabs.

[Jo *laughs.*]

Want me to come over before or something? Help you get ready.

Jo   Oh. Sure. Yeah.

Sherry   I gotta good feeling about this.

Jo   I donno. Whenever I get my hopes up too high. It's usually nothing to get excited about.

Sherry   What kinda piss poor attitude is that?

Jo   I know. I can be really negative.

Sherry   You gotta stop having such a shitty outlook on life.

Jo   I think maybe I'm just a. Negative person.

Sherry   You? Whadya talking about. You're a sweetheart.

Jo   Yeah that's how you see me. But. I can be a real bitch you know? I yell at my mother all the time.

Sherry   Everybody yells at their mother all the time. If I lived with my mother like you do? One of us'd be dead by Christmas. Swearta god.

Jo   [*A little laugh.*] Yeah. That's funny.

Sherry   You know what your problem is, Jo? You're *too* nice.

Jo   I'm telling you./I'm not at all.

Sherry   No it's true. I see you take crap from these guys here. They pay you overtime when you stay late like you do?

Jo   I donno/sometimes?

Sherry   See that's bullshit. Me? I'm outta here by five. I don't give a flying rat's ass. I got my typewriter off and my coat on at five *of* five so I can get the hell outta here. You gotta be more like me.

Jo   I don't have kids.

Sherry   So.

Jo   So they know that. They know there's nothing I gotta be home for.

Sherry   Nothing *I* gotta be home for neither.

Jo   You gotta kid.

Sherry   Yeah but my kid lives with her father so.

[*Beat.*]

Aren't I terrific, huh? Aren't I just a wicked fucking terrific person?

[*Silence.* Jo *sips.* Sherry *smokes—a bit lost in thought.*]

Jo   Why doesn't she live with you.

Sherry   Huh?

Jo   Your kid. Why doesn't she/live with you?

Sherry   Oh I uh. I was having some stuff going on when we got divorced and he. He's a dick as a husband. But. He makes sure she does her homework, you know? Makes her breakfast in the morning. I'm not that kinda person. I wasn't so good at playing house. So. She's better off with him.

[*Beat.*]

Whadya gonna do, right?

[*A sad little laugh.*]

You and me we should get a place together. Be roommates. Maybe even the city or something huh.

Jo   Oh. Uh. Maybe?

SHERRY   You don't wanna live with me?

Jo   No. Maybe I/do. Maybe.

SHERRY   How old are you anyway?

Jo   Thirty-seven. Gonna be thirty-eight.

SHERRY   So listen. In ten years you're gonna be fifty, right?

Jo   More like twelve.

SHERRY   Same difference.

Jo   Not/really.

SHERRY   Look. You don't gotta lotta time left, you know? I'm gonna be thirty-five in a month—and the thought of it makes me wanna kill myself. But what am I gonna do, right? It's happening. It's *on*. And I gotta divorce and a kid and a lousy job but. You know what? I'm lifting myself up outta that cuz. Nobody else is gonna do it. So. Fuck it. Some jerkface wants to break my heart over and over again. Tell me he misses me after he fucks my shit up? Fine. If I'm a shitty mother who can't take care of her own kid. Fine. But. You know what *I'm* doing?

Jo   Huh.

SHERRY   I'm taking *beauty classes* at night. I'm the *oldest* person in the whole freaking school but. I'm doing it! Cuz. I gotta do something, right?

Jo   . . . Yeah . . .

[Jo *starts to cry.*]

SHERRY   Oh. Jeez. I didn't mean to make you cry.

Jo   No! I'm just. Inspired. That was. Inspiring.

SHERRY   [*Pleased with herself.*] Oh yeah?

Jo   Yeah. I.

[*Beat.*]

I gotta do something.

SHERRY   Well, whadya wanna do.

Jo   I donno.

SHERRY   We don't haveta be just secretaries anymore and take this bullshit. It's a different world for us than it was for our mothers, you know? *We* can be. *Anything* we want. Whadya wanna *be* Jo.

Jo   [*Beat.*] I donno.

SHERRY   So. *We* gotta figure it out. OK?

JO   Yeah. Yeah, sure.

SHERRY   [*Beat.*] Listen. After work today? We're gonna go to Loehmann's. And we're gonna pick you out a sexy dress. OK? For the reunion.

JO   Yeah OK.

SHERRY   What're we doing after work today?

JO   We're gonna go to Loehmann's.

SHERRY   And what're we gonna do.

JO   Gonna get me a dress to/wear to the.

SHERRY   A sexy dress. Say it. That part is important.

JO   A sexy dress.

SHERRY   And. We're gonna make something happen for you.

JO   Why are you. Being so nice to me?

SHERRY   [*She shrugs.*] Why the fuck not?

[SHERRY *puts out her cigarette and leaves.*]

TWO

[JO *and* FRANCINE's *living room.*]

[JO *is doing some sort of exercise tape. The faint sounds are heard from the TV.*]

[FRANCINE *watches and smokes.*]

JO   Smoke outside if you're/gonna smoke.

FRANCINE   It's too cold.

JO   Can't you see I'm trying to do/something.

FRANCINE   What's one got to do with/the other.

JO   *Exercise* with you *smoking.*

FRANCINE   You got a television up/in your room.

JO   Ma. Come on.

FRANCINE   This is a common area.

[*She smokes.*]

JO   Where'd you get those anyway. I didn't buy 'em for you.

FRANCINE   Went into town.

JO   Oh you did? How'd you get there?

FRANCINE   Called a taxi.

JO   Very self-sufficient of you.

FRANCINE   It's amazing what you can get yourself to do when you are faced with. *Dire circumstances.*

[*She exhales.*]

Whadya doing that crap for anyway.

JO   I wanna get in shape.

FRANCINE   Whadya care about that all/of a sudden.

JO   Mind your business.

FRANCINE   This cuz of the butcher?

JO   No. It's cuz of *me*. I wanna be healthy.

FRANCINE   [*Beat. Takes a drag on the cigarette.*] What's for dinner.

JO   Lean Cuisine.

FRANCINE   For *me*./What's for *me*.

JO   Lean Cuisine's for both of us.

FRANCINE   You can eat that crap if you want to but I want/real food.

JO   I don't feel like cooking, so I'm gonna have a frozen dinner. You want something different you can. Figure it out.

FRANCINE   [*Beat.*] What about we go to Bailey's and get a sundae! With the fudge sauce dripping off the sides how/they do it.

JO   *You* can go.

FRANCINE   Who wants to go have a sundae all alone? Where's the fun in that, huh?

[*No response.*]

I think you need to stay home from work tomorrow.

JO   *Why.*

FRANCINE   I'm not feeling so good. I need you to take me to see Dr. Elliot.

JO   You took a taxi to get the cigarettes. You can take a taxi to go to/the doctor.

FRANCINE   I need you to be there with me because sometimes he talks and I don't understand what/he's saying.

JO   What's *wrong* with you.

FRANCINE   I'm not breathing so good. I get winded just going from the sofa to/the kitchen.

Jo   Yeah well. Stop *smoking.*

[*Silence.*]

FRANCINE   You got home late today.

Jo   Yeah/I know.

FRANCINE   You go somewhere after work?

Jo   Loehmann's.

FRANCINE   What'd you get at Loehmann's?

Jo   New dress for the reunion.

FRANCINE   You going to that?

Jo   Yeah.

FRANCINE   Who you going with?

Jo   I have a date.

FRANCINE   With who?

[*No response.*]

With the butcher?

[*No response.* FRANCINE *laughs.*]

You going with/the butcher?

Jo   Yeah. With Donny. Yeah.

[FRANCINE *laughs.*]

What're you laughing for?

FRANCINE   [*Laughing.*] Nothing.

Jo   You think it's funny I got a date.

FRANCINE   I'm just laughing. I can laugh if I want to. It's a free country.

[*Pause.*]

You go with that girl Sherry? To/Loehmann's.

Jo   Yeah.

FRANCINE   Why don't you go try on what you got so/I can see.

Jo   Not right now.

FRANCINE   Come on!/I wanna see!

Jo   [*Firmly.*] I *said* not now.

[*She goes into the freezer—takes out two frozen dinners.*]

You want spaghetti with sauce or sweet-and-sour chicken?

FRANCINE   I don't want neither!

JO   Suit/yourself.

FRANCINE   I wanna go to Bailey's for a sundae/I told you!

JO   [*She goes to her purse and gets her keys and throws them to* FRANCINE.] So then get up offa your *ass*! And get in the *car*! And *drive* yourself there!

[*Silence.*]

FRANCINE   That girl Sherry's no good. You've been different since you started spending time with her.

JO   You don't even know her.

FRANCINE   I don't *need* to know her. I'm telling you. She's not a nice girl. She's putting ideas in/your head.

JO   We were talking today about maybe moving in together.

FRANCINE   [*Beat.*] Moving in??? Whadya mean/*moving in???*

JO   Like the two of us getting an apartment together/or something.

FRANCINE   An *apartment???* Where you gonna get/an *apartment???*

JO   Braintree maybe. Brockton. Maybe the city.

FRANCINE   The city??? Two single girls living in the city??? See this is what I'm/talking about.

JO   Last chance Ma. Spaghetti or chicken.

FRANCINE   Chicken.

JO   Chicken it is.

[*She puts the dinners in the microwave and sets the timer.*] I.

[*Pause.*]

I don't.

[*Beat. A confession.*] I don't wanna live here. Anymore.

FRANCINE   Why would you say such/an awful thing.

JO   Whether it's with Sherry or/by myself.

FRANCINE   I'm not listening/to this.

JO   You are *absolutely* going to listen to this!!!

[*Beat.*]

I'm sorry, Ma./I am but.

FRANCINE   You'd leave me? Sick like I am?

JO   You're not. *Sick.* Anymore!

FRANCINE   I'd die if you left me alone here, honey. I don't know how to do/ anything.

JO   So you'll learn!

FRANCINE   I won't I'll die! I won't make it longer than a month Josephine!/ I'll die!

JO   That's garbage!/That's not true!

FRANCINE   You promised your father that you'd look after/me you promised.

JO   Yes yes I know.

FRANCINE   On his deathbed. You said you'd take care of me. So he could go without worrying./You promised him.

JO   That was almost twenty years ago Ma!

FRANCINE   It was a promise! A promise made on a deathbed/Josephine.

JO   *I'm* gonna die if I stay here Ma! I'm dying a little bit every day and I. I don't wanna *die* anymore. So please. Please just. Give me your blessing.

FRANCINE   Whadya need that for. You don't care/what I think.

JO   Ma *please.*

FRANCINE   You said yourself. You're a grown woman. Do what you want. You don't wanna live here. Don't you stay for my sake. Whatever you decide I'll be fine. I'll. I'll make do.

[*Pause.*]

We're a good team./You and me.

JO   I *know* Ma. I just.

FRANCINE   Not a lotta mother and daughters got we what we got.

[*Beat.*]

That butcher. He's just looking for a good time/with you.

JO   He's *nice* to me.

FRANCINE   He's taking *advantage* of you, sweetheart. So's that girl Sherry. People see your sweet nature and they take advantage. You'll see. You'll move out and you'll see. The world's. Not so nice. But.

[*Beat.*]

Family. Family loving you. *That* you can count on. *That's* the only thing you know for sure. But.

[*Beat.*]

But you go on head and *go*. If that's what you need to do. Don't you worry/
about me.

Jo   I'm not going Ma.

Francine   Honey you can/if you want.

Jo   I'm not going anywhere.

[*Jo goes and gets the frozen dinners out of the microwave and brings them
back to the table. They eat.*]

Three

[Sherry, Jo, *and* Francine *in the living room.* Jo *is wearing a low-cut dress.*
Sherry *is doing her hair and makeup.*]

Sherry   Mrs. Rosen you wanna put on some music? While we're getting
ready?

Francine   Do I wanna?

Jo   Ma.

Francine   What kinda question is that?/Do I wanna?

Sherry   I see the record player outta the corner of my eye. Thought
maybe/you like music.

Francine   I don't have anything you two would wanna listen to.

Sherry   What do I wanna listen to?

Francine   I donno. *Disco.*

Sherry   I'll have you know Mrs. Rosen—I like all the old music.

Francine   Like what.

Sherry   All of it. Go on. Put on whatever you like. Just nice to have
something in the background dontcha think?

Francine   Yeah sure why the heck not.

[*She gets up and puts a record on the record player.*]

So is the butcher gonna come inside or what?

Jo   I donno.

Francine   What???

Jo   I said I donno!

[*To* Sherry.]

She needs a hearing aid.

FRANCINE   I absolutely do not.

SHERRY   Oh I like Tony Bennett Mrs. R!

FRANCINE   It's Frank Sinatra.

SHERRY   Oh. Yeah yeah. I hear it now.

FRANCINE   The butcher should come inside.

JO   He has a name and why.

FRANCINE   To meet me.

JO   He's met you already. He's known you since we were kids.

FRANCINE   Still good manners.

[*Beat.*]

Maybe I should put the good candy out/just in case.

JO   Do what you want.

SHERRY   So what're you gonna do tonight?

FRANCINE   Who you talking to?

JO   *You*, Ma. She's talking/to *you*.

FRANCINE   She's mumbling! How the/heck should I know.

JO   Wear your hearing aid!

FRANCINE   I'm gonna watch TV.

SHERRY   You want company?

FRANCINE   No thanks.

JO   Ma!

FRANCINE   What! She asked me do I want and/I don't want.

JO   You're a pain in the ass.

FRANCINE   Why? Cuz I don't want company?

JO   She was being nice/to you.

FRANCINE   What did I say? I said/no thank you.

JO   You should be happy anybody wantsta spend time with/you at all!

SHERRY   You two! You two are *hysterical*. You know that?

JO   A comedy duo.

SHERRY   Yeah. We should get you two on *Carson*.

FRANCINE   Well I do have a background/in show business.

JO   Here we go.

FRANCINE   I could've been a Rockette you know.

SHERRY   You don't say.

FRANCINE   Yeah I took the bus into New York City and outta five hundred girls they wanted me to stay and get fitted for costumes.

SHERRY   So why didn't you do it?

FRANCINE   Because Mr. Rosen begged me to come back and marry him so I did.

SHERRY   Aw that's sweet. Isn't that sweet Jo?

JO   Yeah sure.

FRANCINE   I just wanted to prove to him I could do it. And he called me up at my aunt Shirley's house in Jersey and he said, "Francine, you gotta come back and marry me." And I said, "Only if we don't live with your mother." And he said OK. And so I came back to Boston and I married him.

SHERRY   They blow my mind those Rockettes.

FRANCINE   It takes a lotta concentration. You can't just do whatever you feel like doing.

[*She does a little pose and lifts up her robe.*]

When you dance it's gotta seem like it's one person dancing.

SHERRY   Jeez look at your legs.

FRANCINE   Oh I'm a mess. I got veins popping everywhere.

SHERRY   Not that I can see.

FRANCINE   Cuz I wear the support hose. I weighed ninety-seven pounds before I had kids you know. My waist was nineteen inches around.

SHERRY   How many kids you got?

JO   [*Awkward pause.*] She's just/got me.

FRANCINE   Yeah just Josephine.

[*Beat.*]

I hadda 'nother one/but.

JO   Ma.

FRANCINE   What? It's nothing bad. It happens. It's life.

[*To* SHERRY.]

I had another one before Josephine. A boy. But he was premature.

SHERRY   Oh.

FRANCINE   Yeah poor little guy didn't make it. But. I don't dwell. I'm not a dweller. I was blessed with my Josephine.

SHERRY   Well I gotta say. You're something. You're terrific. I wanna be like you when I'm older. I'm telling you. You still got it.

JO   [*A little laugh.*] She's a shut-in.

[*Pause.*]

She doesn't leave the house unless she's buying cigarettes. Isn't that/right Ma?

FRANCINE   Don't be mean.

JO   But it's true, isn't it? So. Sherry unless you wanna be an old lady who can't hear and won't leave the house when you're almost seventy—you should. Pick a better role model.

[*Silence. A slower and sadder song—like "One for My Baby (And One More for the Road)" begins to play.*]

SHERRY   Aw jeez. This one makes me cry.

FRANCINE   Oh yeah me too.

SHERRY   He sings so pretty.

FRANCINE   Yeah he sure does.

SHERRY   [*To Jo.*] Look up.

[*She puts on mascara.*]

You want I can do your makeup after Mrs. R.

FRANCINE   Yeah maybe.

JO   To watch TV?

SHERRY   Nothing wrong with looking pretty for yourself.

FRANCINE   That's what *I* say.

SHERRY   You ever get your colors done?

FRANCINE   No. But I saw that on the *Today* show. They said Jane Pauley's a Spring.

SHERRY   I can do your colors too if you want. I took the class. I got certified. I got my stuff in the car. It'll change your life.

FRANCINE   [*Beat.*] You're a doer. Aren't you?

SHERRY   I donno. I guess yeah.

FRANCINE   Me too. I'm a doer. Like you.

JO   You're a *sitter.*

FRANCINE   See how she is./How she teases.

SHERRY   I'm telling you. You two need a show.

[*To* JOSEPHINE.]

Okay. Do this.

[*She rubs her lips together—*Jo *rubs her lips together.*]

And then do this.

[*She flips her hair.* JOSEPHINE *flips her hair.*]

You need a little something a little sparkle.

[*She puts lip gloss on* JOSEPHINE.]

Yeah that's good. I think you're done. Take a look in the mirror.

FRANCINE   You look like a streetwalker.

JO   Ma!

FRANCINE   Just saying my opinion/that's all.

SHERRY   Shut your mouth she looks beautiful.

JO   [*Looking in the mirror.*] I look okay.

SHERRY   *You* look *beautiful.*

[SHERRY *stands behind* JO *in the mirror. She really does look beautiful.* SHERRY *gives her hair one last big spray of hairspray to finish her off. The doorbell rings.*]

FRANCINE   I gotta put out the good candy.

JO   Ma! Enough with the/goddamn candy!

SHERRY   You guys got a camera?

FRANCINE   In the linen closet/top of the stairs.

[*Doorbell.*]

JO   No pictures!

[*She smooths her dress and her hair.*]

Okay. Here/goes nothing.

SHERRY   I'm getting the camera!

[*She heads upstairs.*]

JO   I *said*/no pictures!

FRANCINE   Lemme put the candy/in the dish!

JO   He's not staying!

[*She opens the door.* DONNY *stands there with a slightly awkward corsage.*]

Sorry that/took so long.

DONNY   No it's uh.

JO   Hi.

DONNY   Hey.

[*Awkward pause.*]

DONNY   Can I. Can I come/in maybe?

JO   Oh! Jeez. Sorry.

DONNY   Don't worry/about it.

FRANCINE   Hi I got candy.

JO   Sorry sorry.

[*He enters.*]

DONNY   Hullo Mrs. Rosen. Not sure if you remember me/but I.

FRANCINE   I remember you.

DONNY   Nice to see/you again.

FRANCINE   Josephine said you weren't gonna be coming in. Or we woulda fixed up/the house.

DONNY   I thought better to come to the door than honk the horn/you know?

FRANCINE   Uh-huh.

DONNY   S'what my mother always says. So.

[*Beat. He holds out the corsage.*]

I uh. I got you this?

JO   Oh! Thank you.

DONNY   You want me to pin it/on you?

JO   Sure. Sure.

FRANCINE   I gotta get a picture of you two./Where's the camera!

SHERRY   Coming!

JO   No! Pictures!

[SHERRY *enters with the Polaroid camera and hands it to* FRANCINE.]

SHERRY   Here/you go!

JO   Donny this is my friend Sherry from work.

[SHERRY *and* DONNY *see each other.*]

SHERRY   Hi.

DONNY   Oh hey/hi.

SHERRY   Nice to meet you!

DONNY   Yeah/you too.

FRANCINE   Lemme get a picture.

DONNY   We should really/get going.

FRANCINE   Just one picture!

JOSEPHINE   Oh for chrissake, Ma, fine, make it quick.

[DONNY *and* JOSEPHINE *stand and pose. A strange middle-aged prom picture.* FRANCINE *takes the picture with the Polaroid. And then starts waving the picture around.*]

FRANCINE   It's gonna be a gorgeous/picture of you.

DONNY   [*To* JOSEPHINE.] Ready to go?

FRANCINE   Don't you wanna see how/it turns out?

JO   I'll see it later.

[DONNY *helps* JOSEPHINE *on with her coat.*]

SHERRY   Have a good time you two!

DONNY   It was nice/meeting you.

JO   [*To* FRANCINE.] Don't wait up.

SHERRY   Yeah you too.

DONNY   Nice seeing you/Mrs. Rosen.

FRANCINE   The picture's/almost ready!

JO   I said I'll see it later, Ma!/We gotta.

FRANCINE   One more minute!

JO   We gotta go.

[*They exit.* SHERRY *watches them go—and stares at the door. She begins to cry quietly.*]

FRANCINE   I'm telling you. I don't trust him.

SHERRY   [*A little laugh.*] Oh yeah? Why's that.

FRANCINE   He doesn't look you in the eye when he talks to you.

SHERRY   [*A little laugh.*] Yeah. Yeah, he sure doesn't.

[*Beat.*]

You're a smart woman. I mean it. I hope I grow up to be just like you someday. If I ever. Grow up.

[*Beat.*]

Can I. I know you said you didn't want company Mrs. Rosen but. You think I could stay here? For maybe just a little bit?

FRANCINE   You OK hon?

SHERRY   Oh yeah I just. I. I don't wanna go home yet? So.

[*A laugh/cry.*]

I donno where to go?

FRANCINE   [*Beat.*] Why don't you come over here, huh? Sit next to me on the couch.

SHERRY   Yeah OK.

[SHERRY *curls up next to* FRANCINE *and* FRANCINE *wraps her arms around her as if she was a young girl.* SHERRY *begins to fully cry.*]

FRANCINE   You stay long as you like honey. You hear me?

SHERRY   Uh-huh.

FRANCINE   [*She kisses the top of her head.*] Long as you like.

Four

[*The porch.* DONNY *and* JO *sit side by side on the glider drinking out of big cups.*]

DONNY   I'm *really* sorry/about that.

JO   S'OK.

DONNY   I thought I was gonna be/up to it.

JO   Yeah sure.

DONNY   But when I saw her in the parking lot/I donno I.

JO   I get it.

DONNY   I just. Froze?

[*Pause.*]

It's not like I don't see her. I mean I see her all the time cuz of the kids but *seeing* her. Around everybody we useta know. All our friends. With a *date*. With that freaking douche bag she's *dating*. Having to sit there like a jerk *knowing* some other guy's banging my wife it's. I'm sorry I'm just. I'm not a big enough man I guess to/put up with that.

Jo   Uh-huh.

DONNY   So. I'm sorry. I. Know you were looking forward.

[*Silence.*]

Jo   I liked the movie.

DONNY   Yeah? Yeah it was great. Eddie Murphy he's real hysterical funny, right?

Jo   Yeah.

DONNY   Yeah. [*They sip.*] You uh. You coulda gone in without me./I woulda understood.

Jo   No. No I didn't wanna go that bad to begin with/to be honest.

DONNY   Yeah OK.

Jo   I wanted to go cuz. I was gonna be going with. You.

DONNY   Oh.

Jo   Yeah.

DONNY   Huh.

[*Awkward pause.*]

Jo   Oh! I forgot! I still got your jacket./Damnit.

DONNY   What jacket?

Jo   The one you gave me the other night when you/took me home.

DONNY   Oh right.

Jo   I should/go get it.

DONNY   It's fine, I'll get it later I.

[*Teasing.*]

I know where you live.

Jo   Ha. Yeah you do.

DONNY   So I . . . know where to find you.

[*Slightly awkward laugh. Pause.*]

Do you uh. Do you think less of me cuz of how I couldn't go?

Jo   I already told/you no.

DONNY   Yeah but not cuz you're being polite. I wanna know really.

Jo   Why.

DONNY   Cuz I care about what you think about me.

Jo   [*Beat.*] I think that. If I'm speaking true from my heart? I think I. Understand? Why you couldn't go I. I do but.

[*Beat.*]

I wish that you didn't care. I wish that being with me? Was. Enough. And.

[*Beat.*]

Part of me thinks that you're not being truthful to me right now.

DONNY   Oh yeah?

Jo   Yeah part of me feels like it didn't have anything to do with seeing Kathy. Part of me thinks that you didn't want all of them seeing you with. Me.

[*No response.*] I know I'm not the prettiest girl we went to school with. Or the most/interesting or.

DONNY   No it's not that.

Jo   Not like Kathy. Kathy was. A prize. You got the prize. And so. I'd understand if being with me was more like a letdown? Cuz. If we were reversed I'd probly feel that way too.

DONNY   Feel what way?

Jo   Feel like. If I can't walk in there with a girl like Kathy next to me. I wouldn't wanna walk in at all.

DONNY   [*Beat.*] What would you say if I told you that.

[*Beat.*]

That a part of that was true.

Jo   I would. Thank you for your honesty.

DONNY   Jeez now I feel like a shitball.

Jo   No/no.

DONNY   I am I'm a shitball.

Jo   No/you're not.

DONNY   It's just sometimes. I feel like I'm following some kinda invisible rulebook. Telling me what to do. And I don't even know why but sometimes? I feel like I gotta follow it. And other times? I feel like I wanna fucking pulverize it. You ever feel like that?

Jo   Nah I always feel like on the day they passed out the rulebook I was in the bathroom.

Donny   [*A little laugh.*] That's funny.

Jo   [*A little laugh.*] Yeah?

Donny   You're funny a lot.

Jo   I sometimes think I make jokes and I don't even know I'm doing it. Like people are laughing at me and I don't get it.

Donny   I'm not laughing. *At* you.

Jo   OK.

Donny   You're a. You're funny. And you're. You're a pretty girl, Jo.

Jo   No I'm not.

Donny   You are. You're pretty in your own way.

Jo   Well. Isn't that terrific.

Donny   Fuck. I didn't mean it like that/I meant it like.

Jo   Yeah, I know.

Donny   You're *different*.

Jo   Yeah that's true.

Donny   I *like* that. You're different.

Jo   [*A little laugh.*] What's wrong with you?

Donny   [*A little laugh.*] Why's there gotta be something wrong with me? Why can't I just like you cuz I like you?

[*Beat.*]

Look I always did. What I was supposed to do. Marry the girl I was supposed to marry. Be a butcher cuz my father was a butcher. But.

[*Beat.*]

I wish I'd been in the bathroom too when they passed out the rulebooks Jo. Cuz I did all the things I was supposed to do? And. I'm not sure I'm too happy.

Jo   I did everything wrong and I'm not happy either so.

[*Beat.*]

You know what I think? Donny Moretti?

Donny   Whadya think Josephine Rosen.

Jo   I think. I think nobody's happy. I think that's the big joke. From God. Being happy doesn't really exist. Or it does but it's like a scratch-off lottery ticket. And most people don't hit the jackpot. I think you get stuff you think you want and you want something else. I think you never get what you think you want and that sucks too. I think life's about always wanting. Something.

DONNY   So whadya want, Jo.

JO   [*Sincerely.*] I really wish I knew.

[*Beat.*]

I don't know that I've ever wanted anything. Or if I did? It was so long ago. I don't even remember what it felt like. And so. Maybe I'm not even alive. Maybe I'm dead and just. Walking around. And I don't even know it.

[*Beat.*]

You ever feel like that? You ever feel like you're walking around dead? Sometimes. Sometimes I pinch myself over and over and over again. Just so I can feel something to remind myself I'm not dead yet. Or I bite my tongue on purpose. Or I stick my finger with a pin just to see it bleed. Something. Anything. Because otherwise I got no solid proof that I. Actually exist.

[*Beat.*]

Whadya think of that. Huh? Tell me I'm not fucked in the head after hearing *that.*

[*Silence.*]

DONNY   You wanna. Come home. With me?

JO   [*Beat.*] I don't. Think I can.

DONNY   OK.

JO   What kinda fucked up person are you wants to spend the night with me after what I just/said?

DONNY   I donno.

JO   Maybe you're right. Maybe you are just as crazy in the head as I am.

DONNY   [*Laughs.*] Yeah maybe.

JO   [*A little laugh.*] Am I making jokes again?

DONNY   Yeah.

JO   I wish I was making 'em on purpose. I think it'd be a whole lot more. Satisfying.

[*Beat.*]

I was hoping so bad you were gonna save me. Like at the end of some kinda romance movie. Where you'd swoop me up and. Take me away. But the truth is. I'd wake up tomorrow in your rented room. And you'd make me a scrambled egg on your hot plate. And maybe you'd call me again. And maybe you wouldn't. But it's not gonna be a romance movie cuz. I'd still haveta come back. Here. I always gotta come back. *Here* and. Just the thought of *that* is enough to make me. Never wanna leave in the first place.

[*Beat.*]

And so. Thank you for your. Invitation. But I/think I'll just.

DONNY   What if it's. What if you just. What if you just come home with me. And maybe it's tonight. And maybe it's another but. I donno. Sometimes. Sometimes *I* feel dead too. Not in the same way *you're* talking about. But. Yeah. I feel dead. A *lot* lately and. For whatever reason I don't feel that way when. When I'm around. You.

[*Beat.*]

Even if you're not somebody I'm supposed to be with. Even if you're fucked in the head. I'm fucked in the head. Everybody's fucked in the head. Doesn't mean. Doesn't mean they don't want someone to just. To just be *nice* to them. Sometimes. You know? I.

[*Beat.*]

I mean I.

[*Beat.*]

I don't.

[*Beat.*]

I fuck I don't wanna go back to my fucking sad fucking awful rented room by myself OK? So. So if you'd just come *home* with me? If you could just if you could do that/for me I'd.

Jo   I think I should go in.

DONNY   [*Beat.*] Yeah okay.

Jo   I got work/tomorrow so.

DONNY   Yeah. Yeah OK sure.

Jo   G'night.

[JOSEPHINE *turns to go. He stays on the porch.*]

DONNY   Hey so/listen.

Jo   Huh?

DONNY   You maybe you wanna go to Paragon Park this weekend?

Jo   [*A little laugh.*] The amusement park?

Donny   [*A little laugh.*] Yeah. Could be fun maybe?

Jo   I think I read in *The Ledger* that they're tearing it down. Making condominiums.

Donny   Fuck really?

Jo   . . . Yeah . . .

Donny   Me and my uncle useta go there all the time.

Jo   Yeah well. S'too bad.

[*She turns to go again.*]

Donny   Well what/about.

Jo   Huh?

Donny   Just hold on a/second.

Jo   . . . OK . . .

Donny   What about. What about I. Hey! I could make you those veal chops we were talking/about.

Jo   [*A little laugh.*] Oh.

Donny   Whadya/think.

Jo   I forgot about that.

Donny   I mean, I got my kids next weekend but. *This* weekend? If you want. I could make you those chops.

Jo   OK.

[*Beat.*]

I'll uh. Try not to cry.

Donny   Huh?

Jo   Over the baby cows.

Donny   Oh yeah right.

[*Beat.*]

You can if you want.

[*Laughs.*]

Jo   [*A little laugh.*] OK.

Donny   Saturday.

Jo   Sure.

Donny   I'll pick you up.

Jo   I can/drive.

DONNY   No, I'll pick you up. At. Seven o'clock.

Jo   OK.

DONNY   OK.

[*He hesitantly steps forward. A tentative kiss.*]

Five

[*The meat counter.* SHERRY *and* DONNY.]

SHERRY   Yeah hey.

DONNY   . . . Hey . . .

SHERRY   Yeah I'd like. I'm not sure what/I'd like.

DONNY   . . . OK . . .

SHERRY   I'd like. I'd like four chicken breasts, a rump roast, and about a pound and a half of motherfucking liar dirtbag/that's what I'd like.

DONNY   Hey can you keep it down.

SHERRY   Did you just ask me to *keep it down*? Did you? Cuz you know what happens when somebody says/that to me?

DONNY   Oh jeez.

SHERRY   Tells me to *keep it down*? You know what I do? I GET. FUCKING./LOUDER.

DONNY   Yeah if you could just.

SHERRY   If I could just what.

DONNY   I don't wanna start a scene.

SHERRY   Oh really? Cuz. That's exactly what *I* wanna do.

[*Silence.*]

DONNY   How'd you figure out where I worked.

SHERRY   Whadya mean how'd I figure it out. My *good friend* Josephine told me/you dickhead.

DONNY   Could you please.

SHERRY   Next time you wanna lie all over the place you should plan better. You should dot your i's and cross your t's and only pick girls who live in fucking *Ohio* so you don't cross-pollinate/with coworkers!

DONNY   Sherry, I.

SHERRY   You know how much of an asshole I felt last night when this guy I've been hearing about walks through the door and the motherfucker is *you*???

[*Beat.*]

How's your *wife*.

DONNY   If you'd/let me explain.

SHERRY   She good? You two working it out?

DONNY   If you'd/let me talk I'd.

SHERRY   How's *urology* dickhead???

DONNY   Can't even get a/word in edgewise.

SHERRY   Fuck. You.

DONNY   Sherry. Come on. Babe.

SHERRY   Did you just call me *babe*?

DONNY   Slipped/out.

SHERRY   You don't get to call me that no more!!! You don't get to Sherry babe me! You. Fucking.

[*She starts to cry.*]

Ugh! Don't cry Sherilyn. Don't you/fucking cry.

DONNY   You're making me feel awful.

SHERRY   Good!

[*Silence.*]

DONNY   I'm . . . I'm sorry.

SHERRY   What're you *sorry* for?

DONNY   I'm/just saying.

SHERRY   The fact that everything you said to me was a lie? Or/the fact that I.

DONNY   That's not true.

SHERRY   Or the fact that I found out.

DONNY   A little of both.

[*Pause.*]

It wasn't all a lie.

SHERRY   How do you figure?

DONNY   I'm not divorced yet. Kathy and I could still/get back together.

SHERRY Are you really so freaking deluded that you think *that's* the thing I'm most/upset about???

DONNY I'm just saying that part of it wasn't that far from the truth/that's all!!!

SHERRY You said you were a *doctor*!

DONNY Yeah.

SHERRY Buddy look around. You're not a freaking doctor.

DONNY I *could've* been.

SHERRY Yeah and I coulda been Miss America, but last I checked I'm not.

DONNY Would you've gone out with me if you knew I was a butcher?

SHERRY Do I look like a girl who's got high standards.

[*Beat.*]

God I feel like such a freaking chump.

DONNY I wanted to tell you.

SHERRY Yeah so why didn't you.

DONNY I donno. At some point it just it was too late.

SHERRY You said you wanted to marry me? And have babies with me? You said you wanted us to start over together? Was that all bullshit?

DONNY No/no.

SHERRY Cuz it felt real.

DONNY It was. I meant every single word.

SHERRY So what happened?

DONNY It's messed up getting a maybe divorce/you know that.

SHERRY It's not about your wife! That was one thing. But you got three of us???

DONNY It's not/really like that.

SHERRY So first you break my heart and then you hadda go and call me like you did. And tell me/you miss me?

DONNY I don't know why I did that.

SHERRY You call me tell me you're missing me all the while you're seeing my *friend*?/My *coworker*?

DONNY I didn't know you two knew each other! How was I to/know that???

Sherry   You *knew* I work at an accountant firm just like her! You *knew* I work a mile away from here/just like her!

Donny   I mean. I didn't think it all through so good. I got a lot going on in my head right now.

Sherry   [*A little laugh.*] Wow. Really? Wow. Cuz from where I'm looking at you? You got nothing going on in there. That shit's *empty.*

[*Beat.*]

So whadya want. You want me you want her you want/your wife?

Donny   I donno.

Sherry   That's real articulate.

Donny   I don't know what/to tell you!

Sherry   I am not gonna wait while you dick around with me and my friend and/your fucking wife!

Donny   Yeah I know.

Sherry   So you gotta choose. Who's it gonna be.

[*No response.*]

Huh? Shithead. Who do you want outta the three of us cuz I'm not gonna do bigamy with you.

Donny   [*Beat.*] I think I gotta. Give it a try with Josephine.

Sherry   [*Starts to cry.*] OK.

Donny   I'm/sorry.

Sherry   She prettier/than me?

Donny   No. No.

Sherry   She got something I don't have cuz. I'll *be* that./For you.

Donny   I don't know what it is. But if you're gonna stand here, make me choose right now, my gut just says I gotta choose Josephine.

Sherry   Oh, god, that fucking hurts.

Donny   I've been being a real dirtbag. Just thinking about myself. But. I wanna try and maybe stop being that way. I wanna be. Better than I am. And I think I can be better with/Josephine.

Sherry   OK. OK.

[*Pause.*]

You gotta tell her/about us.

DONNY   Yeah I know.

SHERRY   Even though she's gonna hate me for it and not wanna be my friend anymore. You gotta tell her or I will fuck/your shit up.

DONNY   I'll tell her!

SHERRY   I will come over here and throw a scene. I will slash the tires on your car. I will send dead animals to your wife.

DONNY   *Please*/don't do that.

SHERRY   *You* are not a nice person. Nice people? Don't go around treating everybody like garbage. And so. Think about it. Before you go down that road/with her.

DONNY   Yeah okay.

SHERRY   Think about what you're *capable* of. And if you decide that you can't show up for her? Like you're gonna string her along and then break her heart like you broke mine? Leave her the fuck alone and just. Don't even show up to begin with. Because she *is* a nice person and. She deserves better than/your bullshit.

DONNY   Yeah. Yeah okay.

[*Beat.*]

Sherry I'm.

SHERRY   What.

DONNY   I mean it I'm really. Sorry.

SHERRY   [*A small laugh.*] Yeah. Fuck you.

[*She turns and goes.*]

Six

[*Nighttime.* JOSEPHINE *sits on the porch.* DONNY's *jacket is beside her.* FRANCINE *opens the door.*]

FRANCINE   Honey?

JO   Yeah Ma.

FRANCINE   What are you sitting out all by/yourself for?

JO   Somebody's picking me up.

FRANCINE   Where you going?

[*No response.*]

You've been out here since seven o'clock. Almost nine/now.

Jo   Whadya want, Ma.

FRANCINE   I got heartburn. I can't find the Tums.

Jo   Drawer next to the fridge.

[*Beat—*FRANCINE'*s still there.*]

You need me to get them/for you?

FRANCINE   No.

Jo   Okay then.

[*Silence.*]

FRANCINE   You never told me how the reunion/went.

Jo   I know.

FRANCINE   You have fun?

[*No response.*]

See anybody interesting/or anything.

Jo   We didn't go.

FRANCINE   Didn't go??? After all that??? Why would/you not go.

Jo   I don't think either of us really wanted to go in the first place Ma, so. We didn't.

[*Beat.*]

The Tums are in the kitchen. You need/something else?

FRANCINE   You trying to get rid of me?

Jo   No. I just. Don't feel like talking that's all.

FRANCINE   [*Beat.*] Looks like whoever's supposed to come and get you isn't coming.

[*No response.*]

It's late to be going out.

Jo   It's Saturday. People go out later on Saturdays.

FRANCINE   What're you doing.

Jo   Somebody's making dinner for me.

FRANCINE   Who?

[*No response.*]

If they don't come you wanna go get an ice cream?

[*No response.*]

Remember when we useta come out here in the summer? Get an ice cream from the/truck?

Jo   . . . Yeah. . .

Francine   He doesn't come by anymore in the summer. Why do you think that is.

[*No response.*]

Maybe it's cuz there aren't kids here anymore. Useta be so many kids. Now you're the youngest person lives here.

[*She laughs.*]

Jo   It's cuz Mr. Braverman's dead, Ma.

Francine   Huh?

Jo   Mr. Braverman. Who drove the ice cream truck. He's dead. You know that.

Francine   When he die?

Jo   More than ten years ago. So. That's why there's no ice cream man anymore.

Francine   [*Beat.*] I went to school with Morty Braverman.

Jo   Yeah./I know.

Francine   How'd I forget he *died*?

[*Beat.*]

Oy veh iz mir. Whatever you do. Stay young honey. Don't get old like me.

Jo   [*A little laugh.*] Like I have a choice? Can't stop time.

Francine   I/guess.

Jo   It does what it wants.

[*Pause.*]

Every night when I get into bed and I'm lying there. Waiting to fall asleep. I think. There went another day. I got up and I made a bagel and I went to work and I came home and now it's gone. Just. Slipped through my fingers.

[*Beat.*]

One of these days I think I'm gonna fall asleep. And when I wake up. I'll look in the mirror. And I'll be an. Old woman.

Francine   [*A little laugh.*] What kinda crazy talk is that. Who goes to sleep and wakes up an old woman/all of a sudden???

Jo   Not *literally*, Ma! I'm just trying to explain/how I feel.

FRANCINE   I don't understand.

JO   Ten years ago I was only twenty-eight. In ten more years I'm gonna be almost *fifty*!

FRANCINE   So I'll be almost eighty!/That's worse!

JO   This isn't the life I thought I'd be living, Ma! That's. That's all I'm. Trying to say.

[*Silence.*]

FRANCINE   What's so bad about your life.

JO   Forget I said anything/about it.

FRANCINE   No, really. I want to know. What is so *bad* about/your life?

JO   Are you kidding me? I'm a spinster who lives at home with her mother! I had a scholarship to Radcliffe and I'm a secretary! I'm almost forty and I've never been anyplace/but *here*!!!

FRANCINE   That's not true. We went to Florida lots of times when/you were little.

JO   I mean somewhere without *you*! I have never been anywhere/without *you*!

FRANCINE   Oh for Chrissake.

JO   *You* shoulda told me to go back to school! After Daddy died. When I still hadda chance to make something/of myself.

FRANCINE   Oy we're back to/this again.

JO   *You* shoulda forced me!

FRANCINE   *Forced*/you?

JO   You shoulda wanted more for me than I wanted/for myself.

FRANCINE   *You* didn't wanna go back/Josephine!

JO   Says you.

FRANCINE   No it's the truth! You were a scared little girl back then. *You* don't remember. *I* do. And so. Even if I *had*. *Pushed* you out the door and changed all the locks behind you—*you* woulda found a way to come back home because *that's* who you were. So.

[*Beat.*]

Don't you try and blame your life on me honey. Because whatever you got? That's all on *you*.

[*Silence.*]

JO   I tried once. To leave. Five years ago. I went to a travel agent and I bought a one-way plane ticket to Arizona. I hadda go two towns over because I was scared somebody would find out.

FRANCINE   Why Arizona.

JO   It was February. I wanted to go someplace warm.

[*Beat.*]

Every day I'd look at that goddamn ticket like it was gold. Pull it out of its little paper wrapper. Seat 24C. I'd say those words to myself over and over. Delta flight 362 from Boston to Phoenix. Seat 24C.

FRANCINE   So why didn't you go?

JO   [*A confession.*] I chickened out.

[*Beat.*]

I sat there in my room with my bags all packed and my stomach tied in knots. And I heard you watching TV downstairs. And I. I just couldn't get myself out the door. I stood there like an idiot in my room with all my packed bags. Frozen. Until it was too late and I thought. "I missed my goddamn plane. Right now Delta Air Lines's gotta plane flying to Phoenix outta Logan with an empty seat 24C on it." So.

[*Beat. A sad little laugh.*]

Maybe you're right. Maybe I never wanted to go anyplace. Maybe I wanted this shitty life I got.

FRANCINE   There is nothing *shitty* about/your life.

JO   Come on.

FRANCINE   You got a roof over your head. You got your health. You got people/who love you.

JO   Yeah all right.

FRANCINE   What's with you that you need more than that? Huh?

[*Beat.*]

Listen to me. Are you/listening?

JO   I'm listening!

FRANCINE   Be *happy* sweetheart.

JO   Yeah/sure.

FRANCINE   You *choose* to be unhappy. You *choose* to live in sadness. Girls today—you all think you should get everything. *Nobody* gets to have everything/honey.

JO   I *know* that.

FRANCINE   Do you?

[*Pause.*]

Look. When I was younger than you—and your brother died when he was just two days old. And your father took him out of my arms and had him buried without a stone like he was nothing. *I* didn't mope around feeling sorry for myself. I didn't even cry. I just picked myself up and I moved on and I had. *You.* And I. I was just so *grateful.* For what I had. And I loved you. More than anything. But you?

[*Beat. A sad little laugh.*]

All you'd ever do was run away from me. Other mothers they would hold their babies. Cuddle them close. I would try as hard as I could to hold you tight to me. But you'd always just. Wiggle away.

[*A little shrug.*]

You never wanted anything to do with me. Even then. So.

[*Beat.*]

So. *Go.* Josephine. Go if you wanna go so bad honey. Go. I'm not gonna force you to be here.

[*Silence.*]

JO   If I leave Ma. I'm not coming back.

FRANCINE   OK.

[*She kisses her on the forehead.*]

OK.

[FRANCINE *goes back inside and shuts the door behind her.* JOSEPHINE *sits—frozen in a moment of unknown. It is both terrifying and exciting. She sits for a very long time like this. And then. The sudden sound of car on gravel. Headlights illuminate her face. A moment of hope. Blackout.*]

Permissions

British Commonwealth), the Berne Convention, the Pan-American Copyright Convention and the Universal Copyright Convention as well as all countries with which the United States has reciprocal copyright relations. All rights, including professional/amateur stage rights, motion picture, recitation, lecturing, public reading, radio broadcasting, television, video or sound recording, all other forms of mechanical or electronic reproduction, such as CD-ROM, CD-I, information storage and retrieval systems and photocopying, and the rights of translation into foreign languages, are strictly reserved. Particular emphasis is laid upon the matter of readings, permission for which must be secured from the Author's agent in writing.

Inquiries concerning rights should be addressed to:
William Morris Endeavor Entertainment, LLC.
11 Madison Avenue
New York, New York 10010
Attn: Scott Chaloff